D0206128

Local Population and Employment Projection Techniques

Local Population and Employment Projection Techniques

Michael R. Greenberg, Donald A. Krueckeberg,
and Connie O. Michaelson,
with assistance from Richard Mautner
and Nancy Newman

THE CENTER FOR URBAN POLICY RESEARCH
RUTGERS UNIVERSITY
BUILDING 4051 KILMER CAMPUS
NEW BRUNSWICK, NEW JERSEY 08903

Second Printing

Cover Design by Francis G. Mullen
Copyright, 1978, Rutgers—The State University of New Jersey
All Rights Reserved.
Published in the United States of America
by the Center for Urban Policy Research,
New Brunswick, New Jersey 08903
Manufactured in the United States of America

Library of Congress Cataloging in Publication Data

Greenberg, Michael R
  Local population and employment projection techniques.

  Bibliography: p.
  1. Population forecasting—Mathematical models. 2. Employment forecasting—Mathematical models.
  I. Krueckeberg, Donald A., joint author. II. Michaelson, Connie O., 1947-
joint author. III. Title.
  HB885.G69   301.32′01′82   78-1294
  ISBN 0-88285-049-0

To Heather and John

Contents

Acknowledgments

The authors would like to thank Daniel Travers, graduate student in the Department of Urban Planning and Policy Development, for checking the hand calculations.

Michael Greenberg
Donald Krueckeberg
Connie Michaelson

Introduction

This monograph presents a set of programmed models that project the populations of minor civil divisions (MCDs) up to fifty years and employment of counties up to twenty-five years. Three classes of MCD population models are presented, each of which is constrained at the county scale by county projections that are, in turn, constrained by state and national projections. The simplest MCD model extrapolates a trend in the historical growth rates of each MCD. A second method is based on the distributional properties of projections made by regional or county agencies. The most complex type increases or decreases the MCD populations on the basis of density limits. A procedure is provided for allocating the projections to an alternative set of spatial units.

The second part of this book provides employment projection methods. Four models are presented. One is a simple regression model. Three are step-down models: one of which is a constant share model; a second model weights the constant share projections by population projections; and a third includes a competitive component.

Each part of the monograph contains three major pieces: (1) an overview of available projection models; (2) state, county, and, in the case of population projections, minor civil division models; (3) computer programs, user's instructions, and the input and output of a sample problem.

We followed the advice of readers of the predecessor to this volume (Greenberg, *et al.*, 1973) which focused on population projection only, by including hand calculations for those users who might choose to perform the calculations by hand.

Population and employment projections have been most accurate when extended only five, ten, or fifteen years into the future. Longer-run extensions, such as those produced by the following models, must be regarded as grossly speculative. Forecasting populations, especially of small areas, beyond fifteen years ideally requires an encyclopedic knowledge of the national, regional, and local socioeconomic, political, and physical environments, combined with a large measure of imagination. The difficulty of assembling this combination of attributes and the inherent caution of planners, statisticians, economists, and demographers have resulted in a dearth of long-range projections. However, projections of this type are increasingly required by private and public decisionmakers. While the accuracy of such forecasts and projections does not present an impressive record, their development at the county and minor civil division scales has become imperative for the rational planning of projects of long-term investment and impact.

Part I
Population Projections

Chapter One
An Overview of Population Projections Methods

Most projection methods can be applied at several geographical scales. The discussions that follow emphasize the utility of different methods for local level projections.

Definitions: Estimates, Projections, Forecasts

Before comparing the noncomponent and component methods some basic terminology must be reviewed. We will distinguish between "estimate," "projection," and "forecast." Following the lead of Pittinger (1976), an *estimate* refers to current population. Estimates are calculated in lieu of an actual census count and are used to update population figures of the last census. A *projection* refers to future population levels. Population projections indicate what population changes might occur, given assumptions inherent in the projection method and data. Analysts typically develop more than one set of projections, each set embodying a different set of assumptions. Projection sets may represent minimum, maximum, and midpoint growth rates, but all projections are plausible. A population *forecast*, on the other hand, is judgmental. It is the set of projections deemed most likely to occur.

Population projections do not necessarily lead to population forecasts. Agencies often prepare sets of projections ranging from slow growth to rapid growth so that users may select the forecasts that most closely approximate their needs. Deliberately using projections which are on the high or low side of the spectrum can provide a margin of safety in projecting future municipal services or revenues.

Alternative projections may be based on the same method, differing only in their designated growth rates, birth rates, population density ceilings, etc., or they may be the result of different methods. All projection methods have weaknesses and strengths. Some analysts attempt to mitigate the weak points by averaging together projections obtained by two or three different methods to produce a set of most likely projections.

An Overview of Component and Noncomponent Models

Population change involves three separate components: births, deaths, and migration. Models that consider the separate effects of each of these components are known as component models. Component models require comprehensive and detailed data sets which are usually not available at the local government scale. Models that directly use the net effects of the three components are noncomponent models. Because of data limitations, most models that project population at scales below the state scale are noncomponent models.

Noncomponent models may be based on past patterns of net population growth or they may relate net population growth to indicator information, such as changes in housing or voter registration. Noncomponent methods lack detailed age-sex breakdowns which are useful in planning for schools, community services, and different types of housing units. Overall, it is desirable, though not always possible, to consider the three components of population change separately and combine, not average, their effects. This is particularly true for mid- and long-range projection periods because the forces driving births, deaths, and migration may not be correlated.

Births and deaths are referred to as vital events. The numerical difference between births and deaths is called natural increase or decrease. Death rates in urban industrial nations at peace tend to be fairly stable over time and space. Therefore, age-specific mortality rates for the nation as a whole normally can be applied to local area population projections. Death rates are also available by sex. A crude death rate is a gross statistic which indicates only the number of deaths per 1,000 of population. It provides no age-sex detail. Similarly, a crude birth rate indicates births per 1,000 population, but provides no age-sex information. The ratio of births to women of childbearing age (defined as fifteen to forty-four years of age) is a fertility rate. Birth rates and fertility rates change slowly, and they are subject to regional, racial, and ethnic differences. Birth rates used in population projections are often determined empirically for the area under analysis. Morrison notes the importance of allocating births to the mother's city of residence. Otherwise, the "births" assigned to the city's hospitals will not materialize as school children, and this will lead to erroneous conclusions suggesting outmigration (Morrison, 1971).

Migration is the most difficult component to estimate or project at the local level. Migration is subject to relatively rapid fluctuation and is influenced by the size and shape of the locality. Isard (1960) mentions three general observations pertinent to migration. He notes that many moves cover only short distances; thus a large county or town will have a lower proportion of migrants than will a small one. Similarly, a narrow geographic entity will experience more migration across its boundaries than will a wide one. Third, when major population and employment centers are located close to state boundaries there is more migration across the state boundaries than there is when these centers are centrally located within the state.

Morrison (1975) divides the population of a region into stayers and chronic immigrants, e.g. middle management executives. The second group accounts for about half of the moves and its movements appear to be relatively insensitive to local employment conditions. In short, migration is extremely difficult to project at the smaller political entity scales.

Elements Affecting the Choice
and Accuracy of Models

Although no particular projection method is consistently more accurate than others, some methods provide more detailed consideration of factors affecting population growth. The choice of a model is best made by considering its relative accuracy, the type of population data available, the quality of available data, the scale of the analysis, the length of the projection period, the purpose of the projections, and the budget and time frame implications of the projection study.

Types of population data used in estimating and projecting include the following: records of historical population growth in the study area; zoning and density constraints; records of historical population growth in similar geographical areas or in larger ones of which the study area is part; crude birth and death rates; age-sex population breakdowns; fertility rates; and symptomatic data. Symptomatic data are useful because there is a correlation between population size and various other events, objects, or services, such as births and deaths, tax returns, voter registration, school enrollment, telephone installations, utility meter connections, occupancy permits issued, and motor vehicle licenses. Emigration and immigration data are available for the nation as a whole, but must be estimated for state, county, and local levels. The federal government provides specific information on population at military bases in the United States and abroad.

The quality and availability of basic population information are quite variable. The United States Bureau of the Census develops and maintains data solely to provide population statistics and is, therefore, the most reliable source. Symptomatic data, which are utilized at county and local levels, are usually maintained by various public agencies for their own purposes. As such, the data are much more subject to bias, gaps, inaccuracies, or sudden changes in recording procedures that make their use for another purpose—population estimates and projections—difficult.

The scale of analysis is an important factor affecting the choice and accuracy of models. At the national level, population growth is primarily a matter of births and deaths. The migration component is negligible and is available from immigration data. The importance of the migration component is, with rare exceptions, inversely related to the size of the geographic entity being examined. At the local level, migration changes population more quickly than births and deaths (natural increase) and also affects the size of the childbearing population by altering the age structure of the locality.

The smaller the geographic scale of analysis, the greater the need for various symptomatic data to determine population change. If detailed data inputs were used, however, large-scale studies of, for instance, all minor civil divisions in a state would be bogged in an enormously expensive morass of collection and tabulation tasks. In addition, studies involving numerous entities would have to deal with the variations in availability of symptomatic data or with the methods of recording it.

The accuracy and choice of models are also affected by the length of the projection period. Almost any projection method is suitable for short-term periods of up to ten years. Accordingly, inexpensive extrapolation procedures are frequently used. As the projection period lengthens, the amount of detail that can be used in noncomponent models tends to diminish, because of the problems of projecting the symptomatic data and their relationship to population. In general, as the projection period increases, the components are likely to become more and more important because they may follow independent trends. For long-term projections, these trends may become so divergent that their net effect is quite different from what it was during the base year. For this reason, most long-term projection methods should use some sort of component model. Simple historical extrapolations would be the least effective procedure for long-range projections. The programs presented in this volume combine component base projections at federal and state scales with extrapolation at the local government scale.

The choice and accuracy of models is related to the intended use of the projections. Population projections are used to plan for the demand and supply of water, sewage treatment, food, housing tax revenues, other services and facilities, and government funding. At the local level, selection of a method may depend on whether the planner needs age-sex detail, spatial distribution detail, or both. In some cases, slight overestimation may provide a margin of safety; in other cases, slight underestimation is advantageous.

Occasionally, differences in method or intent lead to conflicts among government officials. A case in point is a controversy noted by the New York Times (20 June 1976) between the Federal Bureau of the Census and the New Jersey Department of Labor and Industry. Federal estimates, which work from the national totals down to the county level, showed a loss of 84,000 persons in eight counties in the northern part of New Jersey from 1970 to 1974. The Bureau of the Census' method was based on births, deaths, employment totals, and school enrollment figures. New Jersey State's figures, based on a summation of minor civil division estimates, indicated a gain of 93,000 persons in those same counties during the same period. The state's method was based on births, deaths, utility connections and residential building permits.

Finally, in addition to data, length, time, and use considerations, the analyst frequently is led to a method by budgetary and research-time considerations. When limited by a small budget or when told that the projections "were needed yesterday," the analyst will often turn to simple and inexpensive extrapolation techniques. While these techniques are not sophisticated and are looked upon with disdain by many, their record for short-term projections is generally no worse than the sophisticated methods.

A classification of well-known projection and estimation methods and the circumstances under which they are best used is provided in Exhibit 1.1. The reader may use it as a summary of the sections on component and noncomponent approaches that follow. For more detailed treatments of these methods, see the excellent books by U.S. Bureau of the Census (1951), Morrison (1971), and Pittenger (1976). Krueckeberg and Silvers (1974), Carrothers in Isard (1960), and Chapin (1965) present brief technical introductions.

A note of caution about Exhibit 1.1. The classification represents our collective judgment. Some of the checks are supported by empirical tests (e.g., Isserman, 1977; Greenberg, 1972). Other checks represent our judgment about the best uses of the method. The absence of a check does not mean that the use is impossible or totally inappropriate. An example should help illustrate how the Exhibit was developed. Extrapolation is checked as a short-term projection method for local and county government scales. Long-term projections for large political regions are feasible. However, we do not recommend extrapolation for long-term projections for large regions because component techniques can be used for these purposes.

Component Methods

RESIDUAL

The residual method is used for estimation. It starts out with a known population usually based on the last census. Records of births and deaths are examined, and the population adjusted accordingly to produce an estimated current population. The difference between this anticipated population and the actual population is assumed to be the result of net migration.

This method is simple and does not call for age-sex breakdowns of population. It is useful for population estimates at all scales of analysis. Isard (1960) notes that this method tends to underestimate migration, particularly in areas of high in- or out-migration, because vital events among the migrants are included in the records of births and deaths.

VITAL RATES

The vital rates method is a ratio technique that relates total population to births and deaths. Ratios are developed between state and local government births and deaths from the historical record (e.g. 1970). Second, birth and death rates for the local government are obtained for the estimation period (e.g., 1978) by substituting the known state rate for 1978 into the ratio and solving for the local government birth and death rates. The rates are used to develop estimated populations based on births and deaths. Then the estimates based on the ratios are averaged to reduce errors involved in each of the projections. This is both an estimating and a projecting technique. The vital rates method assumes that a change in the rate of vital events signals a change in population size (Morrison, 1971).

This method is more complex than the residual method, but is still simple to apply at all scales of analysis. It would not be suitable for long-range projections because of the trend extrapolation inherent in projecting

EXHIBIT 1.1

COMPARISON OF POPULATION PROJECTION AND ESTIMATION METHODS

Type of Model	Relative Complexity			Type of Data That Can Be Used			Estimating or Projecting Technique	
	Simple	Moderate	Complex	Historical Counts	Vital Components	Other Indices	Estimation	Projection
Noncomponent:								
Trend Extrapolation	✓	✓		✓				✓
Comparative Forecast	✓			✓		✓		✓
Ratio Trend	✓			✓				✓
Density Ceiling		✓	✓	✓			✓	✓
Ratio Correlation		✓	✓	✓		✓	✓	
Housing Unit		✓	✓	✓		✓	✓	✓
Market Force		✓	✓	✓	✓	✓		✓
GKM		✓	✓	✓	✓	✓		✓
Component:								
Residual	✓				✓		✓	
Vital Rates		✓			✓		✓	✓
Cohort-Survival		✓	✓		✓		✓	✓
Cohort-Component		✓	✓	✓	✓	✓	✓	✓
Composite		✓	✓		✓	✓	✓	✓

EXHIBIT 1.1 (Continued)
COMPARISON OF POPULATION PROJECTION AND ESTIMATION METHODS

Type of Model	Appropriate Estimation and Projection Period			Appropriate Estimation and Projection Scale				Appropriate for Studies Involving Numerous Entities (assuming computer programming is available)
	Short	Middle	Long	Nation	State	County	Local	
Noncomponent:								
Trend Extrapolation	√					√	√	Yes
Comparative Forecast	√					√	√	Maybe
Ratio Trend	√	√	√		√	√	√	Yes
Density Ceiling		√	√			√	√	Yes
Ratio Correlation	√					√	√	No
Housing Unit	√	√				√	√	No
Market Force	√	√	√	√	√	√	√	No
GKM	√	√	√		√	√	√	Yes
Component:								
Residual	√			√	√	√	√	Yes
Vital Rates	√				√	√	√	Maybe
Cohort-Survival	√	√	√	√	√	√	√	Yes
Cohort Component	√	√	√	√	√	√	√	Depends on migration model
Composite	√	√	√		√	√	√	Yes

the birth and death rates. The assumption that the relationship between the vital events and population remains constant and the difficulty of developing accurate ratios between population and births and deaths are drawbacks to this method. Another drawback is that rapid migration, which affects the age structure, will affect the vital events and produce inaccurate estimates (Morrison, 1971). Therefore, the technique is more appropriately used above the local level and is best confined to estimating. The model is weak in its inattention to a specific migration component.

COHORT-SURVIVAL

The most basic method providing age-sex detail is the cohort-survival model. While it is a component model, it does not account for the migration component. The cohort-survival model projects future population based on growth due to natural increase. It is used both in estimating and projection studies. Population is disaggregated into male and female age cohorts. Each age cohort spans five years. Thus, cohort categories are zero to four years old, five to nine years old, ten to fourteen years old, etc. This is represented graphically as an age-sex pyramid. Age-specific death rates are available for each cohort. Age-specific birth rates are applied to female cohorts between the ages of fifteen and forty-four years. Each cohort group is then aged forward towards the final projection year, with mortality and birth rates applied to the survivors at five year intervals. Births are added to the bottom of the pyramid and aged forward accordingly.

The advantage of this technique is the excellent detail it provides in projecting future demand for age-specific needs, such as schools, jobs, or services for the elderly. It is a fairly accurate forecasting technique when migration is either known or negligible. Therefore, its utility is greatest at national and state levels. At the local level, it is useful as a comparative growth projection when several projection sets are being developed. The method adds greatly to the plausibility of long-term forecasts as well as short-term forecasts. Because of the number of calculations involved, it is not useful for studies involving a large number of geographic or political entities unless it is available as a computer program and all of the birth and death data are readily available.

A disadvantage of the basic cohort-survival model is the lack of a migration component. Various methods of estimating migration can be added to the basic model. The result is then referred to as a cohort-component method.

COHORT-COMPONENT

The Bureau of Census' Component Method I uses school enrollment data to estimate the migration component. Net migration is assumed to be the difference between the growth rate of school-age cohorts at the national level and the growth rate of school-age population at the geographic scale of interest.

Component Method II, currently in use by the Bureau of the Census, also uses school enrollment to estimate migration, but the migration component is assumed to be the difference between the anticipated school-age population, based on natural increase, and the actual population of school age. This is one of the most widely used methods at all levels of government (Morrison, 1971). A variation of the Component II method is the grade progression method that breaks down school enrollment by grades. Cohort component methods are effective in creating alternative projection sets because of the simplicity of varying assumptions. For example, one may use high fertility with low migration or vice versa.

The methods provide good detail but are flawed because, unless specifically modified, they develop migration estimates from data pertinent only to families with school-age children. Young married couples, elderly, and single migrants are underestimated. Many of the migrants may be included by birth and death components, which further underestimate total migration.

Other migration estimates can be obtained by extrapolating migration trends from past decades, or by a ratio-correlation method that relates migration to symptomatic data or dwelling units. The advantages and disadvantages of trend-extrapolation and ratio-correlation methods will be discussed under noncomponent models.

COMPOSITE

The composite model applies different techniques to different segments of the total population. Like the component method, it uses age-specific information on births and deaths. Instead of analyzing and projecting the three components of population change, however, the composite method projects population for different age groups using different methods and then sums them for a total population figure. It takes advantage of the fact that different methods are better focused for estimating population of different age groups. In the Bogue & Duncan method, for example, death rates are used to determine population survivors of forty-five years and over, fertility rates to determine population under five years and the Component II method to determine school-age children of five to fourteen years. Other indicators can be used in other composite methods.

The composite model can be used both for estimating and projecting. Advantages of this method are that it provides good detail and can make use of a variety of available indicators (Morrison, 1971). It may be used at state, county, or local levels, depending upon the particular indicator variables used. It is probably most valuable as an estimation technique at the local level. Like the component technique, the composite projection is well suited for developing several projection sets.

A disadvantage of the Bogue & Duncan method is that the migration component will be underestimated with the use of Component Method II. Another risk, noted by Morrison (1971), is that male cohorts in the fifteen to forty-four age range are estimated from the number of female cohorts aged fifteen to forty-four. This compounds any errors in the original determination of the number of females.

Noncomponent Methods

TREND EXTRAPOLATION

Nearly all projection methods extrapolate past or present trends into the future, to some extent. In most discussions of the subject, however, a trend extrapolation model refers specifically to a naive projection model that uses the historical growth pattern to project the future growth pattern. In particular, the extrapolation model deals with the net effects of births, deaths, and migration rather than with the individual components. After graphing past population growth, (either the actual numbers of people or the rates of growth,) one fits a curve to that growth and extends it into the future. Past growth may show a linear, exponential, or logistic curve over the historic period. Linear and nonlinear regression formulas can also be used. Ordinary graph paper expresses time and population in evenly spaced increments of absolute increase. A semi-log graphing technique expresses population growth in logarithms and time in absolute increments of increase, and double logarithm extrapolation expresses both population and time as logarithms. For each pattern, appropriate mathematical formulas are available for extending the trend into the future.

Extrapolation techniques need not express population as a function of time. For estimation purposes, population can also be related to historic trends in employment, school enrollment, housing units, motor vehicle registrations, or other symptomatic data.

The advantages of the trend extrapolation technique are the simplicity of the basic model and its utility when historic Census counts are the only reliable data available. For slow-growth areas and for short-term estimations and projections of five to ten years, extrapolation methods generally fare no better nor worse than other methods. If the analyst has enough knowledge of local conditions to select the best time-period trend to extend into the future, the method is fairly reliable. Extrapolation can also be used as a point of comparison with other methods or as a measure of what could happen if current trends were to continue into the future. The method is also useful when time and budget limitations call for a single method to be used for a large number of MCDs with varying data bases.

The prime disadvantage of trend extrapolation methods is the lack of component detail. Relationships among births, deaths, and migration are not available, and these components may have diverging trends of their own that will lead to a different net growth pattern in the future. In fact, that a particular curve happens to fit the historic pattern is mere coincidence and may have no relation to future growth. The method is least appropriate in areas where rapid migration is (or has been) the primary component of population change. This often occurs at the minor civil division (MCD) level—the same level of analysis that may have only historic data available for input. Pittenger (1976) notes that using trend extrapolation without an understanding of the factors affecting the migration component has several pitfalls. For instance, rapidly increasing college enrollments during the 1960s produced high population gains in cities near colleges. Other localities experienced rapid growth after the construction of new transportation facilities provided greater access to metropolitan areas.

Another problem with projecting past trends into the future is that future population growth rates become dependent upon the depth of the historical period analyzed (Pittenger, 1976). If the past twenty-five years are examined, for instance, the projections may be influenced by rapid population growth that took place during the 1950s, but if the past five or ten years are used for analysis, projections will be considerably different in many regions. A third and somewhat obvious problem inherent in the extrapolation method is that historically high growth trends will be continued into the future. The resulting projection of population growth may be absurdly high if no limiting factors or subjective judgment are used. Declines may be extrapolated to below zero population growth projections.

Despite their obvious shortcomings, extrapolation methods are the simplest and probably the most cost-effective means of making short-term minor civil division projections. In an effort to improve their accuracy, Isserman (1975) has tried to determine which of twelve extrapolation techniques fit communities with particular characteristics, such as agriculture, decline, small, urban, wealthy, and others. His hybrid model approach casts aside sophistication in favor of finding those models that work best for given situations.

COMPARATIVE FORECASTING

In comparative forecasting, the locality's past growth pattern is examined in conjunction with growth patterns of older, larger, minor civil divisions. The assumption behind this method is that the locality's growth pattern will match that of a community that is currently at a more advanced stage of growth. Ideally, social, economic, political, and other variables should also be matched.

Like trend extrapolation, comparative forecasting is a simple method involving minimal data manipulation, and using only historic data as input. It is a useful method for short-term projections, but it is not used as an estimating mechanism. Isard (1960) notes that this method may work best for areas on the periphery of an expanding metropolitan area. Because of the nature of the technique, it is used only at local and county levels of analysis.

The disadvantages of this method are the same as those for the simple extrapolation method. Only net population growth is observed. There may be no reason to assume that factors currently affecting the components of population will produce the pattern of net growth exhibited by the older MCD. In addition, there may be uncertainty about the kind of MCD the locality will pattern itself after—one that grew slowly or one that grew rapidly.

RATIO TREND

The ratio trend technique assumes that the relationship of a minor civil division to a larger geographic entity will prevail in the future. For instance, if the city had 10 percent of the county's population in 1970, it will have 10 percent of the county's projected population for 1980 and 1990. Or, if the city's share of the county's population has been growing over the years, its share will continue to increase according to the same pattern in the future. This method can also be categorized as a *stepdown* technique. It takes advantage of the fact that population projections at the large scale may represent degrees of reliability and component detail that are not possible to achieve at the small scale of analysis. Thus, the large-scale projections act as a constraint on potential population levels for aggregations of smaller geographic entities. Stepdown methods may have more than one "step." Local population projections have been computed by starting with national level projections. The method is used for long-range as well as short-range projection periods.

As with extrapolation techniques, the method is flawed in that historic trends may not be future trends, and the length of the historical period used for determining the ratios will influence future growth rates. Jerome Pickard (1967) attempted to mitigate the latter shortcoming by using short historical periods for short-term projections and long periods for long-term projections. By transforming a locality's percentage share of population into logarithms, changes in a town's share of population can be expressed as differences between logarithms, or as differences between complements of logarithms in the case of very rapidly growing areas. In this way, the recent past is weighted more heavily (Pickard, 1967; Pittenger, 1976). Of course, the use of longer past periods to project longer future periods is of questionable value. Sometimes, there is no simple historic relationship between, for example, the city and the county. In these cases, the authors suggest that the two entities' growth rates can be averaged and projected into the future.

DENSITY CEILING

The density ceiling model employs capacity constraints. It assumes that when a given density is reached population will either stabilize or decline. The density model may utilize linear, exponential, or logistic curves to express population density growth rates. The modified exponential model uses a predetermined ceiling for potential total population and forces projected growth rates to decrease continually so that the ceiling capacity is never reached. It is included in this category because maximum population levels are typically determined via zoning and land use developments that affect population density.

A density model developed by Bruce Newling (1968) uses an empirically determined set of "critical densities" for urban, rural, and suburban areas. These are determined by linear regression, using logarithms of past population ratios and logarithms of past population densities. When the critical density is reached, further population growth spills over into MCDs that have not reached their critical density. The Newling Model assumes an inverse relationship between growth and density, so growth slows as the critical density is approached. A table for classifying MCDs as rural, suburban, or urban based on the New Jersey experience is also included in Newling's model (Newling, 1968; Greenberg, 1972; Greenberg, Krueckeberg, Mautner, 1973).

The advantages of density ceiling models are that they provide practical means of constraining the levels of population projections, and they provide empirical detail regarding probable distribution and concentrations of people, and allow one to experiment with zoning changes. A community could, for example, examine the public-cost implications of *different housing concentration policies.* The density ceiling models are the reverse of stepdown from larger political to smaller political region methods because the analyst determines county or state level population by aggregating the populations of smaller geographic entities. The density ceiling method may actually be more effective for middle and long-range projection periods than for short-range periods which are too brief to indicate capacity density levels. Density ceiling models are not usually used for estimating current population. Our experience suggests that the Newling Model works best in metropolitan areas.

The obvious disadvantage of the density ceiling methods is the accurate selection of maximum densities. In some cases, erroneous estimating of maximum densities invalidates the projections; in other cases, zoning regulations and land use undergo unexpected changes. The rate at which a locality is projected to reach maximum density appears to be based on trend extrapolation patterns. As such, these methods are subject to the same flaws as methods that extrapolate net population growth. Perhaps this explains why density ceiling methods work best for middle and long-range projection periods. Maximum capacity estimates may be reasonable, but the speed with which they are attained may have been estimated inaccurately. A particular drawback of the Newling Model is that it does not directly incorporate local idiosyncrasies, such as large parks or other undevelopable areas. In cases where these areas exist, if the information is available, the analyst must alter the model by using a reduced land area to represent only the amount of developable or developed land.

RATIO CORRELATION

The ratio correlation method is an estimating technique rather than a projection technique. It is similar to the ratio trend method except that population is treated as a function of some other variable—jobs, housing units, motor vehicle registrations, or other symptomatic data. Multiple regression may be used to determine the population's historic relationship to the independent variables. Current shares or logarithms of past shares may also express the relationships among the variables. Projections of these variables at state or county levels are then applied to the local level. For example, a city with 14 percent of the county's housing units in 1970 will presumably have 14 percent of the county's housing units in 1975. Family-size multipliers determined from the regression equation are used to translate the total housing units into total population.

The advantage of this method is that it uses indicators of actual population to determine growth rates. Depending on the indicator variables used, it provides good detail on spatial or occupational distributions of population. The method is effective at the local level, where it can make use of a wide variety of data types, and is a fairly common method of updating population counts between Censuses.

The ratio correlation method is useful for updating population prior to making population projections, but would be too time consuming if a large number of MCDs were involved. A particular problem with the use of regression, noted by Isard (1960), is that a high degree of statistical correlation between population and some other variable may be coincidental rather than causal. The method is not used for projections unless there is reason to assume that methods used to project the independent variables will be more accurate than methods for projecting the population itself or that the data are more reliable. In such a case, determination of future housing shares or family-size multipliers adds further risk to the accuracy of resulting population projections.

Housing Unit

The housing unit method is a technique used for both projection and estimation purposes. It establishes a relationship between the number of dwelling units and population via a family-size multiplier. Dwelling units can be estimated by utility connections, telephone connections, home interviews, land use surveys, vacancy rates, construction data, building permits, and other local records. Net changes in dwelling units are presumed to indicate net changes in population (Morrison, 1971).

Advantages of the method are that it provides good detail and indicates new geographic areas of growth prior to other records (Morrison, 1971). It is fairly popular among MCDs that develop their own projections, but, at larger scales of analysis, the detailed data needed to determine the multipliers and maintain the housing unit estimates may be derived from the public use sample of the Census (Archer, 1977). The method is best used for short- or mid-term projections. The drawback is the possibility of compounding errors regarding the relationships of variables when housing units are determined from housing indicator variables and then population is determined from housing units (Morrison, 1971). Any time an additional step is required, the chances for data errors to surface is increased.

Market Force

At the local scales, in the last two decades, there have been intensified efforts to control residential land use by relating it to such supply and demand factors as jobs, zoning, the location of transportation nodes, and the development of nonresidential land uses. Included in the broad classification are the following techniques: holding capacity, deterministic regression models, multiplier studies, and mathematical programming (Miernyk, 1970; Brown, Horton, and Wittick, 1970; Herbert and Stevens, 1960; Lakshmanan, 1964; Harris, 1973; Bjornstad, 1975; U.S. Water Resources Council, 1972). Holding capacity studies set limits to population by analyzing zoning ordinances, terrain, and trends in household size. However, zoning ordinances have proven to be quite flexible under the financial and, more recently, legal pressures of developers and highway planners. This technique is generally considered poorly suited for rural areas in the path of suburban development.

The remaining market force methods are much more complex causal models. Linear regression may be used to formulate equations that will relate population distribution to such factors as vacant land, the presence of minority group populations, accessibility to work, land values, and other important variables. Employment forecasts made by shift and share, economic base, and input-output techniques may be converted by the use of multipliers to population forecasts. Finally, the future distribution of population may be treated by a procedure to improve conditions in which an objective such as minimizing travel time to work is sought, subject to equations representing constraints on supply of developable land, demand for land, availability of services, and other factors. There is a greater possibility for successful application of these models, at the state and regional scales, than at the local government scale because more information about causal relationships is available there. Two interesting examples of market force studies will be briefly described. Miernyk and associates used an interindustry analysis of West Virginia (1970) to estimate labor-force requirements by industry group. The labor-force estimates were matched with labor skills possessed by West Virginia citizens. The difference between the supply of and demand for labor was translated into expected migration. Migration, in turn, was converted into population.

The Office of Business Economics (Dept. of Commerce) and the Economic Research Service (Dept. of Agriculture) (OBERS) prepare population estimates for the nation, the states, and metropolitan regions. Employment, income, and other projections are developed by using a variety of simple models, for example, shift and share analysis to estimate employment requirements, and the conversion of these estimates into population projections (U.S. Water Resources Council, 1972).

While population projections are produced by the market force studies, it should be noted that they are usually by-products of studies that are focused on economic growth, transportation, environment, and other concerns. Accordingly, the demographic component of the model is a compromise to financial restrictions on the research.

GREENBERG-KRUECKEBERG-MAUTNER (GKM)

The GKM chain model asks for information for different scales of analysis. It offers historical extrapolation, ratio trend, and density ceiling alternatives at the local government scale and constrains these with federal-state-county population projections developed by component and market force techniques.

The model input begins with federal projections for the national level as a constraint on state growth. These projections are stepped-down to the state level via the states' estimated future share of the national population. Up to six states can be included in the analysis. The model automatically sets up an additional dummy state to hold the remainder of the national population. Instead of stepping-down national projections to the state level, a set of state population projections may be used as input. In this latter case, the national total is not a constraint because the state growth is not held to a particular percentage of the national population. If the user wants to avoid federal projections, the federal input step can be eliminated by using the state's (or states') numbers instead of the federal's. Regional projections may be substituted for federal and state numbers.

The next steps in the model are to step-down the state projections to the county level, and then to step-down the county projections to the minor civil division level. The user must insert data for the county and MCD projections. The model uses these projection values to determine the distribution of population in order to step-down the county projections to the MCD scale.

The model gives the user the option of five separate models to project local population (MCD models 1–5). The first two are Newling models based on critical density. The difference between the two is in the way local growth is adjusted to the county constraints. In Model 1, 1970 density information is used as a starting point for the projections. MCD density-derived projections are adjusted to county totals using either the MCD growth rates or the MCD shares of county population. In Model 2, 1950 density information is used as a starting point. The model projects population for the 1950–70 period and the user can compare the computer results with the actual 1950–70 growth. If the results are accurate the use of the model for projecting future growth is presumed accurate. MCD populations are adjusted to county levels by adding to or subtracting from the MCD's that showed the lowest or highest rates of population to change. Model 1 is recommended because it has produced more accurate results than Model 2.

The other three models (MCD models 3, 4, and 5) are extrapolation methods. Model 3 is based on the availability of continuous projections for the MCDs for every decade from the base year to the target year. Model 4 is similar, but is used for MCDs that have discontinuous projections—for example, projections that jump from 1970 to 1990 with no intervening projection figures. Models 3 and 4 extrapolate the projection of the population of the MCDs implied in projections made by county planners. Briefly, we do not accept the actual projections made by county and local planners; however, we do use the distributional properties of their projections.

Model 5 is an historical extrapolation model and is used when no MCD projections are available. It develops projections by extrapolation of five censuses of historical data (e.g. 1930 to 1970). The GKM model demands that all MCDs within any single county have the same type of projection data—continuous, discontinuous, or historical—so that the same submodel can be used. However, different submodels can be used for different counties.

The methods involved appear quite involved compared to some of the other projection methods, but can be explained by the intent of the model. The Greenberg-Krueckeberg-Mautner model is designed for use by state or regional level agencies in projecting populations for numerous civil divisions. At this scale of analysis, it is necessary to use data sources and methods that apply equally to all of the towns and cities involved. Since the quantity and quality of detail regarding housing-unit updates, age-sex distributions, etc., will vary among the minor civil divisions, historical data projections at the federal, state, and county level represent the only data sources that are typically available. Therefore, the step-down approach is appropriate. Finally, the model is replicable and easily altered. Different development policies at the federal, state, regional, and county scales may be studied. If the density ceiling model is used, the implications of different density strategies can be examined.

Potential disadvantages of this model can be ascertained from previous discussions of extrapolation, step-down (ratio), and density ceiling methods. One additional disadvantage is that, whereas state and county projections are usually available, the agencies that produce the minor civil division and county projections use different methods and data. Accordingly, in the worst case, this complex chain model may compound inaccurate projections at each step rather than reduce the differences among projections made by different methods for different geographical scales.

Chapter 2
The Overall,
State, and County Models

An Overview of Programmed Population Models
Presented in this Section

The previous section briefly weighed the relative advantages of alternative techniques for making small area projections. The authors are convinced that the most rational, though far from the most simple, procedure for making projections for numerous entities requires the use of a combination of models, each of which alone has one or more weaknesses, but which taken together are sound. Exhibit 2.1 presents a flow diagram of the population projection procedures presented in this volume.

The State Model

A major objective of the state population model, as well as all models described in this and subsequent chapters, is to utilize as fully as possible the best existing projections available at each geographic level of the problem, i.e., the nation, states, counties, and MCDs. We believe that the cohort-survival models of the U.S. Bureau of the Census are the most appropriate to the nation as a whole and to the states. The model assumes a set of national projections for the full projection period, from 1980 to

2020. These estimates of national growth may be selected from among the various projection series available. (See, for example, U.S. Bureau of the Census, April 1972; December 1972; and others in bibliography.) These inputs act as a growth ceiling for the state projection models in that the sum of projection for all states must equal the given national total for each decade.

The following notation will be used throughout the chapter:

$$
\begin{aligned}
S &= \text{State Population} \\
N &= \text{Nation Population} \\
C &= \text{County Population} \\
i &= \text{State } i \\
j &= \text{County } j \\
\ell &= \text{Number of States} \\
\ell + 1 &= \text{Dummy state} \\
t &= \text{Base time period} \\
d &= \text{Last time period} \\
g &= \text{Growth series (H = high series, M = medium series)} \\
r &= \text{Growth ratio for a decade} \\
\bar{r} &= \text{Average growth ratio for a state or county for each growth series} \\
S^* &= \text{Unadjusted state population} \\
N^* &= \text{Unadjusted nation population}
\end{aligned}
$$

The inputs for the states consist of the population size of each state for each decade, beginning with 1930 up to and including the last decade of available projections, which might be the year 1990 based on current U.S. Bureau of the Census projections for the states. (See, for example, U.S. Bureau of the Census, March 1972.) At this point, two time series of projections are introduced and carried through the state model and all subsequent county and MCD models of growth. These two series may represent two alternative sets of assumptions concerning migration, birth rate, or other variables. Thus, from this point on, one projects *two values* for every state, county, or MCD, for each point in time. The basis for selecting and specifying these alternative time series is discussed later in this chapter.

The principal tasks of the state model are to extend the state projections to the year 2020 (if they do not extent that far in the input data) and to adjust the various series and states to the given national constraint.

We are restricted to handling six states in the program.

The user must specify in the option control card, discussed in Chapter 6, the year that marks the last decade of state projections in the input

EXHIBIT 2.1

FLOW DIAGRAM OF ALTERNATIVE PROJECTION MODELS

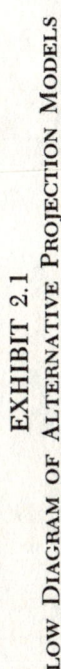

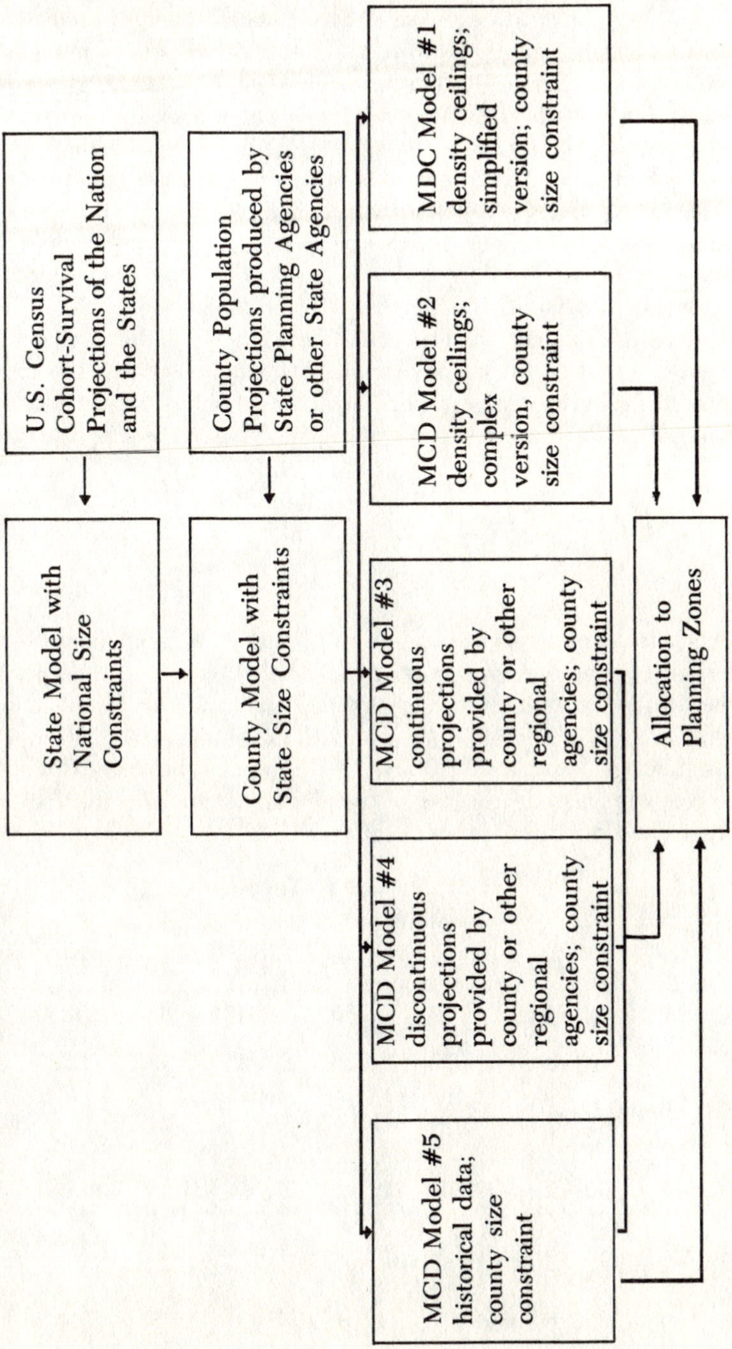

U.S. Census Cohort-Survival Projections of the Nation and the States

County Population Projections produced by State Planning Agencies or other State Agencies

State Model with National Size Constraints

County Model with State Size Constraints

MDC Model #1 density ceilings; simplified version; county size constraint

MCD Model #2 density ceilings; complex version, county size constraint

MCD Model #3 continuous projections provided by county or other regional agencies; county size constraint

MCD Model #4 discontinuous projections provided by county or other regional agencies; county size constraint

MCD Model #5 historical data; county size constraint

Allocation to Planning Zones

data. This year must be the same for all states. Thus, if projections to the year 2000 are put in for one state, all other states must also have projections to 2000. Furthermore, all state projections put in must be consistent with the national projections put in, for the program will not alter and adjust the state projections that are given by the input data.

The first step in the program is to determine if the last decade of input projections "d" is 2020. If so, the program moves on to the county model, accepting as given the full range of the state projections series. If, however, (d) is less than 2020, say 1990, then the state series must be extended to 2020. This extension is made as follows.

Since the number of states (ℓ) is limited to six, a dummy state must be created to represent the balance of the nation, so that the projections, after they have been extended, can be adjusted proportionally to the national total. Thus, a dummy state $(S^{\ell+1})$ is created in Equation (2.1).

$$\text{Eq. (2.1)} \qquad S_t^{\ell+1,g} = N_t - \sum_{i=1}^{\ell} S_t^{i,g}, \quad t = (1, \ldots d).$$

This calculation first sums the given (input) state populations $(S^i, i = 1. \ell)$ for each of the two growth series $(g = H, M)$, and each time period (t). It then finds the difference between this sum and the given national total (N_t) and assigns the difference to the dummy state. Throughout this program $t = 1$ implies 1930 and $t = 10$ implies the year 2020.

We will illustrate the use of the dummy state with some hypothetical data, omitting specification of (g).

POPULATION (Thousands)

(Projected)

	1930	1940	1950	1960	1970	1980	1990
S^1	700	740	760	800	810	850	900
S^2	940	1,052	1,333	2,052	2,182	2,220	2,351
S^3 (dummy state)	?	?	?	?	?	?	?
Nation	73,922	79,298	90,795	107,594	121,944	140,279	161,804

Eq. (2.1) $S^3_{1930} = 73,922 - (700 + 940) = 72,282$

$S^3_{1940} = 79,299 - (740 + 1052) = 77,507$

Other calculations of S^3 made as above follow:

POPULATION (Thousands)

	1930	1940	1950	1960	1970	1980	1990
S^3	72,282	77,507	88,702	104,742	118,949	137,209	158,553

Next we extrapolate the growth of each state, including the dummy state, based on the trend from 1930 to (d), the end of available projections. For this purpose we use an exponential model (the rationale is explained in Chapter 3) with constrained ratios that works as follows:

Eq. (2.2)
$$r_t^{ig} = \frac{S_t^{ig}}{S_{t-1}^{ig}}, \quad t = (2, \ldots d)$$

The ratio of growth for each decade is calculated as in Equation (2.2). For example, if the population of a state in 1940 was 400,000 and in 1930 was 300,000, then the rate, for 1940, would be 1.33.

Eq. (2.2) for S^1

$$r_{1940/1930} = \frac{740}{700} = 1.0571$$

$$r_{1950/1940} = \frac{760}{740} = 1.0270$$

The r values for S^1 for all the time periods are produced below:

r VALUES

State	1940/1930	1950/1940	1960/1950	1970/1960	1980/1970	1990/1980
S^1	1.0571	1.0270	1.0526	1.0125	1.0494	1.0588

Values for S^2 and S^3 are also calculated in the program.

The next step is to find the mean of all rates for each state, by growth series (g), as

Eq. (2.3)
$$\bar{r}^{ig} = \frac{\sum_{t=2}^{d} r_t^{ig}}{d-1}.$$

To diminish the effects of extreme and unusual values of (r) on the calculated mean, two constraints are placed on Equations (2.2) and (2.3). First, where either the numerator or denominator of $r = 0$, (r) is not calculated. Second, where (r) is calculated and found to be greater than 1.5 or less than .5, it is constrained to equal 1.5 and .5, respectively. These limits can, of course, be raised or lowered by the program user by the simple alteration of the two statements in the program (see statements 36000 and 37000). We calculate the $\bar{r}$ value for S^1

Eq. (2.3) $\bar{r}$ for S^1 = (1.0571 + 1.0270 + 1.0526 +
$\qquad\qquad\qquad$ 1.0125 + 1.0494 + 1.0588)/6 =

$$\frac{6.2574}{6} = 1.0429$$

The $\bar{r}$ values for S^1, S^2, and S^3 are as follows:

$\bar{r}^1 = 1.0429$
$\bar{r}^2 = 1.1710$
$\bar{r}^3 = 1.1404$

Next, the mean (r) values are used to extend the population projection for each series as Equation (2.4), where the asterisk (*) implies an unadjusted projection.

Eq. (2.4) $\qquad\qquad S_t^{ig*} = \bar{r}^{ig}(S_{t-1}^{ig})$, $\quad t = (d+1 , \ldots 10)$

$$S_{2000}^{1*} = 1.0429(900) = 938.6$$

UNADJUSTED PROJECTIONS (Thousands)

	$\bar{r}$	2000	2010	2020
S^{1*}	1.0429	938.6	978.9	1,020.9
S^{2*}	1.1710	2,753.0	3,223.9	3,775.2
S^{3*}	1.1404	180,813.8	205,200.1	235,150.6

Finally, all projections from 1980 to 2020 are adjusted proportionally to the given national totals. This is done by first summing the unadjusted projections in Equation (2.5), and then by adjusting them proportionally in Equation (2.6).

Eq. (2.5) $\quad N_t^{g*} = \sum\limits_{i=1}^{\ell+1} S_t^{ig*}$, $t = (6, \ldots 10)$.

Eq. (2.5) $\quad N_{1980}^{*} = 938.6 + 2753.0 + 180,813.8 = 184,505.4$

The other preliminary nation values follow:

	2000	2010	2020
N*	184,505.4	210,402.9	239,946.7

Eq. (2.6) $\quad S_t^{ig} = N_t \left[\dfrac{S_t^{ig*}}{N_t^{g*}} \right]$, $t = (6, \ldots 10)$.

Equation (2.6) is used to adjust the difference between the federal projections that have been given to 2020 and the sum of state projections.

We will assume that the federal projections for the nation in comparison to the sum of preliminary state projections are as follows:

	2000	2010	2020
N	183,067.0	209,848.0	238,298.0
N*	184,505.4	210,402.9	239,946.7

Using Equation (2.6) for S^1

$$S_{2000}^1 = 183,067 \ \frac{938.6}{184,505.4} = 931.3$$

$$S_{2010}^1 = 209,848 \ \frac{978.9}{210,402.9} = 976.3$$

$$S_{2020}^1 = 238,298 \ \frac{1,020.9}{239,946.7} = 1013.9$$

The following are the final projections for S^1, S^2 and S^3 for 2000–2020:

	2000	2010	2020
S¹	931.3	976.3	1,013.9
S²	2,731.5	3,215.4	3,749.3
S³	179,404.2	205,656.3	233,534.8
N	183,067.0	209,848.0	238,298.0

County Projection Model

The county projection model has the same general structure as the state model, but in this case it is the state projections to 2020, generated by the state model, that are given and to which the various counties must be adjusted.

The input data for this program are the population histories of all counties (a maximum number of 100) plus available projections for the counties. A good source of these projections may be state or regional planning agencies (U.S. Bureau of the Census, P-25, No. 454, 1970). The objective is to make use of the distributional properties of state and regional projections, while constraining them by national population totals and a state total generated by analysis at the national scale. Overall, we seek to take advantage of local knowledge of the spatial distribution of growth while avoiding local boosterism and exclusionary biases.

This model is executed on a state-by-state basis, and data sets for all counties in a state must be consistent and complete. By *consistent* we mean that, for our reasoning about the distributional properties to be meaningful, all projections entered for counties of a single state should represent a consistent set emanating from one source or procedure. Also, they should all cover the same projection period, which may reach all the way to 2020. By *complete* we mean that all counties of each state must be accounted for, just as all states of the nation had to be accounted for in the state model. Every county within which MCD projections are going to be made must be separately represented. All others may be aggregated into a dummy county, but this must be done by the user in the county model, whereas in the state model it is done by the program.

After determining the latest year of projections (d), rates of change are calculated, the mean rate is determined, and the projections are extended to 2020, as in Equations (2.7), (2.8), and (2.9).

Eq. (2.7)
$$r_t^{ij} = \frac{C_t^{ij}}{C_{t-1}^{ij}}, \quad t = (2, \ldots d).$$

Eq. (2.8)
$$\bar{r}^{ij} = \frac{\sum_{t=2}^{d} r_t^{ij}}{d-1}.$$

Eq. (2.9)
$$C_t^{ij*} = \bar{r}^{ij}(C_{t-1}^{ij}), \quad t = (d+1, \ldots 10).$$

The calculation of (r) and its mean ($\bar{r}$) is subject to the same two constraints as apply to the states model regarding zero terms and extreme values.

We will illustrate the county calculations with two counties composing sample state 1 (S^1).

	1930	1940	1950	1960	1970	Projected 1980	1990	2000	2010	2020
C^1	207	209	227	246	291	330	370			
C^2	493	531	533	554	519	526	533			
S^1	700	740	760	800	810	850	900	931.3	976.3	1013.9

Counties 1 and 2 have projections to the year 1990; the state projection is taken from our work in the previous step.

Eq. (2.7) for C^1

$$r_{1940/1930} = \frac{209}{207} = 1.010$$

$$r_{1950/1940} = \frac{227}{209} = 1.086$$

The remaining r values for C^1 and the values for C^2 are as follows:

r VALUES

County	1940/1930	1950/1940	1960/1950	1970/1960	1980/1970	1990/1980
C^1	1.010	1.086	1.084	1.183	1.134	1.121
C^2	1.077	1.004	1.039	0.937	1.013	1.013

Next, we calculate the $\bar{r}$ for C^1 and C^2. For C^1 equation (2.8) $= \bar{r} =$

$$\frac{(1.010 + 1.086 + 1.084 + 1.183 + 1.134 + 1.121)}{6} = 1.103$$

Thus for C^1; $\bar{r}^1 = 1.103$
and for C^2; $\bar{r}^2 = 1.014$

Equation (2.9) is applied to the 1970 totals to derive preliminary estimates.

$$C^{1*}_{1980} = 1.103 \ (291) = 321.0$$
$$C^{1*}_{1990} = 1.103 \ (321) = 354.1$$

The unadjusted projections for C^1 and C^2 are as follows:

	r	1980	1990	2000	2010	2020
C^{1*}	1.103	321.0	354.0	390.5	430.7	475.1
C^{2*}	1.014	526.3	533.6	541.1	548.7	556.4

The full set of projections is then adjusted to the state growth series via Equations (2.10) and (2.11).

Eq. (2.10)
$$S_t^{i*} = \sum_{j=1}^{m} C_t^{ij*}, \quad t = (6, \ldots 10).$$

Eq. (2.11)
$$C_t^{ijg} = S_t^{ig} \left[\frac{C_t^{ij*}}{S_t^{i*}} \right], \quad t = (6, \ldots 10).$$

Eq. (2.10) $S_{1980}^{1*} = 321.0 + 526.3 = 847.3$

$\qquad\qquad S_{1990}^{1*} = 354.0 + 533.6 = 887.6$

The other preliminary state values follow:

	1980	1990	2000	2010	2020
S^{1*}	847.3	887.6	931.6	979.4	1031.5

Equation (2.11) is used to adjust the difference between the state unadjusted and final projections. The final state projections follow:

	1980	1990	2000	2010	2020
S^1	850.0	900.0	931.3	976.3	1013.9

Using equation (2.11) for C^1

$$C_{1980}^1 = 850.0 \left[\frac{321.0}{847.3} \right] = 322.0; \quad C_{1990}^2 = 900 \left[\frac{354.0}{887.6} \right] = 358.9$$

The following are the final projections for C^1 and C^2 for 1980–2020. (Fractional discrepancies due to rounding errors.)

	1980	1990	2000	2010	2020
C^1	322.0	358.9	390.4	429.3	467.0
C^2	528.0	541.1	541.0	546.7	546.9
S^1	850.0	900.0	931.3	976.3	1013.9

Thus, we have a set of population histories and projections, ranging from 1930 to 2020 ($t = 1\ldots 10$), for separate growth series (g) for each county (j) in each state (i).

Selecting Alternative Projection Series for the Nation, States, and Counties

The chief distinction among alternative national projections cited earlier in this chapter lies in the fertility rates. Bureau of the Census models of the nation tend to make uniform or nearly uniform assumptions regarding the migration and mortality components of demographic change. To make a choice among projection series' fertility rates, we suggest studying the historical record, weighing the factors that will affect the future fertility rates, and considering the risks of making a wrong (too high or too low) choice and its implications concerning the decisions to which the population projections are addressed.

The choice lies finally in the best judgement of the user. In some cases, for decisionmaking purposes, the analyst may prefer to be on the high side. In other cases, a conservative approach may dictate seeking a minimum value, and a low series will be chosen. Some additional references that may be useful in this choice follow: Keyfitz, 1972; U.S. Commission on Population Growth and the American Future, 1972; Bogue, 1969.

For projections of the populations of the states, we again strongly recommend the work of the U.S. Bureau of the Census. It is at this point in our model that the two separate projection series are introduced. These are designated in the programs as Series H and Series M. The two series chosen here may represent a high and a low series, a median and a high, or a median and a low, depending on the decision under consideration. On the other hand, the two choices may simply represent a set of different assumptions based on migration, fertility, or some other basis, which may or may not turn out to represent significantly different numbers for the areas being studied. Indeed, the purpose of the projection may be to determine if two sets of assumptions that seem quite different at the state level will have significantly different impacts on certain subareas of the state.

Furthermore, there is no necessity that the state alternatives be directly consistent with the national series. For example, if an "E" fertility series is chosen for the nation, the state series need not be versions of the "E" series at the state level. Because of the creation of the dummy state, representing the balance of the nation in the program, consistency is forced within the program. In other words, if the state fertility rate series chosen for the states is lower than the national rate chosen, the program will simply impute to the dummy state a compensatingly higher fertility rate than the nation's. The only consistency that seems strongly advisable is that among the projections of the various states themselves.

The choice of a projection series for the counties must similarly be based on judgement with respect to the objectives of the analysis and its decisionmaking implications. In addition to the possibility of using the projected county populations published by state and regional agencies, we would also like to point out the possibility of using the model in a more experimental fashion. For example, one could simulate the long-run implications of certain kinds of public policies, such as county-wide zoning restrictions, by artificially limiting some or all of the counties all the way out to 2020 and allowing the models to work out the impacts of this policy at the MCD level.

Chapter 3
MCD Models 3, 4, and 5; Based on Continuous Projections, Discontinuous Projections, and Historical Data Only

This chapter presents two variations on a model that utilizes the distributional properties of available projections for the MCDs of a county in the same manner that the county model used the distributional properties of available projections of the counties of a state. This chapter also presents an MCD model that projects on the basis of the historical record alone. All the models are tied to the county, state, and federal constraints. However, models 3, 4, and 5 can be used to develop short-range unconstrained projections.

In contrast to available state and county projections made at the national and state levels, respectively, it is somewhat common for available county-wide MCD projections to be one-point projections. For example, we may find a projection for all of a county's MCDs for the year 2000, but not for any intervening decades between 1970 and 2000. MCD Model 4 handles this kind of discontinuous projection with an interpolation routine. Model 3 is used where this interpolation routine for intervening unprojected decades is not required. In effect, the two models are the same, but one requires the use of the interpolation routine, the other does not.

The outputs of the county model described in Chapter 2 are taken as given projections to which the total of all MCDs within a county must conform in each of the following three models described.

The following new notation not used in Chapter 2 will be used throughout the chapter:

M = Minor civil division (MCD) population
k = Community k
M* = Unadjusted MCD population
C* = Unadjusted county population
r* = growth rate for discontinuous projection series
n = number of intervening decades with no projections.
M** = preliminary projections for missing decades in a discontinuous series.

MCD Model 3; Using Continuous Projections

This model first determines the last decade (d) for which projections have been input. Again these data must be consistent and complete as these terms were defined in Chapter 2. Growth rates are then calculated and means found for each MCD, computed subject to the constraints on these calculations described in Chapter 2. The equations are as follows, where (k) is the number of the MCDs in county (j) of state (i).

Eq. (3.1)
$$r_t^{ijk} = \frac{M_t^{ijk}}{M_{t-1}^{ijk}}, \quad \begin{array}{l} t = (2, \ldots d) \\ k = (1, \ldots h) \end{array}$$

Eq. (3.2)
$$\bar{r}^{ijk} = \frac{\sum\limits_{t=2}^{d} r_t^{ijk}}{d-1}$$

Then to project to 2020 we compute unadjusted projections for each MCD as

Eq. (3.3) $\quad M_t^{ijk*} = \bar{r}^{ijk}(M_{t-1}^{ijk}), \quad t = (d+1, \ldots 10).$

All projections are then adjusted as illustrated in Equations (3.4) and (3.5).

Eq. (3.4) $\quad C_t^{ij*} = \sum\limits_{k=1}^{h} M_t^{ijk*}, \quad t = (6, \ldots 10).$

Eq. (3.5)
$$M_t^{ijkg} = C_t^{ijg} \cdot \frac{M_t^{ijk*}}{C_t^{ij*}}$$

Equations (3.1)–(3.5) are duplications of the equations used to match the state preliminary projections to the federal constraints and the county preliminary projections to the state constraints. Nevertheless, we will illustrate their application with the following data set:

	Population					Projected				
	1930	1940	1950	1960	1970	1980	1990	2000	2010	2020
M^1	2000	2100	2200	2400	2700	3100	3600	4200	—	—
M^2	8000	10400	12800	15600	19300	22900	30400	35800	—	—
C^1	10000	12500	15000	18000	22000	25000	33000	38000	40000	44000

For example, Eq. (3.1) for M^1

$$r_{1940/1930} = \frac{2100}{2000} = 1.050$$

$$r_{1950/1940} = \frac{2200}{2100} = 1.048$$

The other r values for M^1 and M^2 appear below:

r VALUES

MCD	1940/1930	1950/1940	1960/1950	1970/1960	1980/1970	1990/1980	2000/1990
M^1	1.050	1.048	1.091	1.125	1.148	1.161	1.167
M^2	1.300	1.231	1.219	1.237	1.187	1.328	1.178

Using Equation (3.2), we get the following:

$\bar{r}$ values for M^1 and M^2

$$\bar{r} \text{ for } M^1 = \frac{7.790}{7} = 1.113$$

$$\bar{r} \text{ for } M^2 = \frac{8.680}{7} = 1.240$$

Applying Equation (3.3) we obtain unadjusted projections for M^1 and M^2 for 2010 and 2020.

$$M^{1*}_{2010} = 1.113 \, (4200) = 4675$$
$$M^{1*}_{2020} = 1.113 \, (4675) = 5203$$

The unadjusted projections for M^1 and M^2 are summarized below:

	1980	1990	2000	2010	2020
M^{1*}	3100	3600	4200	4675	5203
M^{2*}	22900	30400	35800	44392	55046

Next, following Equation (3.4) we add the MCD unadjusted projections to obtain an unadjusted county projection.

For $C^{1*}_{1980} = 3100 + 22900 = 26000$

UNADJUSTED AND FINAL COUNTY PROJECTIONS

	1980	1990	2000	2010	2020
C^{1*}	26000	34000	40000	49067	60249
C^1	25000	33000	38000	40000	44000

Finally Equation (3.5) is used to adjust the preliminary MCD projections. For example, for M^1:

$$M^1_{1980} = 25000 \left[\frac{3100}{26000} \right] = 2981$$

$$M^1_{1990} = 33000 \left[\frac{3600}{34000} \right] = 3494$$

The final Model 3 projections for M^1 and M^2 are as follows:

	1980	1990	2000	2010	2020
M^1	2981	3494	3990	3811	3800
M^2	22019	29506	34010	36189	40200
C^1	25000	33000	38000	40000	44000

Notice that, because the preliminary projections for M^2 were relatively high in comparison to the total final projection for C^1, the projections for M^1 and M^2 for 2010 and 2020 were drastically reduced. M^1's population was projected to decline in 2010 and 2020. Clearly, a lack of agreement between analysts at two or more geographical scales will probably result in unsatisfying projections at the smaller area scale.

MCD Model 4; Using Discontinuous Projections

The MCD Model 4 first interpolates projection values for intervening blank decades in the input data. The latest projection decade (d) is located. Then the next latest projection (d-n), and the number of intervening unfilled decades (n) are determined. The model then calculates the growth rate for the period (n) as:

Eq. (3.6)
$$r_n^{ijk**} = \frac{M_d^{ijk}}{M_{d-n}^{ijk}}$$

The implicit growth rate per decade is thus found as:

Eq. (3.7)
$$r^{ijk*} = \sqrt[n+1]{r^{ijk**}}$$

This rate is then used to fill in the intervening empty projection decades, as in:

Eq. (3.8)
$$M_{(d-n)+1}^{ijk} = M_{d-n}^{ijk} \cdot r^{ijk*}$$

The model then proceeds, as MCD Model 3 did, through Equations (3.1), (3.2), (3.3), (3.4), and (3.5).

To illustrate Model 4, suppose the input data were identical to the Model 3 example input data with one exception. The exception is that no initial MCD projections were made for 1980.

Using Equation (3.6), we calculate r* for the 1970 to 1990 period.

$$r_{1990\text{-}1970}^{1*} = \frac{3600}{2700} = 1.333$$

$$r_{1990\text{-}1970}^{2*} = \frac{30400}{19300} = 1.575$$

The implicit growth rate for the 1970–1980 and 1980–1990 decades is calculate' from Equation (3.7).

$$r^{1*} = (\text{\textsubscript{} } 333)^{1/2} = 1.155$$
$$r^{2*} = (1.\text{\textsubscript{} } 75)^{1/2} = 1.255$$

Equation (3.8) is then used to fill in the 1980 projection.

$$M^{1**}_{1980} = 2700 \, (1.155) = 3119$$
$$M^{2**}_{1980} = 19300 \, (1.255) = 24222$$

The preliminary figures for M^1 and M^2 are summarized below:

						Projected		
	1930	1940	1950	1960	1970	1980	1990	2000
M^{1**}	2000	2100	2200	2400	2700	(3119)	3600	4200
M^{2**}	8000	10400	12800	15600	19300	(24222)	30400	35811
C^1	10000	12500	15000	18000	22000	25000	33000	38000

The model returns next to Equations (3.1)–(3.5) used for the continuous projection case. Equation (3.1) yields the r_t^{ijk} values.

MCD	1940/1930	1950/1940	1960/1950	1970/1960	1980/1970	1990/1980	2000/1990
M^1	1.050	1.048	1.091	1.125	(1.155)	(1.155)	1.167
M^2	1.300	1.231	1.219	1.237	(1.255)	(1.255)	1.178

Equation (3.2) yields the $\bar{r}^{ijk}$ values

$$\bar{r} \text{ for } M^1 = 1.113$$
$$\bar{r} \text{ for } M^2 = 1.239$$

Equation (3.3) estimates the unadjusted projections for 2010 and 2020. The unadjusted projections are as follows:

	1980	1990	2000	2010	2020
M^{1*}	3119	3600	4200	4675	5203
M^{2*}	24222	30400	35800	44356	54957

Next, using Equation (3.4) an unadjusted county total is obtained and compared to the constrained county total.

	1980	1990	2000	2020	2020
C^{1*}	27341	34000	40000	49031	60160
C^1	25000	33000	38000	40000	44000

Equation (3.5) adjusts the MCD projections.

For $M^1_{1980} = 25000 \left[\frac{3119}{27341} \right] = 2852$

$$M^1_{1990} = 33000 \left[\frac{3600}{34000} \right] = 3494$$

The final population projections for MCD Model 4 are summarized below:

	1980	1990	2000	2010	2020
M^1	2852	3494	3990	3814	3805
M^2	22148	29506	34010	36186	40195
C^1	25000	33000	38000	40000	44000

The final projections from Models 3 and 4 are quite similar, though they will not be in all cases, particularly if two or more decades are missing in sequence (e.g. 1980, 1990, 2000).

MCD Model 5; Based on Historical Data Only

Model 5 is, in a sense, our model of last resort. It assumes that no projections are available and that the density constraint models are not appropriate. Projections for 1980 to 2020 must then be made on the basis of the historical record alone and adjusted to the county projections. Where the other MCD models are viable options, this model can still be computed and used for comparative purposes.

Of the various demographic trend models (as discussed in Chapter 1), the exponential growth-rate model was chosen for use here in MCD Model 5, as well as in the state, county, and MCD Models 3 and 4. First, we desired a simple consistent technique throughout. Experimentation showed that due to the nature of the successive constraints applied from the national to state, from state to county, from county to MCD, it made little difference in most cases which trending technique was used, particularly where extrapolation was required for only two or three decades.

The most significant difference caused by the trending technique seemed to be the effect it had on places with declining populations. The advantage of the exponential model in comparison to an arithmetic change increment model is that no entity, e.g. MCD, is ever forced to zero population. This seemed desirable for two reasons. First, we wished to be on the conservative (high) side of any projection made for our particular application to nuclear power plant siting. This is particularly important where the power plant site may be located in one of these declining-population locations. The siting-decision process is particularly sensitive to populations located near the plant. Second, although ghost towns exist, they are unusual, and there have been historically many behavioral factors that retard outmigrations from declining areas.

The procedures of MCD Model 5 are the same as those previously described. The latest decade (d) is set at 1970 (t = 5) and rates are calculated and their means found. These rates are then used to construct unadjusted projections to the year 2020, and these are then adjusted to county totals as in Equation (3.5).

Once again returning to Equations (3.1)–(3.5), we illustrate the use of MCD Model 5.

	1930	1940	1950	1960	1970
M^1	2000	2100	2200	2400	2700
M^2	8000	10400	12800	15600	19300
C^1	10000	12500	15000	18000	22000

Equation (3.1) produces r^{ijk} values.

MCD	1940/1930	1950/1940	1960/1950	1970/1960
M^1	1.050	1.048	1.091	1.125
M^2	1.300	1.231	1.219	1.237

Equation (3.2) produces $\bar{r}$ values.

$\bar{r}$ for M^1 = 1.079

$\bar{r}$ for M^2 = 1.247

Equation (3.3) yields preliminary unadjusted MCD projections and, when added, equation (3.4) yields an unadjusted county projection.

	1980	1990	2000	2010	2020
M^{1*}	2913	3143	3392	3660	3949
M^{2*}	24067	30012	37425	46668	58195
C^{1*}	26980	33155	40817	50328	62145
C^{1}	25000	33000	38000	40000	44000

Equation (3.5) is used to produce the final projections:

	1980	1990	2000	2010	2020
M^{1}	2699	3128	3158	2909	2796
M^{2}	22301	29872	34842	37091	41204
C^{1}	25000	33000	38000	40000	44000

Chapter 4
Minor Civil
Division Projections:
Two Versions Based
On Density Ceilings

The projections of the county model described in Chapter 2 are accepted as given. As alternatives to MCD Models 3, 4, and 5, we offer in this chapter two additional models that project population on the basis of density ceilings. One (MCD Model 2) consists of a model developed by Newling and two additional steps based on correcting MCD projections and then on assigning or subtracting additional increments based on either the projected growth rates or the MCD share of the county population. The other (MCD Model 1) uses the Newling model and either the growth rates or the MCD proportion of the county population to add or subtract increments.

These complex methods are useful because they present a more theoretically comprehensive perspective than Models 3, 4, and 5. While Models 3, 4, and 5 are simpler, systematic, and replicable, their use at this scale at best relies on MCD projections produced at the county level and below. Usually, projections by local planning boards are prepared for only one or two decades into the future and are renowned for their unreliability. County produced projections, and projections from other local sources, tend to either overproject, thereby reflecting a policy of local boosterism, or, more recently, to underproject, thereby reflecting an exclusionary or no-growth policy. "Available forecasts by chambers of commerce are notoriously overoptimistic and projections reported by city planning commissions are seldom an improvement." (Schmitt and Crosetti, 1953). In either case the distinction between projection and policy statement is often muddled.

The Newling Model

The combination of procedures that we chose to use can be applied in a completely systematic manner, but they also allow for some judgment to be exercised. The Newling method involves the derivation of critical population densities for urban, suburban, and rural MCDs. All communities are classified and will converge to one of the critical densities, some like older central cities by losing population, others, like former farmlands adjacent to central cities, by gaining population. Eventually, all of the MCDs in the region will approach a steady state of clearly defined rural, suburban, or urban densities.

Newling originally developed his model after observing an inverse relationship between relative population growth from 1950 to 1960 and population density in 1950 (Newling, 1968). This relationship is expressed in Equation (4.1).

Eq. (4.1) $\quad (1 + r_{d_t}) = A d_t^{-k}$

where $(1 + r_{d_t})$ is the growth ratio, i.e., rate of growth at each density for a given density ceiling group (e.g., urban, rural, suburban.

         A is a constant, for each density ceiling group; it is the growth ratio when the density is one person per unit area,

         k is a constant, for each density ceiling group; it is the ratio of the rate of change of growth to the rate of change of density, and

         d_t is the density at time t.

The density at one time period forward (d_t may be expressed as

Eq. (4.2) $\qquad\qquad d_{t+1} = (1 + r_{d,t})d_t$

$$\text{or,} \qquad = A d_t^{-k} d_t$$

which may be simplified as

Eq. (4.3)
$$d_{t+1} = Ad_t^{1-k} .$$

Equation (4.3) may be generalized for time (t+m) where (m) is any number of intervals.

Eq. (4.4)
$$d_{t+m} = \sqrt[k]{A} \left[\frac{d_t^{(1-k)^m}}{\left(\sqrt[k]{A}\right)^{(1-k)^m}} \right] .$$

The expression in brackets approaches unity as (m) becomes very large. Thus $(A^{1/k})$ is the critical density. Each MCDs future densities are related to its initial density (d_t), the critical density $(A^{1/k})$ of its density ceiling group, and the rate (k) at which all members of the group approach the critical density.

Newling determined the parameters (A) and (k) for three groups of counties by least squares. All communities were classified with reference to their density in 1950 and growth rate from 1950 to 1960 by partitioning the scattergram into segments equally removed from the regression lines. The density of each unit is projected by substituting in Equation (4.4) the appropriate (A) and (k) values and its population density in 1960 is provided as the value of (d_t).

In essence, density acts as a surrogate for a host of previously cited factors responsible for the suburbanization process. For example, the procedure can subsume the decline of old densely developed central cities, the rapid increase and then the leveling off of suburbs, the preservation of lands in rural uses, and other commonly observed phenomena. Tests of the Newling model and of several other previously mentioned techniques showed that in the New York-New Jersey region the Newling model was the most accurate model at the MCD scale (Greenberg, 1972). However, some other potential users have told us that they could not use the model because the density ceiling groups were not distinct in their study regions. The following two sections explain the use of the Newling Model.

Derivation of (A) and (k) Parameters

The parameters are calculated in two steps. First, a scattergram of population densities and growth ratios is prepared. Secondly, regression lines are fitted where distinct linear clusters are formed by the data.

Where the clusters do not appear, the models should not be used to simulate trends. They could, however, be used to estimate the implications of alternative target densities on land use. The above two steps require detailed explanations because the user of the computer programs must estimate these equations.

Exhibits 4.1 and 4.2 present an idealized set of input data for the calibration of the equations. The thirty-two observation units are counties for the time period 1950 to 1970 and the first thirty counties form three distinct linear arrays.

SPATIAL SCALE OF THE INPUT DATA

The county unit rather than the MCD is utilized for devising the parameters because the county should be far more representative of general regional trends and should therefore be less likely to exhibit a unique pattern. In two applications of the Newling model, we have found that more than 90 percent of the counties have fallen into distinct linear clusters.

By contrast, attempts to develop scattergrams from sample MCD data have demonstrated that outliers appear which complicate the process of separating the groups. Statistical techniques for identifying and excluding outliers may be applied to such a classification problem. One experiment indicated, however, that when the outliers were removed, the resulting groups formed linear arrays that closely resembled those developed from the county data. Therefore, we suggest that the user attempt to derive the equations from county data. Procedures for calibrating the parameters when the county data are inadequate are discussed later.

TIME SPAN OF THE INPUT DATA

The two decades 1950–1970 have been selected for the input data based upon our studies in the Northeast United States. These two decades include most of the period of substantial population suburbanization and are therefore a convenient period upon which to base a study of the relationship between growth and population density. A decade may prove to be sufficient in some cases. The longer temporal span, however, has the advantage of including more MCDs that have experienced a steady state. For example, a forecast of the likely transformation of farmland to urban land uses by the planned unit development and the continued thinning out of portions of the central city may be made with slightly more confidence from a longer perspective. A thirty- or forty-year span would presumably increase this perspective further. However, experiments indicate that this longer time span creates intolerably high deviations in MCD Model 2. In general, the user, supported by knowledge of regional growth trends, should be able to identify the appropriate time span by inspection of alternative scattergrams.

AN EXAMPLE

The calculation of the parameters will be illustrated by the data presented in Exhibits 4.1 and 4.2. The first ten observations form a linear cluster of counties that are, or are becoming, densely urbanized. The second set (counties 11-20) might be categorized as suburban and exurban. Finally, the third linear cluster (counties 21-30) consist of low-density rural counties.

EXHIBIT 4.1
ILLUSTRATIVE INPUT DATA

County	Population Density 1950	Average Decade Growth Ratio 1950–70	Log X Population Density 1950	Log Y Average Decade Growth Ratio 1950–70	Classification
1	1,857	1.638	3.2688	0.2143	
2	5,058	1.214	3.7040	0.0842	
3	5,850	1.267	3.7672	0.1028	
4	6,361	1.167	3.8035	0.0671	Urban or
5	8,111	1.019	3.9091	0.0082	Rapidly
6	6,034	1.321	3.7806	0.1209	Urbanizing
7	20,000	1.001	4.3010	0.0004	
8	950	1.900	2.9777	0.2788	
9	2,211	1.580	3.3446	0.1987	
10	16,802	0.968	4.2254	−0.0141	
11	889	1.141	2.9489	0.0573	
12	573	1.383	2.7582	0.1408	
13	86	1.912	1.9345	0.2815	
14	344	1.592	2.5366	0.2019	Suburban
15	506	1.532	2.7042	0.1853	or
16	324	1.453	2.5105	0.1623	Exurban
17	472	1.484	2.6739	0.1714	
18	1,004	1.296	3.0017	0.1126	
19	1,702	1.210	3.2309	0.0828	
20	2,016	1.159	3.3045	0.0641	

EXHIBIT 4.1 (Continued)
ILLUSTRATIVE INPUT DATA

County	Population Density 1950	Average Decade Growth Ratio 1950–70	Log X Population Density 1950	Log Y Average Decade Growth Ratio 1950–70	Classification
21	65	1.431	1.8129	0.1556	
22	82	1.283	1.9138	0.1082	
23	97	1.266	1.9868	0.1024	
24	106	1.212	2.0253	0.0835	
25	168	1.287	2.2253	0.1096	Rural
26	182	1.207	2.2601	0.0817	
27	150	1.163	2.1761	0.0656	
28	251	1.050	2.3997	0.0212	
29	86	1.512	1.9345	0.1796	
30	32	1.783	1.5051	0.2512	
31	50	1.150	1.6990	0.0607	Outlier
32	25	1.500	1.3979	0.1761	Outlier

EXHIBIT 4.2
COUNTY DENSITY AND GROWTH RATIO

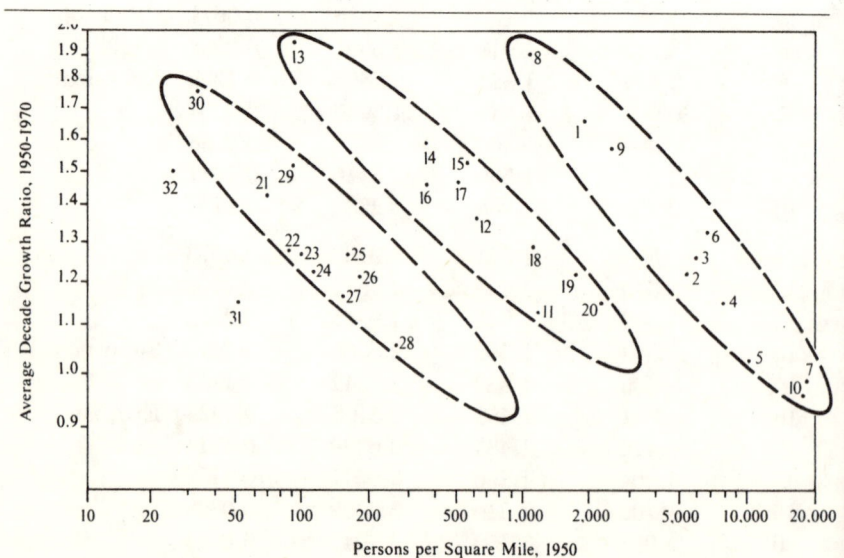

The names of the three groups should be regarded only as a necessary evil intended to aid in the description of the results. The distinction between some counties in different groups may not always be great. For example, counties classified as urban or rapidly urbanizing may, by census definition of urban densities, be rural (density less than 1,500 per square mile) in the base period (e.g., county 8), while counties classified as suburban by the scattergram because of a reduced-growth rate may, by census definition, be urban (e.g., counties 19 and 20).

Least square regression equations are fitted to the logarithmically transformed density and population ratio data in Exhibit 4.1. The (k) and (A) parameters are respectively the slope (with sign changed) and antilog of the intercept of the regression equation. The critical density is derived by solving for the antilogarithm of the expression $(A^{1/k})$. The (A) and (k) parameters, critical density, and Pearsonian correlation coefficient are listed in Exhibit 4.3.

EXHIBIT 4.3
PRELIMINARY PARAMETERS FOR PROJECTING
THE POPULATION OF MINOR CIVIL DIVISIONS

	Urban and Rapidly Urbanizing	Suburban and Exurban	Rural
No. of Counties	10	10	10
A	9.16707	3.96323	3.76920
k	0.23087	0.16376	0.22747
Critical density (persons/sq. mile)	14,718	4,487	341
r	−.967	−.933	−.902

In comparison to Newling's study of New Jersey and the authors' previous studies, this urban critical density is higher and the suburban and the rural densities are relatively low.

The rural critical density was deliberately set lower in order to illustrate one of the decisions that must be made when calibrating the equations. Exhibits 4.1 and 4.2 list and illustrate the positions of two rural counties, 31 and 32. County 31 is clearly an outlier and can be removed by statistical testing for outliers. County 31 may be in reality geographically isolated with few transportation routes linking it to the remainder of the region, or it may be an unfavorable climatic anomaly (e.g., a desert). Local knowledge is most important in deciding how to treat a particular county. County 32 is not so easily dismissed as an anomaly. It may be a large, formerly rural, and isolated county that is rapidly developing in the portion nearest the spreading metropolis.

Exhibit 4.4 illustrates the alternative equations developed by including the two additional counties in the rural group.

EXHIBIT 4.4
ALTERNATIVE PARAMETERS FOR THE RURAL COUNTY GROUP

	With 10 Rural Counties	With County 32	With Counties 31 and 32
No. of Counties	10	11	12
A	3.76920	2.96606	2.58369
k	0.22747	0.17836	0.15219
Critical density persons/sq.mile	341	444	511
r	−.902	−.857	−.727

The differences in this illustrative case, and in many actual cases, are clearly significant enough to warrant great care in making the decision about which counties to include in the model, especially because the user will probably be dealing with small sample sizes. Two guidelines are recommended. First, a selective analysis may be made of growth rate and density characteristics at the MCD scale. Such an analysis may, however, cloud rather than clear the picture. Second, the user, perhaps with the assistance of a local expert, should establish how typical and important the outlier is. For example, if the county is an artifact caused by a political boundary that includes both densely populated and completely undeveloped areas in mountains, then the user should exclude the county. On the other hand, if the unusual county, in the eyes of the user, is a signal of an emerging land use pattern, then the county should be included. For purposes of the illustrative examples that follow, the rural equation has been calculated including county 32.

The Fortran programs include six equations structured in the form of Equation (4.4). Three of the six contain the parameters calibrated in the example: (1) urban, (2) suburban, and (3) rural. When the parameters are redefined and should the need for more than three equations arise, the user need only change the parameters presently in the program. Four constants derived from the Newling model (4.4) must be changed to redefine each equation. The calibration of the constants is illustrated with the urban equation developed in the manual and listed in the program.

const $(1,1)$ = 1/k log A = 4.1678

const $(1,2)$ = $(1 - k)$ = .7691

const $(1,3)$ = (k) = .2309

const $(1,4)$ = log A = .9622

The remaining pieces of equation (4.4) are m and $log\ d_t$. The m denotes the decade. In MCD Model 2, m is 1 = 1960, 2 = 1970, ... 7 = 2020. In MCD Model 1, m is 1 = 1980, 2 = 1990, ... 5 = 2020. d_t is the initial density of the MCD: the 1950 density in MCD Model 2; the 1970 density in MCD Model 1.

INCOMPLETE DATA AND UNCLEAR RELATIONSHIPS

We have suggested that the user should derive the equations from county data. However, if an insufficient number of counties are available, or if the county data do not present a clear array, then MCD data drawn on a random or a stratified random basis (if one pattern is not clear) should be used. Two regions that are likely to present an unclear pattern are the dense urban region that has rural MCDs but few distinctive rural counties and the rural region spotted with periodic, small, but dense, urban developments.

A sample size cannot be specified. Our tests indicate that the user should expect to plot at least fifty MCDs in order to distinguish three linear groups. It is possible that the user may have to utilize the universe of places if the number of potential observations is especially limited.

In the event that the user is unable to achieve clearly distinct groups without pruning the number of observations to the point that the regression lines become subjective manifestations of the researcher's perceptions of urban growth, then we recommend that the technique not be used for projection unless the specific goal is to test a hypothesized pattern of growth and density ceilings.

Classification of the MCDs

All MCDs must be classified with regard to their average decade population growth rate between 1950 and 1970, and their population density in 1950. The classificatory procedure is illustrated in Exhibit 4.5. Dashed lines were drawn on both sides of the suburban regression line

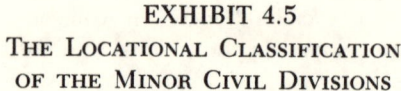

EXHIBIT 4.5
THE LOCATIONAL CLASSIFICATION
OF THE MINOR CIVIL DIVISIONS

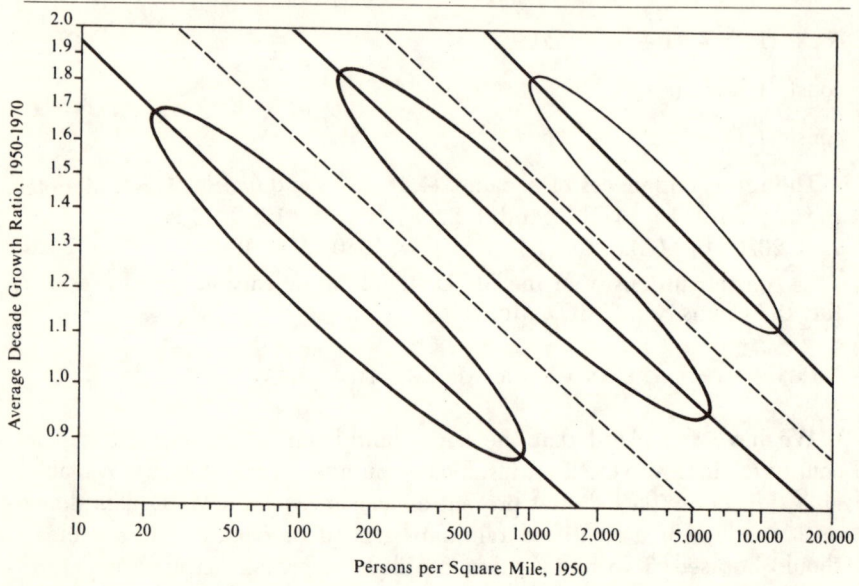

equidistant from the suburban and the urban on the right side and equidistant from the suburban and the rural on the left side.

The dashed lines were used as class boundaries. Each community's 1950 population density and 1950–1970 average decade growth rate were plotted. An MCD found to the right of the right-hand dashed line was classified as urban; it was classified as rural if its coordinates fell to the left of the left-hand boundary; and it was classified as suburban if it fell between the two dashed lines.

This mechanical procedure should be modified if the 1960–1970 growth rate was very different from the 1950–1970 rate, and if specific information regarding an MCD indicates that an important change in its development is likely. For example, if development in a township is legally forbidden because of potential environmental impact (e.g., extremely wet or dry lands), or if a mass transit facility or highway is likely to be constructed within several decades, then the MCD classification should be modified to reflect this knowledge.

The scattergram will identify the anomalous MCD. The town may be an industrial park, or an undevelopable mountain region with no population, or a military base, resort, lighthouse, or a borough of 0.1 square miles with two high-rise structures. In the above cases the user should utilize the net instead of the gross areas or remove the anomalous MCDs from the counties, being sure that the appropriate subtractions are made from the county and state input data.

A second group of counties that are difficult to classify are those falling immediately adjacent to the classification boundary (e.g., MCD 0101002 in the sample problem of Chapters 7 and 8). In such cases we recommend that a local expert be consulted. Overall, both in the calculation of the parameters and in the classification of the MCDs, we cannot overstate the need to utilize special information and local expertise.

Column 10 of the input card is reserved for the classification of the MCDs: (1) urban, (2) suburban, and (3) rural, in this particular case. Numbers 4–6 are also available in the event that more than three equations are developed.

A Brief Example of the Results
Produced by the Newling Model

Projections of population density are obtained from a combination of the community's population density and the appropriate (A) and (k) values. Exhibit 4.6 illustrates how urban MCDs approach an urban critical density derived in prior study.

At this point it is important to distinguish between two versions we have developed. The simpler model uses 1970 as the base density; the more complex form uses 1950 as (d_t). Also, the more complex version predicting from 1950 requires an additional step in adjusting the difference between the Newling model and the county size constraint. The advantages of this more involved version are that by simulating from a 1950 base the user obtains an internal test of the results in the 1970 projection and a spacing out of growth over a longer projection period. A weakness of the more complex model is that accuracy may be lost in the early decades because communities that grew at extraordinarily high rates between 1950 and 1970 as the result of PUDs, for example, will be underprojected by the model for at least two decades or until the model can grow these MCDs up to denser levels. In short, projecting from an earlier base results in deviations from the actual 1970 projections that sometimes will not be completely eliminated in the later decades. By examining the projections in Chapter 8, the reader will note that over the decades the gap between the two versions of the projection model tends to decrease because, as the critical density is approached, the increments of the version closer to the critical density will decrease relative to the second model.

EXHIBIT 4.6
DENSITY PROFILES CALCULATED WITH URBAN PARAMETERS

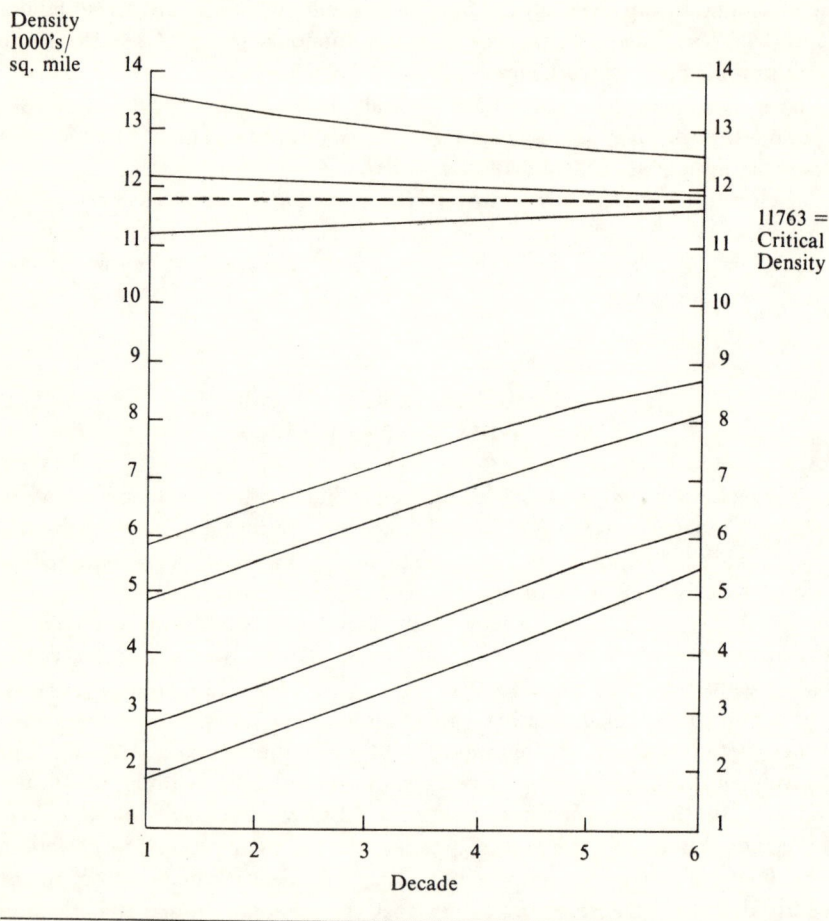

Adjustment of the Preliminary MCD Projections
for MCD Models 1 and 2.

The final steps in MCD Models 1 and 2 require adjusting the preliminary MCD projections to the county projections (constraints). We will be discussing three distinct procedures:

1. Adjustment according to 1970 projection error
2. Adjustment according to comparative growth rate
3. Adjustment according to preliminary projection proportion

We will term them: (1) the 1970 error method, (2) the growth rate method, and (3) the proportion method.

MCD Model 2 always employs the 1970 error method, followed by one of the other two methods. The choice between the other two methods is made by the user and specified in the option card, described in Chapter 6. MCD Model 1 requires the application of only one of the two optional adjustment methods — either the growth-rate method or the proportion method. Whichever of these two is specified by the user will be applied to both MCD Models 1 and 2.

THE 1970 METHOD OF ADJUSTMENT, USED IN MCD MODEL 2 ONLY

MCD Model 1 uses the 1970 actual density in the Newling equations. In contrast, MCD Model 2 begins with the 1950 actual density in order to provide an internal check of the accuracy of the model over a span of two decades. While producing a diagnostic check for the user, overprojection and underprojection errors are accumulated in the 1970 projection. The error method seeks to reduce the difference between the actual and projected populations. The assumption of this first method in MCD Model 2 is that if a model tends to overproject or underproject a known present value, then that same model will tend to also overproject or underproject that value into the future. The first step in this method is to compare each MCD's 1970 preliminary projection with the actual known 1970 population of the MCD. Each MCD is classified as being either overprojected or underprojected by the model, based on this 1970 comparison.

Next the preliminary projections for each decade beyond 1970 are summed for all MCDs within a county and that sum is compared with the two county projections (H) and (M). If the county total has been underprojected by the MCD model (sum of the MCDs < county projection), then an increment up to, but not exceeding, the 1970 underprojection increments of those MCDs classified as being underprojected is added to each MCD so classified (by the 1970 comparison). Likewise, where the MCD model is overprojecting the county (sum of the MCDs > county projection), a subtraction is made from those MCDs classified as overprojected (in the 1970 comparison). If, having made these adjustments, the sums of MCDs do not equal the county projections, then additional increments are added or subtracted by one of the other two methods.

Let us consider an example. Suppose we have a county whos (H) series and (M) series projections for 1980 are those shown in Exhibit 4.7. Suppose, also, that if we sum the 1980 preliminary MCD projections for that county we get 385,000, as shown in Exhibit 4.7. Let us deal only with the

EXHIBIT 4.7
CALCULATION OF COUNTY INCREMENTS

Series	1980 Constraint	Sum of Preliminary MCD Projections for 1980	County Increments (Constraint – Sum of MCDs)
H	400,000	385,000	15,000
M	375,000	385,000	–10,000

(M) series, in which case the county has been overprojected by 10,000. This amount, which is called the "county increment", is subtracted from the MCDs as follows. First, we will not subtract anything from those MCDs that were underprojected by the model in 1970. Thus their preliminary 1980 projections are accepted as suitable for the 1980 (M) series and left untouched by this method. Next, we look at the remaining MCDs that were overprojected in 1970, and sum the total of their overprojection increments and call this total the sum of the (X) vector, say it is 20,000. Now clearly the overprojection in 1980 (10,000) is less than the overprojection (sum of the (X) vector 20,000) in 1970. Since we allow this adjustment procedure to subtract from the 1980 figures an amount up to the amount of the sum of the vector, clearly the entire 10,000 can be subtracted from the overprojected MCDs. Taking, for example, the MCD in Exhibit 4.8, we see that this MCD classified as urban is overprojected

EXHIBIT 4.8
PRELIMINARY PROJECTIONS, MCD MODEL 2
FOR AN OVERPROJECTED MCD

	1950	1970	1980	1990	2000	2010	2020	Land Area (Sq. Mi.)
Actual Population	4,000	8,000	—	—	—	—	—	2.00
Preliminary Projections		9,046	11,880	14,646	17,208	19,478	21,426	

for 1970 by 1,046. We take the ratio of its overprojection to the sum of the (X) vector times the county increment for 1980 to find out how much should be subtracted from 11,880 (the MCDs preliminary 1980 projection). Thus we would calculate

$$\frac{1,046}{20,000} \ (-10,000) \ = \ -523$$

and 11,880 − 523 = 11,357.

The MCDs adjusted 1980 (M) projection is then taken to be 11,357.

Now suppose that, in fact, the sum of MCD projections for 1980 had been 405,000 rather than 385,000. Then the 1980 county increment would have been − 30,000. But this routine could have subtracted only an increment of 20,000. The other 10,000 excess must be subtracted in one of the two remaining adjustment methods.

Underprojections are handled similarly. The 1980 county increment in Exhibit 4.7 of 15,000 associated with series (H) would be compared with the sum of a (Y) vector, consisting of the increments of underprojection associated with MCDs that were underprojected in 1970. If the county increment of underprojection was less than or equal to the sum of the (Y) vector, then all of the increments would be added to those underprojected MCDs in proportion to their share of the sum of the (Y) vector. Any portion of the county increment exceeding the sum of the (Y) vector is held aside to be allocated by a second method.

A flow diagram of this 1970 error method is shown in Exhibit 4.9.

THE GROWTH RATE METHOD OF ADJUSTMENT

The assumption of this method is that systematic models are much more likely to err in projecting the population of an MCD that rose from 1,000 to 10,000 in a recent decade than in projecting the population of an MCD that rose from 9,500 to 10,000 during the same decade. Accordingly, most of the remaining county increments from MCD Model 2 would, under this method, be added to or subtracted from the most rapidly growing MCDs.

If, for example, an MCD is projected to receive 10 percent of the county's growth in a decade, it would then gain 10 percent of the increment to be added or lose 10 percent of the increment that must be subtracted. A general exception is made. MCDs that are projected to decline are not adjusted any further in order to avoid the possibility of unrealistically depopulating central cities and rural areas.

EXHIBIT 4.9
FLOW DIAGRAM OF THE 1970 ERROR
ADJUSTMENT METHOD FOR A COUNTY

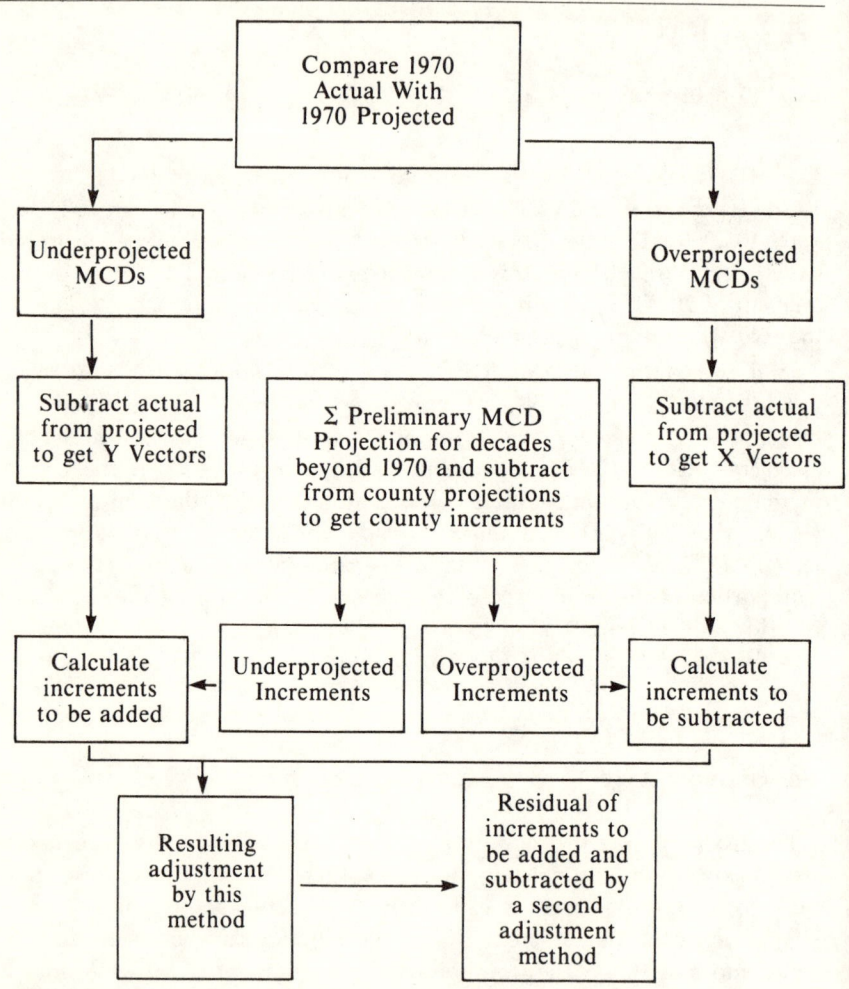

THE PROPORTION METHOD OF ADJUSTMENT

This adjustment process has been developed specifically for those regions in which many of the MCDs have declined and/or in which redevelopment of the central cities with high-rise structures is expected. In such regions, under the adjustment procedure that uses the growth-rates method to adjust the MCD populations, the program will modify the projections of only those MCDs that gained population. The MCDs that lost population are not adjusted. Therefore, in an extreme case (for example, when seven out of a total of ten MCDs have lost population as in county 202 of Chapter 8), the populations of the three MCDs that grew in resident population may be increased or decreased (including negative projections) to unrealistic levels.

This alternate adjustment process uses the absolute population sizes of the MCDs and the counties, and specifically adds or subtracts population from each MCD in proportion to its share of the county population. For example, if an MCD had 20 percent of the preliminary county population projected for 1980, its final 1980 projection would be modified by 20 percent of the population that is to be added or subtracted from the county. If the county increment to be added is 1,000, then the MCD would be allocated an additional 200 persons or $(0.20) \times (1,000)$. The results presented in Chapters 6–8 have been developed with the proportion method of preliminary MCD adjustment.

Exhibits 4.10 and 4.11 are flow diagrams for MCD Models 1 and 2, respectively.

A Detailed Example of the Results Produced by the Newling Model

Newling's model is not easily understood in the abstract. Accordingly, using the parameters derived in this chapter, we will illustrate its use. We begin with a county that has three communities. Each community has 8,000 residents in the initial time period (1970), a land area of four square miles, and a density of 2,000 persons per square mile. However, one of these communities is expected to grow rapidly into an urban community, the second into a suburban community, and the third is expected to decline. Accordingly, we classify the three as urban, suburban, and rural, respectively.

Given these classifications, we can use the Newling's model equations (4.3) and (4.4) to project the population density at any time.

FOR THE URBAN COMMUNITY

Eq. (4.3) $d_{1980} = 9.16707 \, (2000)^{1-.23087} =$

$\qquad$ antilog $(\log 9.16707 + .76913 \log 2000) =$

$\qquad$ antilog $(.9622 + .76913 \, (3.3010)) =$

$\qquad$ antilog $3.5011 = 3170$

Repeating with equation (4.3), we have

$$d_{1990} = 9.16707 \, (3170)^{1-.23087} = 4518$$

Equation (4.3) will calculate successive ($d_{2000} = 5934$) increments into the future.

FOR THE SUBURBAN COMMUNITY

Eq. (4.3) $d_{1980} = 3.96323 (2000)^{1 - .16376} =$

$\qquad$ antilog (log 3.9632 + .8362 log 2000) =

EXHIBIT 4.10
FLOW DIAGRAM OF POPULATION PROJECTIONS: SIMPLER VERSION (MCD MODEL 1)

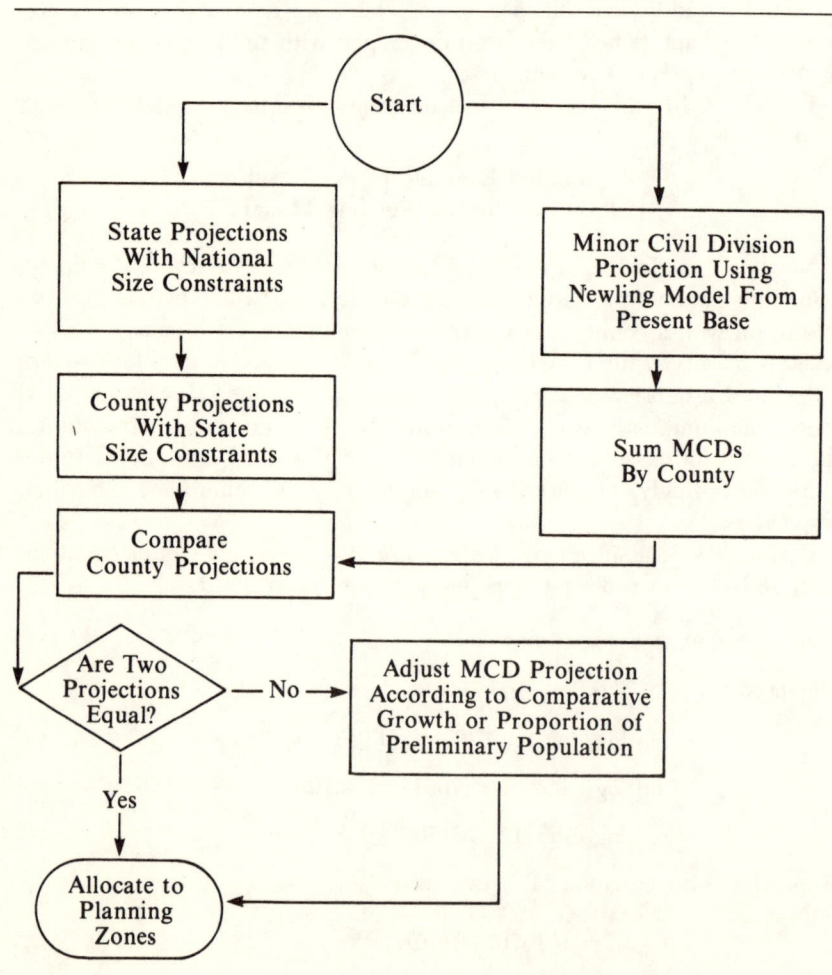

$$\text{antilog} (.5980 + 2.7603) =$$

$$\text{antilog} \ 3.3583 = 2283$$

FOR THE RURAL COMMUNITY

Eq. (4.3) $d_{1980} = 3.76920 \ (2000)^{1 - .22747} =$

$$\text{antilog} (\log 3.76920 + .7725 \log 2000) =$$

$$\text{antilog} (.5762 + 2.5500) =$$

$$\text{antilog} \ 3.1262 = 1337$$

EXHIBIT 4.11
FLOW DIAGRAM OF POPULATION PROJECTIONS:
COMPLEX VERSION (MCD MODEL 2)

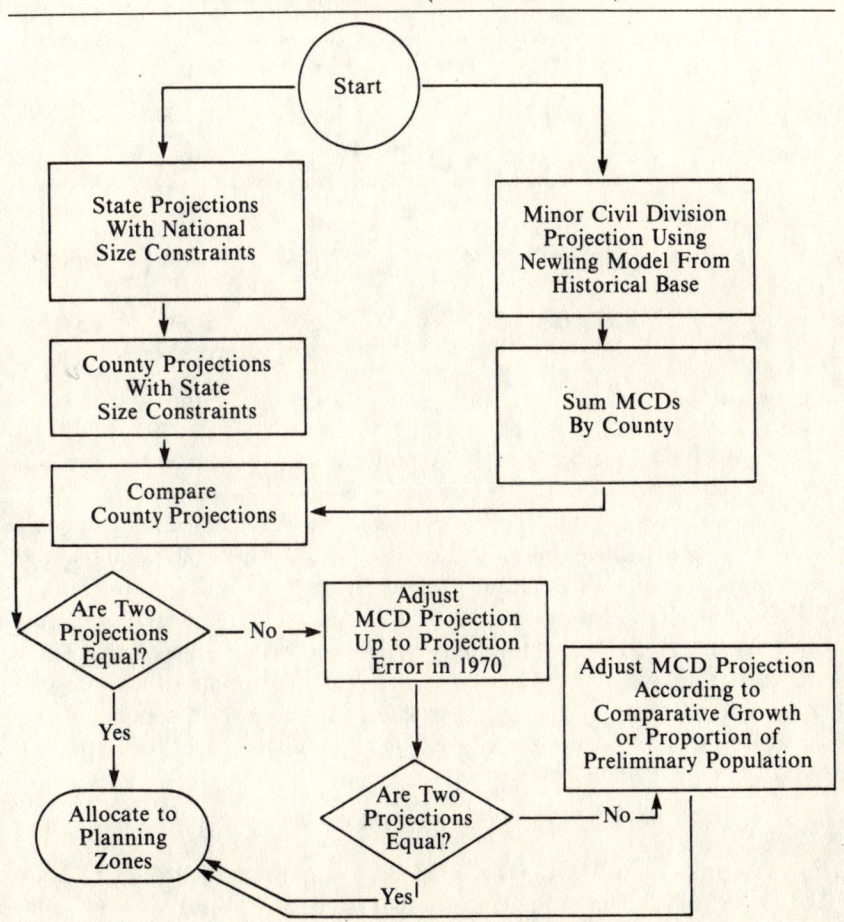

The densities from 1980 through 2020 using equation (4.3) are as follows:

	1970	1980	1990	2000	2010	2020
Urban MCD	2,000	3,170	4,518	5,934	7,318	8,598
Suburban MCD	2,000	2,283	2,550	2,797	3,022	3,224
Rural MCD	2,000	1,338	981	771	641	555

The densities are multiplied by the land area to produce population projections. The preliminary projections for the three communities in County 1 must be adjusted to the final county projections in the stepdown model.

MCD	1960	1970	1980	1990	2000
Urban	4,000	8,000	12,680	18,072	23,736
Suburban	7,000	8,000	9,132	10,200	11,188
Rural	9,000	8,000	5,352	3,924	3,084
County Unadjusted Final	20,000	24,000	27,164	32,196	38,008
County	20,000	24,000	28,000	32,000	36,000
County Increment	0	0	+836	−196	−2,008

The sum of the unadjusted MCD projections does not equal the final county projections. The difference is the county increment.

Three methods of adjusting the preliminary MCD projections for MCD Models 1 and 2 have been presented. MCD Model 1 is suggested. Therefore, the growth rate and proportion methods will be illustrated.

The rural MCD is projected to decline. Accordingly, no further calculations are made on that community. The growth-rate choice allocates or subtracts the remaining population based on the relative projected increases of the two MCDs that are projected to increase in population. For the urban MCD, the projected unadjusted population for 1980 is 12,680, the 1970 population 8,000.

$$12,680 - 8,000 = 4,680$$

For the suburban MCD, the projected unadjusted growth is 1,132 (9,132 − 8,000). The sum of the unadjusted growth for the two communities is 5,812 (4,680 + 1,132). The urban MCD accounted for 80.52 percent, and the suburban community accounted for 19.48 percent, of this projected growth. Accordingly, 80.52 percent of the 836 additional people (the 1980 county increment) are added to the urban community and 19.48 percent are added to the suburban community.

$$M_{1980}^{urban} = 12,680 + (.8052)\ 836 = 13,353$$

$$M_{1980}^{suburban} = 9,132 + (.1948)\ 836 = 9,295$$

$$M_{1980}^{rural} = 5,352 + (0)\ 836 = 5,352$$

The unadjusted projections for 1990 and 1980 are used to subtract 196 people in 1990 (county increment 1990), and the unadjusted projections for the years 2000 and 1990 are used to subtract 2008 (year 2000 county increment) people from the year 2000 projection. The final projections follow:

MCD	1980	1990	2000
Urban	13,353	17,908	22,026
Suburban	9,295	10,168	10,890
Rural	5,352	3,924	3,084
County	28,000	32,000	36,000

The proportion adjustment method prorates the differences on the proportion of the MCD population in the preliminary projection. The unadjusted MCD projections and the proportions they represent are listed below.

	1980	%	1990	%	2000	%
Urban MCD	12,680	46.68	18,072	56.13	23,736	62.45
Suburban MCD	9,132	33.62	10,200	31.68	11,188	29.44
Rural MCD	5,352	19.70	3,924	12.19	3,084	8.11
Unadjusted County	27,164	100.00	32,196	100.00	38,008	100.00
Final County	28,000	—	32,000	—	36,000	—
County Increment	836	—	−196	—	−2,008	—

The adjustments for the urban MCD are illustrated below:

$$M_{1980}^{urban} = 12,680 + .4668\ (836) \quad = 13,070$$

$$M_{1990}^{urban} = 18,072 + .4613\ (-196) \quad = 17,962$$
$$M_{2000}^{urban} = 23,736 + .6245\ (-2008) = 22,482$$

The final projections are as follows:

MCD	1980	1990	2000
Urban	13,070	17,962	22,482
Suburban	9,413	10,138	10,597
Rural	5,517	3,900	2,921
County	28,000	32,000	36,000

Two Alternative Density Ceilings Models

The parameters of Newling models are sometimes difficult, if not, impossible to calibrate. This section explores two simpler density ceiling models. They have not been programmed. These two are a logical extension of MCD Models 3,4, and 5, developed in Chapter 3, which produce unadjusted population projections. In these alternative density ceilings models those projections are converted into densities. The densities are compared to a density ceiling for the community(ies) set by the analyst. If the projected density violates the density ceiling, the population is reduced to the density ceiling value. This procedure will be illustrated with the sample projections developed in Chapter 3. Using MCD Model 3, we prepared unadjusted projections for the population of M^1 and M^2 as follows:

	1980	1990	2000	2010	2020
M^1	3,100	3,600	4,200	4,675	5,203
M^2	22,900	30,400	35,800	44,392	55,046

Assume that M^1 is one square mile and M^2 is twenty square miles. Further assume that M^1 is already largely developed and will not grow much above 4,500 persons per square mile. M^2 is relatively undeveloped and can grow to about 2,000 persons per square mile. The preliminary projections tabulated above imply that M^1 is above 4,500 persons per square mile by the year 2010. M^2 exceeds 2,000 persons per square mile by 2010. Accordingly, if the density ceilings are used, the final projections for M^1 and M^2 are the following:

MCD	1980	1990	2000	2010	2020
M^1	3,100	3,600	4,200	4,500	4,500
M^2	22,900	30,400	35,800	40,000	40,000

A second extension of equations (3.1) − (3.8) is to use the final MCD projections, rather than the unadjusted projections. With respect to MCD Model 3, the final projections for M^1 and M^2 are:

	1980	1990	2000	2010	2020
M^1	2,981	3,494	3,990	3,811	3,800
M^2	22,019	29,506	34,010	36,189	40,200
C^1	25,000	33,000	38,000	40,000	44,000

M^1 does not violate the 4,500 persons per square mile density, but M^2 does exceed the 2,000 persons per square mile density by 2020. To be consistent with the county total for the year 2020, 200 people should be added to M^1. In this case, the addition of 200 people to M^1 does not violate its 4,500 persons per square mile density ceiling. If population must be reallocated, equation (3.5) should be used. The totals of those communities that do not exceed their upper limits constitute a county unit for the reallocation calculations.

It is possible that all of the communities will exceed their density ceilings. In that event, county and community policies are clearly at odds and should be reviewed.

Chapter 5
Apportionment of Population From MCDs To Planning Zones

The user may allocate the projections of population to the planning zones either according to the present spatial distribution—evenly over the land surface—or with the aid of a predetermined land use guide, a mathematical model, or any other method deemed appropriate for the specific application. This chapter suggests procedures for locating the present and projected population in geographic zones that may be service areas, planning districts, market areas, grid zones, river basins, etc. For purposes of an example we will utilize the population rose used for nuclear power plant siting studies. While the allocation procedure will be described specifically to power plant siting, the program will accept any set of one hundred sixty planning areas, each identified by a four digit location code.

Data Sources for Allocating the Present Population

The first suggested step is to assign the existing population to the planning zones. Even if the user does not wish to allocate the projected population according to the base period distribution, this initial step has the advantages of providing a check of the possibility that some population has been omitted from the input data and of presenting a perspective of the base period distribution against which the projected distribution may be compared.

Three major sources of information are available for doing this: the 1970 U.S. Census Bureau counts, air photos and other maps, and field surveys. All may have to be used in the course of a location survey. As the zones increase in size coarser data may be used. Nuclear power plant siting requires population zones of widely varying sizes. Therefore, the data utilized and procedures suggested in this chapter are likely to be relevant to many other planning units.

The U.S. Bureau of the Census published population counts at five spatial scales relevant to most apportionment problems: county, minor civil division, enumeration district, census tract, and block. In the densely developed Northeast, a circular study region of 50-mile radius may contain as many as thirty to thirty-five counties, 400 to 650 MCDs, 700 to 1,500 census tracts, and 30,000 to 60,000 census blocks.

In nuclear power plant siting studies, estimates and projections are prepared for 160 zones: ninety-six zones within 10 miles of the center of the reactor site, and sixty-four zones lying between 10 and 50 miles from the site. The center of the site is fixed on aerial photographs (scale = 1" = 400 ft. is suggested). Within 10 miles of the center concentric circles are drawn at 1, 2, 3, 4, 5, and 10 miles. Other circles are drawn at 10-mile intervals: 20, 30, 40, and 50 miles from the center.

The circular space is further divided into sectors of 22-1/2 degrees with each of the sixteen segments centered on one cardinal compass point. The resulting population rose contains 160 zones defined by the ten concentric circles and sixteen sectors. The numbering system of circles and sectors referred to subsequently in the text is specified in Exhibit 5.1.

A four-digit combination of two codes was used to number each of the 160 zones of the rose. The first two digits represent the concentric circle; the second two digits represent the sector. For example 3009 represents the zone between 20 and 30 miles (code 30) from the center and due south (code 09). A location 0213 represents a zone between 1 and 2 miles (code 02) from the center and due west (code 13).

We will now consider the appropriateness of alternative data sets for allocating the MCD population to the rose. The MCD is generally the most appropriate scale for the outer 40 miles (10–50), block data is most appropriate inner 10 miles (1–10) because of the increasing number and decreasing size of the population rose zones present in the inner portion of the rose. The inner 10 miles contain ninety-six zones, while the outer region has only sixty-four zones. Using the formula for the area of a circle, the 50-mile area includes 7,854 square miles of which only 4 percent lies in the inner 10 miles. Each of the 40–50-mile zones contains 176 square

ALLOCATION ZONES FOR A NUCLEAR POWER SITING EXAMPLE:
THE INNER TEN MILES

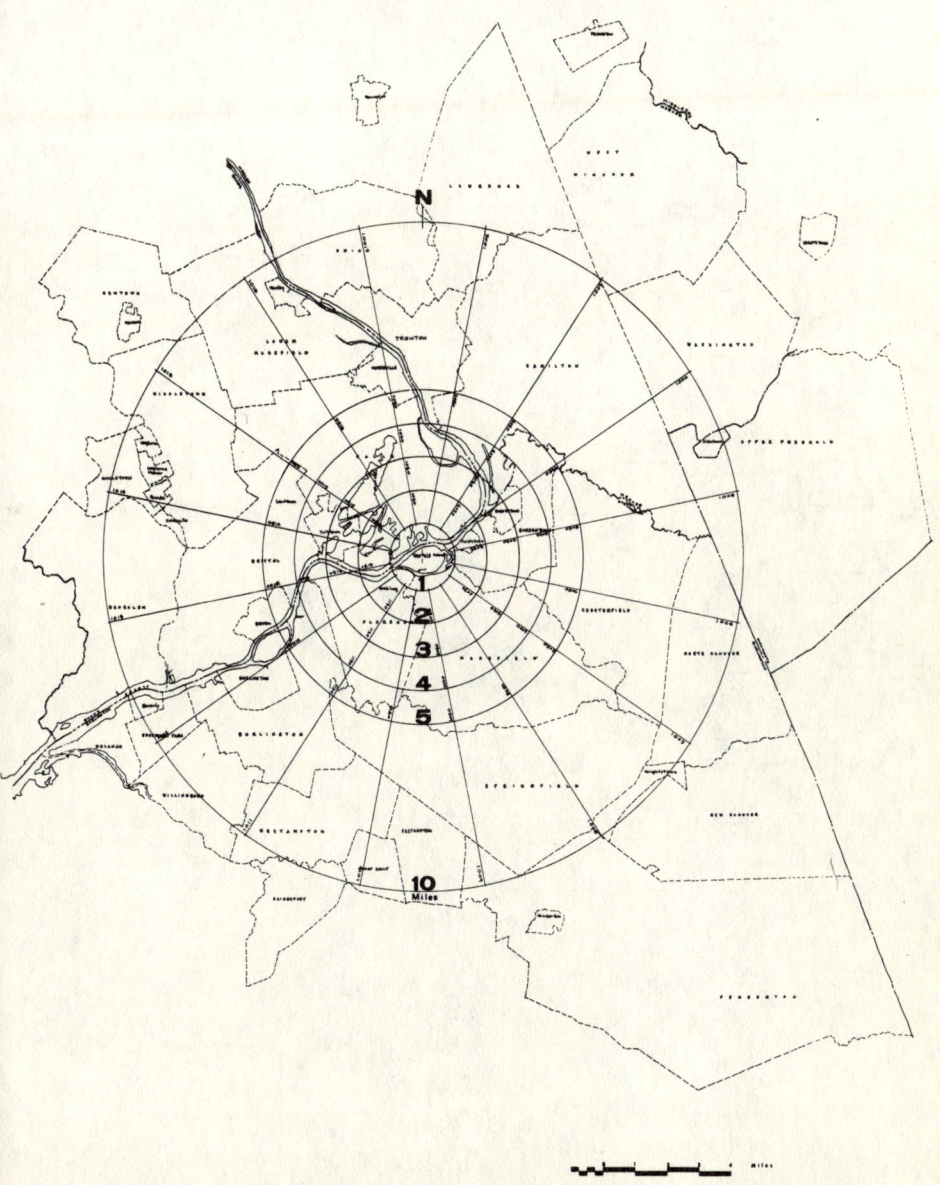

ALLOCATION ZONES FOR A NUCLEAR POWER SITING EXAMPLE: A FIFTY MILE REGION

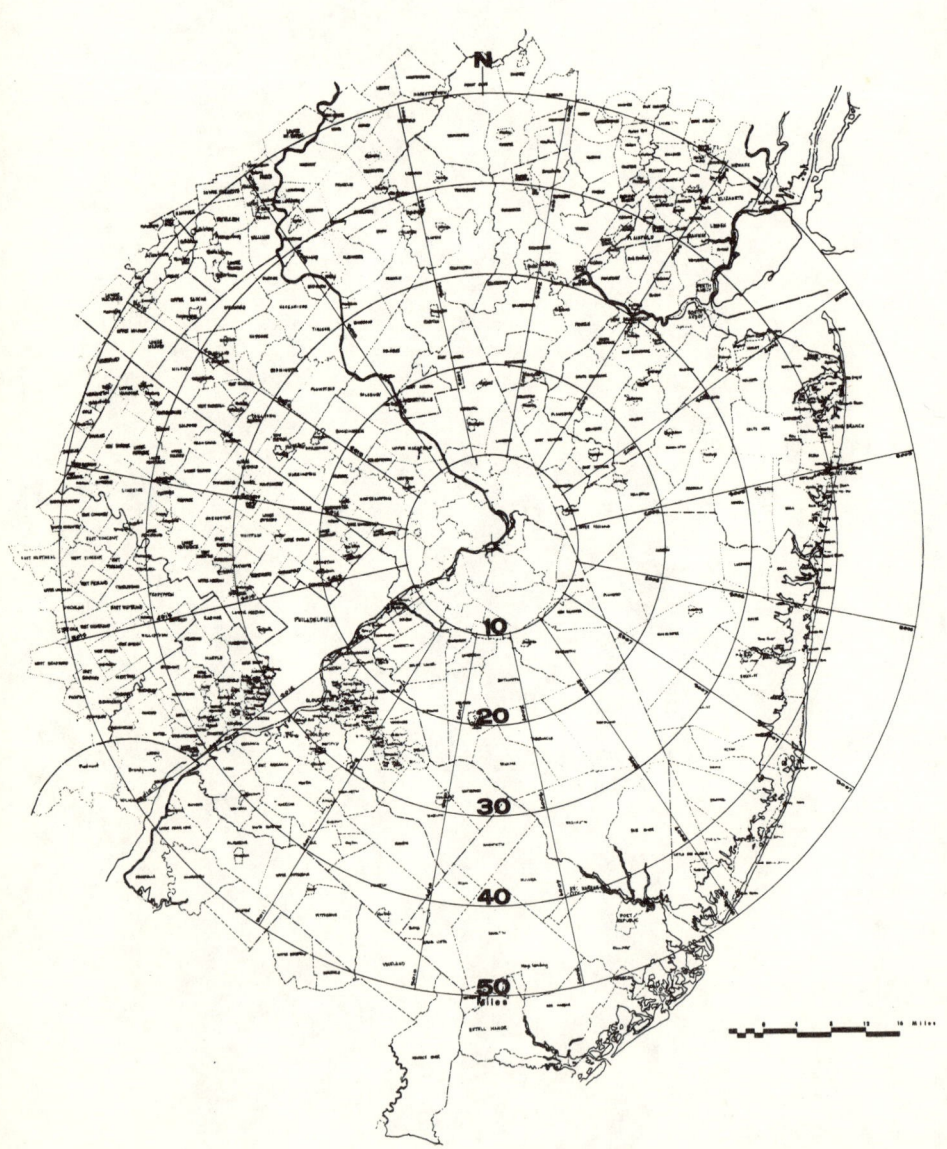

miles, compared to 59 square miles for the 10–20-mile zones, 14.7 square miles for the 5–10-mile zones, and 0.196 square miles for the 0–mile zones. At the outer extreme, the 40–50-mile zones are likely to be larger than any of the MCDs, while at the other extreme, the inner zones are probably smaller than most of the MCDs. While several 40–50-mile sections include more than a score of MDCs, large townships, near the site, may each span more than twenty zones of the rose.

Within the inner 10 miles and especially within the inner 5 miles, block data may not be available and may not always be sufficiently accurate. Nuclear power plants have frequently been sited in relatively unpopulated areas. The Census Bureau does not tabulate block data for rural areas, although it will under special contract.

The following combinations of techniques are suggested in the inner 10 miles. A dwelling unit count should be made in the inner 1 mile by field surveys and verified by examination of block census data and aerial photos. Each dwelling unit is multiplied by an average number of persons per unit drawn from local data. The population in the remainder of the inner 10 miles is apportioned by U.S. Census block data if available. Counts for the rural areas not included in the Census Bureau block counts may be made with the use of air photos and U.S. Geological Survey (U.S.G.S.) maps. The total number of dwelling units in each zone is used to apportion the 1970 MCD census counts. For example, if 2,000 of an MCD's 3,000 dwelling units lie in one zone of the rose and the other 1,000 in a second zone, two-thirds of its 1970 population is assigned to the first zone, and one-third to the second zone of the rose.

In contrast to the ninety-six small zones in the inner 10 miles of the rose, the majority of the MCDs in the sixty-four zones of the outer 40 miles of the rose are likely to fall in only one zone and the vast majority in only one or two sections of the rose. MCD data should be used for those MCDs that fall in only one zone.

Census tract and enumeration district data should provide a more precise location pattern than the MCD for apportioning the population of those MCDs in the outer rose that fall into two or more zones. However, rather than the indiscriminate use of tract data, we advise the user to identify crucial areas to which the application of tract data will significantly improve the allocation results. For example, a city of 500,000 residents having 20 square miles and 100 census tracts should probably be apportioned with census tract data if it lies in the 10–20-mile ring. However, it might not be necessary to use tract data if the city lies in one of the outer zones and if the population distribution within the city is presently moving toward a relatively even pattern. In addition, prior work dealing with the allocation of MCD populations to water and sewerage

EXHIBIT 5.1
CODE USED FOR NUMBERING THE ZONES
OF THE POPULATION ROSE

A. Concentric Circles

Numbering Code for First Two Digits	Distance in Miles from Center
01	0–1
02	1–2
03	2–3
04	3–4
05	4–5
10	5–10
20	10–20
30	20–30
40	30–40
50	40–50

B. Sectors

Numbering Code for Last Two Digits	Compass Direction
01	N
02	NNE
03	NE
04	ENE
05	E
06	ESE
07	SE
08	SSE
09	S
10	SSW
11	SW
12	WSW
13	W
14	WNW
15	NW
16	NNW

service areas in the New York Metropolitan Region suggests that assignment errors are compensatory rather than additive in dense urban areas (Carey, et. al. 1972). Finally, before using tract and enumeration district data, the authors suggest that the user validate the accuracy of the base maps.

The location assignments in the 10–50-mile area should normally be made according to the following procedure. The proportion of land area of each of the MCDs lying in two or more zones of the population rose is measured by a planimeter. Population is allocated according to the percentage of the MCD land falling in each section of the rose. For example, assume a community of 10,000 persons and 10 square miles, where 60 percent of the land lies in one section of the rose and 40 percent of the land lies in an adjacent section. Accordingly, 6,000 persons would be allocated to the first section and 4,000 persons to the second section of the rose. The user may, of course, use any method he considers appropriate, as long as the result is in terms of a percentage which is in the form of the input utilized in the computer program. The program includes a summation check of the allocation in shares and will identify any MCD that is not between 98 and 102 percent allocated. The user should note that final projected and allocation totals may differ by 0.00001 percent, about ten persons per million. (Single precision is utilized in the computer program in order to save core.)

Overall, as the number of zones per unit of planning area increases, as the areas become less urbanized, and as accuracy within the zones becomes more important, the user should progress the method of apportioning the population from the MCD to the enumeration district and the census tract, to the block, to the air photo and geological survey map, and finally to a field survey.

Impact of the Choice of Allocation Method on the Remainder of the Study Region

The use of block, air photo, and U.S.G.S. map data in the inner 10 miles to allocate the existing population has two direct impacts on the remainder of the study. First, MCDs that were partially apportioned by block data because they were partially located in the inner 10 miles should be completely apportioned with block data in order to be consistent.

Secondly, and quite important, the allocation of projections in the inner zones may be significantly affected by the change from the land area to the subsequent block method of allocation. The difference between the two methods of apportioning the 1970 population decreases as one moves further away from the central site. In the inner five miles especially, the difference may be substantial when unoccupied rural areas and industrial and commercial sites are allocated population by the land area method.

The increased accuracy of using the block data, air photos, and maps in the inner portion of the rose is obvious. However, the choice of the block method of apportionment also tends to apportion the projected growth into the already developed zones. At this point a most extreme specific example will illustrate the potential effect of this choice. Village Q occupies 10 percent of the area of Township A, but had more than one-third of the township's population in 1970. By allocating the population growth on the basis of the present actual distribution, based on that block data, we will, in turn, allocate one-third of the projected population to the Village Q area. This result does agree with the observed tendency for development to occur at the fringes of preexisting nodes. However, not recognized is the coexisting tendency for development to fill in present rural areas rather than to redevelop older nodes at higher densities. In short, within some MCDs the use of present block data to allocate future growth will tend to concentrate the projected population with the existing population, while the land area apportionment will disperse population equally over the land. This choice of method has little consequence in the outer zones of the rose because the vast majority of the MCDs lie only in one or two zones. However, within the inner 5 miles of the rose, the choice could seriously affect the projected population distribution.

One solution to this problem, which has not been incorporated into the program, is as follows:

The present population could be allocated on the basis of the present resident distribution. Then increments could be apportioned according to the land area method—land area representing developable residential land, excluding at a minimum those lands committed to non-residential uses. In addition to the optional land survey, the added requirements of this approach are: (1) a projection matrix dichotomized into present and expected absolute change submatrices which could be produced by subtracting from each projection the population of the previous decade; and (2) an allocation matrix split into present distribution and available land area submatrices. A satisfying addition to the above model would utilize a gravity model to apportion the increment on the basis of developable land, public service, and transportation factors.

If all five MCD models are used, the final projection results will consist of four allocation matrices: (1) for MCD Model 1; (2) for MCD Model 2; (3) for MCD Models 3, 4, and 5; (because the MCD data input sets for 3 and 4 are mutually exclusive and not necessarily exhaustive and Model 5 projections are used as a supplement where MCD Models 3 and 4 cannot be applied) and (4) for MCD Model 5.

Chapter 6
The Population Program: Job Deck Set-up and Input Formats

Job Deck Set-Up

The program, reproduced in Chapter 7 and demonstrated in Chapter 8, is written in Fortran IV and all construction and testing were run at the Center for Computer Information and Services at Rutgers University, New Brunswick, New Jersey on an IBM 360/67.

The job deck set-up has ten components which are listed below and illustrated in Exhibit 6.1 in their mandatory order. The system cards, sets 1, 3, and 10, may vary from system to system, but it is imperative that the input data, sets 4-9, be in strict order.

Set 1, System Cards. These cards are written in Job Control Language (JCL).

Set 2, Main Program and Subroutine. These are written in Fortran IV and exhibited in Chapter 7.

Set 3, System Cards. These JCL cards set up two utility or scratch files: one for MCDs and one for the allocation proportions.

Set 4, Option Card. This is one card, whose format is later specified.

Set 5, Nation Data. These are always two cards, whose format is later specified.

Set 6, State Data. There will be either two or four cards for each state: the first one or two will be read by the program as H series (originally standing for High) and the second one or two cards for each state will be read by the program as the M series (originally standing for Median). Data for each state must begin with the same decade (e.g., 1930) and end with the same decade (e.g., 1990). The states must be in numerical order. This format is later specified.

EXHIBIT 6.1
JOB-DECK SET-UP:
POPULATION PROJECTIONS

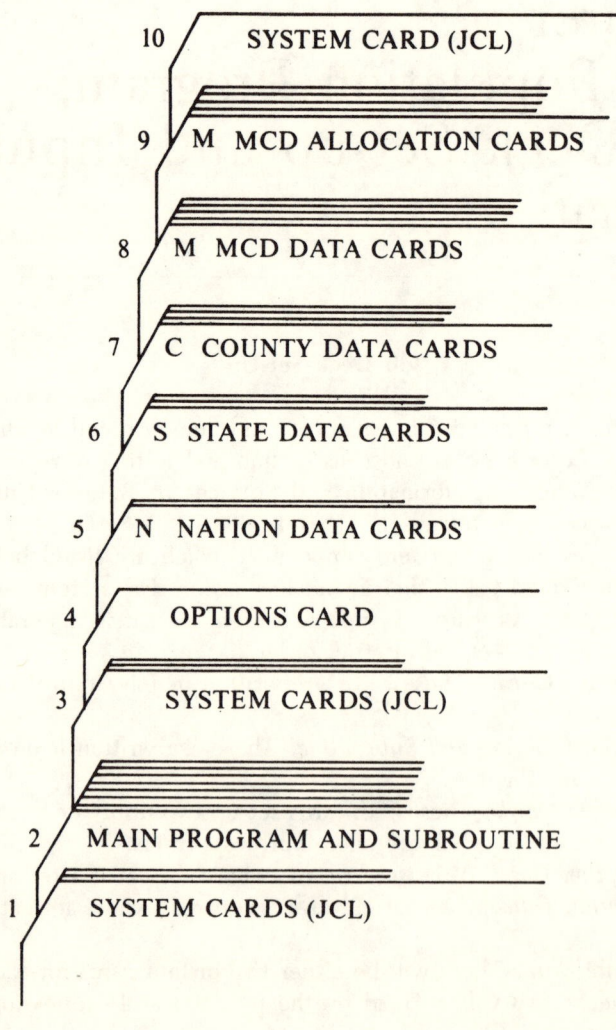

10 / SYSTEM CARD (JCL)

9 / M MCD ALLOCATION CARDS

8 / M MCD DATA CARDS

7 / C COUNTY DATA CARDS

6 / S STATE DATA CARDS

5 / N NATION DATA CARDS

4 / OPTIONS CARD

3 / SYSTEM CARDS (JCL)

2 / MAIN PROGRAM AND SUBROUTINE

1 / SYSTEM CARDS (JCL)

Set 7, County Data. There will be one or two cards for each county. These must be in numerical (ID) order within each state, and ordered by state; e.g., State 1, County 1; State 1, County 2; State 2, County 1; State 2, County 2; etc.

Set 8, MCD Data. There will be only one card for each MCD. These must be ordered within their respective counties, and by respective states: e.g.:

State 1	County 1	MCD 1
State 1	County 1	MCD 2
State 1	County 2	MCD 1
State 1	County 2	MCD 2
State 2	County 1	MCD 1

Any MCD that is or might be projected to exceed a population of 1,000,000 persons, such as a large city like Philadelphia, should be broken down into several parts to be handled as separate MCDs in the program. The format is later specified.

Set 9, MCD Allocation Cards. There may be several cards for some MCDs. The number of cards per MCD will vary. Their format is specified below.

Set 10, System Card. This card signals the end of the job.

Input Formats

PROGRAM OPTIONS CONTROL CARD FORMAT

Columns

1–4	Value of "d" for state data—year of last input data; e.g., 1990
5	ℓ = number of states; $1 < \ell < 6$
6, 7	m = number of counties $1 \leq m \leq 100$
8–10	h = number of MCDs $1 \leq h \leq 700$
11	Blank if MCD Model 1 is to be utilized; "1" if MCD Model 1 is to be skipped
12	Blank if MCD Model 2 is to be utilized; "1" if MCD Model 2 is to be skipped

13	Blank if MCD Model 3 is to be utilized; "1" if MCD Model 3 is to be skipped
14	Blank if MCD Model 4 is to be utilized; "1" if MCD Model 4 is to be skipped
15	Blank if MCD Model 5 is to be utilized; "1" if MCD Model 5 is to be skipped
16	Blank if densities of MCD Models 1 and 2 are to be printed; "1" if densities of MCD Models 1 and 2 are not to be printed
17	Blank if adjustment option according to comparative growth is to be applied to MCD Models 1 and 2; "1" if adjustment option according to percent of preliminary population projections is to be applied to MCD Models 1 and 2
18–80	Blank

NATION DATA CARDS FORMAT

Card 1

Columns

1	"N", indicating nation
2	"O"
3–10	Blank
11	"1", indicating card 1
12–20	Population for year 1930
21–29	Population for year 1940
30–38	Population for year 1950
39–47	Population for year 1960
48–56	Population for year 1970
57–65	Projection for year 1980
66–74	Projection for year 1990
75–80	Blank

Card 2

Columns

1	"N"
2	"O"
3–10	Blank
11	"2", indicating card 2
12–20	Projection for year 2000
21–29	Projection for year 2010
30–38	Projection for year 2020

STATES DATA CARDS FORMAT

Card 1

Columns

1	"S", indicating states data
2	Identifying number of the state
3–9	Blank
10	"H" for H growth series
11	Blank if data does not exist beyond year 2000, in which case only one card will be required for each series; "1" if a second data card for this *series* exists (see note below)
12–19	Population for year 1930
20–27	Population for year 1940
28–35	Population for year 1950
36–43	Population for year 1960
44–51	Population for year 1970
52–59	Projections for year 1980
60–67	Projections for year 1990
68–75	Projections for year 2000
76–80	Blank

Card 2

Columns

1	"S"
2	Identifying number of the state
3–9	Blank
10	"M" for M growth series
11	Blank if data does not exceed year 2000; "1" if it does (see note below)
12–19	Population for year 1930
20–27	Population for year 1940
	etc., as on Card 1

NOTE: If there are no given projections for 2010 and 2020, then there will be two cards for each state, as above. Column 11 will be blank in both cards.

If there are projections for 2010 and 2020 then a second card for each series, four cards all together for each state, are required. In that case cards one and three will have the formats of one and two above with "1" in Column 11; cards two and four will have the same format with the 2010 projection in Columns 12–19, and the 2020 projection in Columns 20–27.

Counties Data Cards Format

Card 1

Columns

1	"C", indicating county data
2	Identifying number of the state
3–5	Identifying number of county within the state
6–10	Blank
11	Blank if data does not exist beyond year 2000, in which case only one card will be required for each county; "1" if a second data card for this county exists

12–19	Population for year 1930
20–27	Population for year 1940
28–35	Population for year 1950
36–43	Population for year 1960
44–51	Population for year 1970
52–59	Projection for year 1980
60–67	Projection for year 1990
68–75	Projection for year 2000
76–80	Blank

Card 2

Column

1	"C"
2	Identifying number of state
3–5	Identifying number of county within the state
6–10	Blank
11	"2", indicating second card
12–19	Projection for year 2010
20–27	Projection for year 2020

MCDs Data Cards Format

Columns

1	"M", indicating MCD data
2	Identifying number of state
3–5	Identifying number of county within the state
6–8	Identifying number of MCD within the county
9	"3" if this data is of the continuous projection series appropriate to MCD Model 3; "4" if this data is of the discontinuous projection series appropriate to MCD Model 4; "5" if this data is only historical data of the type appropriate to MCD Model 5 (see note below)

10	Classification number for MCD Models 1 and 2 enter 1, 2, 3, 4, 5, or 6
11	Blank
12–17	Population for year 1930
18–23	Population for year 1940
24–29	Population for year 1950
30–35	Population for year 1960
36–41	Population for year 1970
42–47	Land Area in square miles. A decimal point must be punched in Column 45. There are then two places to the right of the decimal
48–53	Projection for year 1980
54–59	Projection for year 1990
60–65	Projection for year 2000
66–71	Projection for year 2010
72–77	Projection for year 2020
78–80	Blank

Note: All MCDs of a county must have the same number in Column 9

ALLOCATION DATA CARDS FORMAT

Card 1

Columns

1	"M"
2	Identifying number of state
3–5	Identifying number of county within the state
6–8	Identifying number of MCD within the county
9, 10	Blank
11	Card number for this MCD
12–15	A four-digit zone number

16–20 A portion of the population of the MCD to be allocated to the zone just mentioned (Column 12–15). This proportion is expressed as a percentage where the decimal is *not punched*, such that 100 percent is punched "10000" and 4.25 percent is punched "00425"

21–24 A zone number

25–29 A proportion to be allocated to zone mentioned in Columns 21–24

30–33 A zone number

34–38 A proportion

•

•

etc.

•

•

75–80 Blank

Cards 2, 3, . . .

All subsequent cards follow the same format as Card 1, altering of course the card number in Column 11.

Chapter 7
The Population Program:
Input, A Listing
of the Program and
A Sample Problem Data Set

This chapter consists of a listing of the input deck for a sample problem. The job set-up is as described in Chapter 6, including the complete set of models presented in Chapters 3, 4, and 5. The data set consists of two states with projections to 1990, with three counties in the first state and two in the second. MCDs are projected on all five MCD models for forty MCDs — ten each in the first two counties of the first state, and ten each in the counties of the second state. The numbers used in the sample problem to represent the Nation and the states are modeled on, but do not replicate, the actual population histories of the United States and specific states. The counties and the MCDs used in the sample problem are modeled on the type of demographic patterns we have observed in previous studies. The programs were also tested with MCDs having anomalous population profiles.

```
//MAUTNERG JOB (3367003,H018,-40,20,2,B,6),'GREEN/KRUECKE BERG',
//      TIME=2,CLASS=L
//STEP     EXEC FORTGCLG,REGION.FORT=125K,PARM.LKED='MAP',
//      REGION.GO=215K
//FORT.SYSIN DD *
C                                                                      100
C        LONG-RANGE POPULATION PROJECTIONS FOR MINOR CIVIL DIVISIONS   200
C        BY MICHAEL R GREENBERG, DONALD A KRUECKEBERG, & RICHARD MAUTNER 300
C             RUTGERS UNIVERSITY, NEW BRUNSWICK, NEW JERSEY            400
C                           MARCH 1, 1973                             500
C                                                                      600
      DIMENSION NN(700,4), FP(700,10), XCRD(20)                        1000
      DIMENSION CTOT(100,9), CONST (6,4)                               2000
      DIMENSION HM(2,100,10), CNCR(2,100,5), CVECT(100,2), VECT(700,2) 3000
      DIMENSION XP(700,5,2), NT(10), CTOTA(100,5,2), YP(2,700,10)      4000
      DIMENSION PCT(700), TP(187,11), NP(187), NR(10), NS(16)          5000
      DIMENSION RPCT(9), NRNG(9), NSECT(9), NQ(11)                     6000
      DIMENSION NOYES (5), NMST (7),              KYRS (10),  NTS (10) 7000
      DOUBLE PRECISION XNATN (10), STATES (8,2,10), RIG(7,2)           8000
      DOUBLE PRECISION SRIG                                            9000
      DIMENSION CMRIG (700),       NMCTY(100,3), DENS(9)               10000
C     NMST  - STATE NUMBERS AS THEY APPEAR IN STATES MATRIX.           11000
C     NMCTY - STATE #, CTY #, STATE/CTY # IN HM MATRIX                 12000
      COMMON PK, TP, FP, XP, K, NP,                                    13000
     1      NITER, ZP(187,11),NMOD,YP                                  14000
      EQUIVALENCE (YP(1),CTOTA(1))                                     15000
      EQUIVALENCE (PCT(1),CMRIG(1))                                    16000
C     SNAME - SUBDIVISION (MUNICIPALITY) NAMES                         17000
C     NN    - INTEGER INPUT DATA:  1 - COUNTY, 2 - ID,                 18000
C             3 - 1950 DENSITY, 4 - CLASS                              19000
C             ALTERNATELY 3 -D, 4 - MODEL #                            20000
C     FP    - FLOATING POINT INPUT AND COMPUTED DATA:                  21000
C             1,2,3 - 1950, 1960, 1970 ACTUAL                          22000
C             4-9   -   1970 - 2020 COMPUTED                           23000
C             10    - LAND AREA IN SQUARE MILES                        24000
C     CNAME - COUNTY NAMES                                             25000
C     CTOT  - COUNTY TOTALS      1-3  -  1950 - 1970 ACTUAL            26000
C                                4-9  -  1970 - 2020 COMPUTED          27000
C     HM    - COUNTY MATRIX: 1 H H, 2 - M; 1-10 - 1930-2020            28000
C     CNCR  - COUNTRY INCREMENTS: SEE HM ABOVE                         29000
C     VECT  - SUBDIVISION VECTORS FOR DIFFERENCE BETWEEN 1970A AND     30000
C             1970E: 1 - X; 2 - Y                                      31000
C     CVECT - COUNTY TOTALS FOR VECT (ABOVE)                           32000
C     XP    - PHASE II RESULTS. 1-5 - 1980-2020                        33000
C                               1-2 - H-M                              34000
C     CTOTA - PHASE II COUNTY RESULTS                                  35000
      RIGMAX = 1.5                                                     36000
      RIGMIN = 0.5                                                     37000
      READ(5,2000)LDEC,NST,NCTY,NMCD,NOYES,NPDENS,LADJ                 38000
 2000 FORMAT(I4,I1,I2,I3,7I1)                                          39000
      NITER = 1                                                        40000
      KDDD  = (LDEC - 1930) / 10 + 1                                   41000
      KOPO  = KDDD + 1                                                 42000
      DO 2002 ND = 1,10                                                43000
 2002 KYRS (ND) = 1920 + 10 * ND                                      44000
      DO 2005 J = 1,187                                                45000
      DO 2005 N = 1,11                                                 46000
 2005 ZP(J,N) = 0.0                                                    47000
```

```
C      STATE PROJECTIONS WITH NATIONAL SIZE CONSTRAINTS                47500
       READ(5,2010) XNATN                                              48000
2010 FORMAT(11X,7F9.0,/,11X,3F9.0)                                     49000
       DO 2015 KS = 1,2                                                50000
       DO 2015 KQ = 1,10                                               51000
       STATES(8,KS,KQ) = 0.0                                           52000
2015 STATES (NST+1,KS,KQ) = 0.0                                        53000
       DO 2040 KD = 1,NST                                              54000
       DO 2040 KS = 1,2                                                55000
       RIG(KD,KS) = 99999.9                                            55500
       READ(5,2020)NMST(KD),KTRAIL,(STATES(KD, KS,KQ),KQ=1,8)          56000
2020 FORMAT(1X,I1,8X,I1,8F8.0)                                         57000
       STATES(KD,KS,9) = 0.0                                           58000
       STATES(KD,KS,10) = 0.0                                          59000
       IF(KTRAIL.EQ.0) GO TO 2030                                      60000
       READ(5,2025) (STATES(KD, KS,KQ),KQ=9,10)                        61000
2025 FORMAT(11X,2F8.0)                                                 62000
2030 DO 2035 KQ = 1,10                                                 63000
2035 STATES   (NST+1,KS,KQ) = STATES (NST+1,KS,KQ) + STATES(KD, KS,KQ) 64000
2040 CONTINUE                                                          65000
       NMST(NST+1) = NST + 1                                           66000
       DO 2124 KS = 1,2                                                67000
       DO 2124 KQ = 1,KDDD                                             68000
2124 STATES (NST+1,KS,KQ) = XNATN (KQ) - STATES (NST+1,KS,KQ)          69000
       DV = FLOAT(KDDD - 1)                                            70000
       NDM = NST + 1                                                   71000
       IF(KDDD.EQ.10) GO TO 2146                                       72000
       DO 2134 KD = 1,NDM                                              73000
       OO 2134 KS = 1,2                                                74000
       RIG (KD,KS) = 0.0                                               75000
       SRIG = 0.0                                                      75500
       DV = 0.0                                                        75600
       DO 2130 KT = 2,KDDD                                             76000
       IF (STATES(KD,KS,KT).EQ.0.0.OR.STATES(KD,KS,KT-1).EQ.0.0)GOTO2130 76500
       SRIG = STATES (KD,KS,KT) / STATES (KD,KS,KT-1)                  77000
       DV = DV + 1.0                                                   77500
       IF (SRIG.GT.RIGMAX) SRIG = RIGMAX                               78000
       IF (SRIG.LT.RIGMIN) SRIG = RIGMIN                               79000
2130 RIG(KD,KS) = RIG(KD,KS) + SRIG                                    80000
       RIG (KD,KS) = RIG (KD,KS) / DV                                  81000
2134 CONTINUE                                                          82000
       DO 2144 KD = 1,NDM                                              83000
       DO 2144 KS = 1,2                                                84000
       DO 2144 KT = KDPO,10                                            85000
2144 STATES(KD,KS,KT) = RIG(KD,KS) * STATES (KD,KS,KT-1)              86000
2146 DO 2148 KD = 1,NDM                                                87000
       DO 2148 KS = 1,2                                                88000
       DO 2148 KT = 1,10                                               89000
2148 STATES(8,KS,KT) = STATES(8,KS,KT) +STATES(KD,KS,KT)              90000
       DO 2154 KD = 1,NDM                                              91000
       DO 2154 KS = 1,2                                                92000
       DO 2154 KT = KDPO,10                                            93000
2154 STATES(KD,KS,KT) = XNATN (KT) * (STATES(KD,KS,KT) /              94000
     1    STATES(8,KS,KT))                                             95000
       WRITE(6,2160)KYRS                                               96000
2160 FORMAT('1',40X,'STATE PROJECTIONS',/,' STATE.   R-BAR',10I10)    97000
       DO 2170 KD = 1,NDM                                              98000
       DO 2170 KS = 1,2                                                99000
```

```
      DO 2165 KT = 1,10                                              100000
      STATES(8,KS,KT) = 0.0                                          101000
2165  NTS (KT) = STATES (KD,KS,KT)                                   102000
2170  WRITE(6,2167)NMST(KD),RIG(KD,KS),NTS                           103000
2167  FORMAT(I6,F8.5,10I10)                                          104000
      DO 2168 KD = 1,NDM                                             105000
      DO 2168 KS = 1,2                                               106000
      DO 2168 KT = 1,10                                              107000
2168  STATES(8,KS,KT) = STATES(8,KS,KT) +STATES(KD,KS,KT)           108000
      DO 2175 KS = 1,2                                               109000
      DO 2173 KT = 1,10                                              110000
2173  NTS (KT) = STATES (8,KS,KT)                                    111000
2175  WRITE(6,2177) NTS                                              112000
2177  FORMAT('0NATION       ', 10I10)                                113000
C     COUNTY PROJECTIONS WITH STATE SIZE CONSTRAINTS                 113500
      DO 2230 KD = 1,NCTY                                            114000
      READ(5,2210) NMCTY(KD,1),NMCTY(KD,2),KTRAIL,   (HM(1,KD,KQ),   115000
     1    KQ=1,8)                                                    116000
2210  FORMAT(1X,I1,1X,I2,5X,I1,8F8.0)                                117000
      HM(1,KD,9) = 0.0                                               118000
      HM(1,KD,10) = 0.0                                              119000
      IF(KTRAIL.EQ.0) GO TO 2220                                     120000
      READ(5,2215) (HM(1,KD,KQ),KQ=9,10)                             121000
2215  FORMAT(11X,2F8.0)                                              122000
2220  DO 2225 KQ = 1,10                                              123000
2225  HM(2,KD,KQ) = HM (1,KD,KQ)                                     124000
      NMCTY (KD,3) = NMCTY(KD,1) * 100 +  NMCTY(KD,2)                125000
2230  CONTINUE                                                       126000
      KD = 0                                                         127000
      KC = 1                                                         128000
2240  KSTD = KC                                                      129000
      KD = KD + 1                                                    130000
2241  DO 2242 J = 1,10                                               131000
2242  XNATN(J) = 0.0                                                 132000
      IF(KD.GT.NST) GO TO 2288                                       133000
2244  IF(NMST(KD). LT.NMCTY(KC,1)) GO TO 2288                        134000
      IF(NMST(KD).EQ.NMCTY(KC,1)) GO TO 2250                         135000
      WRITE(6,2245)                                                  136000
2245  FORMAT(' CARDS OUT OF SEQUENCE ')                             137000
      CALL EXIT                                                      138000
2250  NDC = 10                                                       139000
      CMRIG(KC) = 99999.9                                            139500
2260  IF(HM(1,KC,NDC).NE.0.0) GO TO 2270                             140000
      NDC = NDC - 1                                                  141000
      IF(NDC.NE.0) GO TO 2260                                        142000
      WRITE(6,2265)NMCTY(KC,3)                                       143000

2265  FORMAT(' COUNTY ',I3, 'HAS NO DATA')                           145000
      CALL EXIT                                                      146000
2270  IF(NDC.EQ.10) GO TO 2286                                       147000
      DV  = 0.0                                                      148000
      CMRIG(KC) = 0.0                                                149000
      DO 2274 KT = 2,NDC                                             150000
      IF (HM(1,KC,KT).EQ.0.0) GO TO 2274                             150500
      IF (HM(1,KC,KT-1).EQ.0.0) GO TO 2274                           151000
      CRIG = HM(1,KC,KT) / HM(1,KC,KT-1)                             152000
      IF (CRIG.GT.RIGMAX) CRIG = RIGMAX                              153000
      IF (CRIG.LT.RIGMIN) CRIG = RIGMIN                              154000
```

```
      CMRIG(KC) = CMRIG(KC) + CRIG                                 155000
      DV  = DV  + 1.0                                              156000
2274 CONTINUE                                                      157000
      CMRIG(KC) = CMRIG(KC) / DV                                   158000
      MQ  = NDC + 1                                                159000
      DO 2284 KT = MQ,10                                           160000
      HM(1,KC,KT) = CMRIG(KC) * HM(1,KC,KT-1)                      161000
2284 HM(2,KC,KT) = HM(1,KC,KT)                                     162000
2286 DO 2285 MQ = 1,10                                             163000
2285 XNATN(MQ) = XNATN(MQ) + HM(1,KC,MQ)                           164000
      KC = KC + 1                                                  165000
      IF(KC.GT.NCTY) GO TO 2288                                    166000
      GO TO 2244                                                   167000
2288 KLST = KC - 1                                                 168000
      WRITE(6,2289)KYRS                                            169000
2289 FORMAT('1',40X,'COUNTY PROJECTIONS',/,' COUNTY   R-BAR',10I10) 170000
      DO 2294 KX  = KSTD,KLST                                      171000
      DO 2294 KS  = 1,2                                            172000
      DO 2292 KT  = 6,10                                           173000
      HM(KS,KX,KT) = STATES (KD,KS,KT) * (HM(KS,KX,KT) / XNATN (KT)) 174000
      NTS (KT-5) = HM(KS,KX,KT-5)                                  175000
2292 NTS (KT)  = HM(KS,KX,KT)                                      176000
2294 WRITE(6,2167) NMCTY( KX,3),CMRIG(KX), NTS                     177000
      DO 2298 KS = 1,2                                             178000
      DO 2296 KT = 1,10                                            179000
2296 NTS (KT) = STATES (KD,KS,KT)                                  180000
2298 WRITE(6,2299) NMCTY(KC-1,1),RIG(KD,KS),NTS                    181000
2299 FORMAT('0',I5,F8.5,10I10)                                     182000
2300 IF(KD.GT.NST) GO TO 2305                                      183000
      IF(KC.GT.NCTY) GO TO 2305                                    184000
      GO TO 2240                                                   185000
2305 M = NMCD                                                      186000
      DO 2440 KC = 1,M                                             187000
      READ(5,2435)XCRD                                             188000
2435 FORMAT(20A4)                                                  189000
2440 WRITE(4,2435)XCRD                                             190000
      END FILE 4                                                   191000
      REWIND 4                                                     192000
2450 READ(5,2435,END=2460) XCRD                                    193000
      WRITE(3,2435) XCRD                                           194000
      GO TO 2450                                                   195000
2460 END FILE 3                                                    196000
      REWIND 3                                                     197000
2500 IF (NITER.LE.5) GO TO 2520                                    198000
      WRITE(6,2510)                                                199000
2510 FORMAT ('1END OF PROJECTIONS  ')                             200000
      CALL EXIT                                                    201000
2520 IF(NOYES(NITER).NE.1) GO TO 2530                              202000
2525 NITER = NITER + 1                                             203000
      GO TO 2500                                                   204000
2530 GO TO (2600,2600,3000,3000,3000),NITER                       205000
C     MCD MODEL 1 AND 2 PRELIMINARY PROJECTIONS                   205500
2600 M = NMCD                                                      206000
      DO 1 LA = 1,NCTY                                             207000
      DO 1 LB = 1,9                                                208000
      IF (LB.GT.5) GO TO 1                                         209000
      CTOTA(LA,LB,1) = 0.0                                         210000
      CTOTA(LA,LB,2) = 0.0                                         211000
```

```
    1 CTOT (LA,LB) = 0.0                                                212000
      CONST(1,1) =    4.1678                                            213000
      CONST(1,2) =    .7691                                             214000
      CONST(1,3) =    .2309                                             215000
      CONST(1,4) =    .9622                                             216000
      CONST(2,1) =   3.6520                                             217000
      CONST(2,2) =    .8362                                             218000
      CONST(2,3) =    .1638                                             219000
      CONST(2,4) =    .5981                                             220000
      CONST(3,1) =   2.6473                                             221000
      CONST(3,2) =    .8216                                             222000
      CONST(3,3) =    .1784                                             223000
      CONST(3,4) =    .4722                                             224000
      CONST(4,2) =   1.0000                                             225000
      CONST(4,1) =   1.0000                                             226000
      CONST(4,3) =   1.0000                                             227000
      CONST(4,4) =   1.0000                                             228000
      CONST(5,1) =   1.0000                                             229000
      CONST(5,2) =   1.0000                                             230000
      CONST(5,3) =   1.0000                                             231000
      CONST(5,4) =   1.0000                                             232000
      CONST(6,1) =   1.0000                                             233000
      CONST(6,2) =   1.0000                                             234000
      CONST(6,3) =   1.0000                                             235000
      CONST(6,4) =   1.0000                                             236000
      IF (NPDENS.EQ.1) WRITE(6,2605)  NITER                            237000
 2605 FORMAT('1       MCD MODEL', I2    /  ' DENSITIES - 1950 - 2020 AS B 238000
     1ELOW '/)                                                          239000
      NCT = 1                                                           240000
      DO 2720   KC  = 1,M                                               241000
      READ(4,2610)KST,KCTY,KMCD,NCLASS,(FP(KC,J),J=1,3),AREA            242000
 2610 FORMAT(1X,I1,1X,I2,I3,1X,I1,13X,3F6.0,F6.2)                       243000
      NN (KC,2) = 100000 * KST + 1000 * KCTY + KMCD                     244000
      NN (KC,4) = NCLASS                                                245000
      IF(NITER.EQ.1) PCT(KC) = FP(KC,3) / AREA                         246000
      IF(NITER.EQ.2) PCT(KC) = FP(KC,1) / AREA                         247000
      MSTC = 100 * KST + KCTY                                           248000
      FP(KC,4) = 0.0                                                    249000
 2650 IF (MSTC - NMCTY(NCT,3)) 2652,2680,2670                           250000
 2652 WRITE(6,2655) NN(KC,2)                                            251000
 2655 FORMAT('1MCDS OUT OF SEQUENCE WITH COUNTYS ',I6)                  252000
      CALL EXIT                                                         253000
 2670 NCT = NCT + 1                                                     254000
      IF(NCT.GT.NCTY) GO TO 2652                                        255000
      GO TO 2650                                                        256000
 2680 NN(KC,1) = NCT                                                    257000
      AL = ALOG10 (PCT(KC))                                            258000
      IF(NITER.EQ.1) NCOL =5                                            259000
      IF(NITER.EQ.2) NCOL =4                                            260000
      IF(NITER.EQ.1) NMAX = 5                                           261000
      IF(NITER.EQ.2) NMAX = 7                                           262000
      DO 2690 N = NITER,NMAX                                            263000
      CC = CONST (NCLASS,2) ** N                                        264000
      X = CONST (NCLASS,1) - ((CC / CONST (NCLASS,3))* CONST (NCLASS,4)) 265000
     1    + CC * AL                                                     266000
      Y = 10 ** X * AREA                                                267000
      FP(KC,NCOL) = Y                                                   268000
      CTOT(NCT,NCOL) = CTOT(NCT,NCOL) + Y                               269000
```

```
2690 NCOL = NCOL + 1                                                270000
     DO 2695 N = 1,3                                                271000
2695 CTOT(NCT,N) = CTOT(NCT,N) + FP(KC,N)                           272000
     IF(NPDENS.NE.1) GO TO 2720                                     273000
     DO 2700 N = 1,9                                                274000
2700 DENS(N) = FP(KC,N) / AREA                                      275000
     WRITE(6,2705) NN(KC,2),( DENS(N),N=1,9)                        276000
2705 FORMAT( I8,9F9.2)                                              277000
2720 CONTINUE                                                       278000
     REWIND 4                                                       279000
     N = 1                                                          280000
 200 LCT = 0                                                        281000
     WRITE(6,199) NITER                                             282000
 199 FORMAT('1      MCD MODEL', I2,': PRELIMINARY PROJECTIONS '/)   283000
     WRITE(6,201)                                                   284000
 201 FORMAT('          MCD     1950     1960     1970A     1970E    19   285000
    180     1990     2000     2010     2020',/)                     286000
 202 LCT = LCT + 1                                                  287000
     DO 204 L = 1,9                                                 288000
 204 NT(L) = FP(N,L)                                                289000
     WRITE(6,205)NN(N,2),(NT(K),K=1,9)                              290000
 205 FORMAT( 8X,I7,9I9)                                             291000
     IF (N.EQ.N)GO TO 220                                           292000
     N = N + 1                                                      293000
     IF (LCT.EQ.55)GO TO 200                                        294000
     GO TO 202                                                      295000
 220 WRITE(6,221) NITER                                             296000
 221 FORMAT('1            MCD MODEL',  I2,  ': SUM OF PRELIMINARY PRO   297000
    1JECTIONS   ',/,                                                298000
    1      '          NO     1950     1960     1970A     1970E    19   299000
    180     1990     2000     2010     2020',/)                     300000
     DO 225 N = 1,NCTY                                              301000
     DO 222 L = 1,9                                                 302000
 222 NT(L) = CTOT (N,L)                                             303000
 225 WRITE(6,205) NMCTY(N,3),(NT(K),K=1,9)                          304000
C    COUNTY INCREMENTS                                              305000
     DO 305 J = 1,NCTY                                              306000
     DO 305 MM = 6,10                                               307000
     CNCR(1,J,MM-5)=HM(1,J,MM) - CTOT(J,MM-1)                       308000
     CNCR(2,J,MM-5)=HM(2,J,MM) - CTOT(J,MM-1)                       309000
 305 CONTINUE                                                       310000
     WRITE(6,307)  NITER                                            311000
 307 FORMAT('1        MCD MODEL', I2, ': COUNTY INCREMENTS '/       312000
    1' COUNTY     1980H     1980M     1990H     1990M     2000H     2000M   313000
    22010H     2010M     2020H     2020M'/)                         314000
     DO 309 K=1,NCTY                                                315000
 309 WRITE (6,310) NMCTY(K,3),((CNCR(J,K,L),J=1,2),L=1,5)           316000
 310 FORMAT( I7,10F9.0)                                             317000
     DO 320 K=1,NCTY                                                319000
     CVECT(K,1)= 0.0                                                320000
 320 CVECT(K,2) = 0.0                                               321000
C    ADJUST MCD MODEL 2 PROJECTIONS UP TO PROJECTION ERROR IN 1970  321200
     IF(NITER.EQ.1) GO TO 326                                       321500
     DO 325 K=1,M                                                   322000
     XX = FP(K,3) - FP(K,4)                                         323000
     VECT(K,1) = 0.0                                                324000
     VECT(K,2) = 0.0                                                325000
     IF (XX.LT.0.0) VECT(K,1) = -XX                                 326000
```

```
      IF (XX.GT.0.0) VECT(K,2) = XX                                          327000
      NC = NN(K,1)                                                           328000
      IF (XX.LT.0.0) CVECT(NC,1) = CVECT(NC,1) - XX                          329000
      IF (XX.GT.0.0) CVECT(NC,2) = CVECT(NC,2) + XX                          330000
  325 CONTINUE                                                               331000
  326 DO 370 KT = 1,5                                                        332000
      DO 369 KM = 1,2                                                        333000
      N = 1                                                                  334000
      DO 368 KC = 1,NCTY                                                     335000
      KCC = KC                                                               336000
      KNN = N                                                                337000
      CTY = CNCR(KM,KC,KT)                                                   338000
      XMULT = 1.0                                                            339000
      IF (CTY.LT.0.0) XMULT = -1.0                                           340000
      NLR = 2                                                                341000
      IF (CTY.LT.0.0) NLR = 1                                                342000
      IF (CTY.LT.0.0) CTY = - CTY                                            343000
      CLIM = CTY                                                             344000
      IF (CTY.GT.CVECT(KC,NLR)) CLIM = CVECT(KC,NLR)                         345000
  330 KCTY = NN(N,1)                                                         346000
      IF (KCTY.NE.KC) GO TO 360                                              347000
      XP(N,KT,KM) = FP(N,KT+4)                                               348000
      IF(NITER.EQ.1) GO TO 340                                              349000
      AD = XMULT * (VECT(N,NLR) / CVECT(KC,NLR)) * CLIM                      350000
      XP(N,KT,KM) = FP(N,KT+4) + AD                                          351000
      CNCR(KM,KC,KT) = CNCR(KM,KC,KT) - AD                                   351500
C     ADJUST MCD MODELS 1&2 PROJECTIONS ACCORDING TO COMPARATIVE GROWTH     351700
  340 N = N + 1                                                             352000
      IF (N.LE.M) GO TO 330                                                  353000
  360 IF (CTY.LT.CVECT(KC,NLR)) GO TO 368                                   354000
      CLIM = CTY - CVECT(KC,NLR)                                             355000
      LMD = N - 1                                                            356000
      SPT = 0.0                                                              357000
      DO 362 KP = KNN,LMD                                                    358000
      ADJ = FP(KP,KT+4) - FP(KP,KT+3)                                       359000
      IF (ADJ.GT.0.0)SPT= SPT + ADJ                                          360000
  362 CONTINUE                                                               361000
      DO 365 KP = KNN,LMD                                                    362000
      IF (LADJ.EQ.1) GO TO 363                                               363000
      ADJ = FP(KP,KT+4) - FP(KP,KT+3)                                       364000
      IF (ADJ.LE.0.0) GO TO 365                                              365000
      AD = XMULT * (ADJ / SPT) * CLIM                                        366000
      GO TO 364                                                              367000
C     ADJUST MCD MODELS 1 AND 2 ACCORDING TO X OF PRELIMINARY POPULATION    367200
  363 IF(CTOT(KC,KT+4).EQ.0.0) GO TO 365                                    367500
      AD = FP(KP,KT+4) / CTOT(KC,KT+4) * CNCR(KM,KC,KT)                     368000
  364 XP(KP,KT,KM) = XP(KP,KT,KM) + AD                                      369000
  365 CONTINUE                                                               370000
  368 CONTINUE                                                               371000
  369 CONTINUE                                                               372000
  370 CONTINUE                                                               373000
      N = 1                                                                  374000
  500 LCT = 0                                                                375000
      WRITE(6,499) NITER                                                     376000
  499 FORMAT('1           MCD MODEL', I2, ': FINAL MCD PROJECTIONS '/)      377000
      WRITE(6,501)                                                           378000
  501 FORMAT('           MCD    1980H    1980M    1990H    1990M    200     379000
     10H    2000M    2010H    2010M    2020H    2020M',/)                    380000
```

```
502 DO 503 L = 1,5                                                    381000
    NT(2*L-1)= XP(N,L,1)                                              382000
503 NT(2*L)  = XP(N,L,2)                                              383000
    WRITE(6,504) NN(N,2),NT                                           384000
504 FORMAT( 8X,I7,10I9)                                               385000
    NC = NN(N,1)                                                      386000
    DO 508 L = 1,5                                                    387000
    CTOTA(NC,L,1) = CTOTA(NC,L,1) +XP (N,L,1)                         388000
508 CTOTA(NC,L,2) = CTOTA(NC,L,2) + XP (N,L,2)                        389000
    IF(N.EQ.M) GO TO 520                                             390000
    N = N + 1                                                         391000
    IF (LCT.EQ.54) GO TO 500                                          392000
    LCT = LCT + 1                                                     393000
    GO TO 502                                                         394000
520 WRITE (6,521) NITER                                               395000
521 FORMAT('1       MCD MODEL', I2,': FINAL COUNTY PROJECTIONS',/)    396000
    WRITE(6,522)                                                      397000
522 FORMAT('         COUNTY    1980H    1980M    1990H    1990M    200 398000
   10H    2000M    2010H    2010M    2020H    2020M',/)              399000
    DO 525  N = 1,NCTY                                                400000
    DO 523 L = 1,5                                                    401000
    NT(2*L-1)= CTOTA(N,L,1)                                           402000
523 NT(2*L)  = CTOTA(N,L,2)                                           403000
525 WRITE(6,504) NMCTY(N,3),NT                                        404000
530 CONTINUE                                                          405000
C   ALLOCATION OF MCD PROJECTIONS TO PLANNING ZONES                   405500
    IF(NITER.GE.3) M = NM                                             406000
    DO 540 K = 1,M                                                    407000
540 PCT(K) = 0.0                                                      408000
    DO 545 K = 1,187                                                  409000
    DO 545 KK = 1,11                                                  410000
545 TP(K,KK) = 0.0                                                    411000
    DO 548 K = 1,16                                                   412000
    NP(K + 170) = K                                                   413000
548 NS(K) = K                                                         414000
    DO 553 K = 1,10                                                   415000
    NR(K) = K                                                         416000
    IF (K.GT.5) NR(K) = (K - 5) * 10                                  417000
553 NP(K + 160) = NR(K)                                               418000
    NP(187) = 9999                                                    419000
    DO 555 K = 1,10                                                   420000
    DO 555 KK = 1,16                                                  421000
    KS = 16 * (K - 1) + KK                                            422000
555 NP(KS) = 100 * NR(K) + NS(KK)                                     423000
565 READ(3,570,END=999) NRA,NRB,NRC,(NRNG(K),NSECT(K),RPCT(K),K=1,7)  424000
570 FORMAT(1X,I1,1X,I2,I3,3X,7(2I2,F5.4))                             425000
    NRC = 100000 * NRA + 1000*NRB + NRC                               426000
    DO 580 K = 1,M                                                    427000
    IF (NRC.EQ.NN(K,2))GO TO 590                                      428000
580 CONTINUE                                                          429000
    IF (NITER.EQ.3.OR.NITER.EQ.4) GO TO 565                           430000
    WRITE (6,585) NRC                                                 431000
585 FORMAT(I8,' BAD ID')                                              432000
    GO TO 565                                                         433000
590 DO 600 KK = 1,7                                                   434000
    KN = 100 * NRNG(KK) + NSECT(KK)                                   435000
    IF (KN.EQ.0) GO TO 565                                            436000
    KR = NRNG(KK)                                                     437000
```

```
            KS = NSECT(KK)                                              438000
            PK = RPCT(KK)                                               439000
            PCT(K) = PCT(K) + PK                                        440000
            NMOD = NN(K,4)                                              441000
            CALL CALC (KN,1,160)                                        442000
            CALL CALC (KR,161,170)                                      443000
            CALL CALC (KS,171,186)                                      444000
            CALL CALC (9999,187,187)                                    445000
   600  CONTINUE                                                        446000
        GO TO 565                                                       447000
   999  N = 1                                                           448000
            IF(NITER.EQ.3.OR.NITER.EQ.4) GO TO   725                    449000
            IF(NITER.LT.6) GO TO 700                                    450000
            DO 699 K = 1,187                                            451000
            DO 699 KK = 1,11                                            452000
   699  TP(K,KK) = ZP(K,KK)                                             453000
   700  LCT = 4                                                         454000
            IF (NITER.EQ.6) WRITE(6,800)                                455000
   800  FORMAT('1',40X,'ALLOCATIONS: MCD MODELS 3, 4, 5  '/)            456000
            IF(NITER.NE.6) WRITE(6,810) NITER                          457000
   810  FORMAT('1',40X,'ALLOCATIONS: MCD MODEL',  I2/)                  458000
            IF (N.EQ.161) WRITE(6,820)                                  459000
   820  FORMAT (41X,'SUMMARY BY RINGS (OR ROWS)'/)                      460000
            IF (N.EQ.171) WRITE(6,830)                                  461000
   830  FORMAT (41X,'SUMMARY BY SECTORS (OR COLUMNS)'/)                 462000
            IF(N.EQ.187) WRITE (6,840)                                  462500
            IF(N.LT.161) WRITE (6,702)                                  463000
            IF(N.GE.161) WRITE (6,701)                                  464000
   840  FORMAT (51X, 'TOTALS   ',/)                                     465000
   701  FORMAT('        1970A      1980H      1980M      1990H      1990M    466000
       1  2000H      2000M      2010H      2010M      2020H      2020M',/)  467000
   702  FORMAT(' ZONE    1970A      1980H      1980M      1990H      1990M    468000
       1  2000H      2000M      2010H      2010M      2020H      2020M',/)  469000
   703  DO 704 L = 1,11                                                 470000
   704  NQ(L) = TP(N,L)                                                 471000
        WRITE (6,705) NP(N),NQ                                          472000
   705  FORMAT( I5,11I10)                                               473000
        LCT = LCT + 1                                                   474000
        N = N + 1                                                       475000
        IF (LCT.EQ.54) GO TO 700                                        476000
        IF(N.EQ.161.OR.N.EQ.171.OR.N.EQ.187) GO TO 700                  477000
        IF(N.LT.188) GO TO 703                                          478000
        IF (NITER.LT.6) WRITE(6,710) NITER                              479000
   710  FORMAT('1 MCD MODEL ', I2, ': CHECK OF ALLOCATION SHARES '/)    480000
        IF(NITER.EQ.6) WRITE(6,712)                                     481000
   712  FORMAT('1 MCD MODELS 3, 4, 5: CHECK OF ALLOCATION SHARES '/)    482000
        DO 720 N = 1,M                                                  483000
        X = PCT(N)                                                      484000
        IF (X.GT.0.98.AND.X.LT.1.02) GO TO 720                          485000
        WRITE(6,715) NN(N,2),PCT(N)                                     486000
   715  FORMAT( I8,' PCT NOT = 1.0 ',F5.2)                              487000
   720  CONTINUE                                                        488000
   725  REWIND 3                                                        489000
        IF(NITER.LT.5) GO TO 2525                                       490000
        NITER = NITER + 1                                               491000
        IF (NITER.EQ.6) GO TO 999                                       492000
        GO TO 2525                                                      493000
   C        BEGIN MCD MODELS 3, 4, AND 5                                493500
```

```
3000 NCT = 1                                                        494000
     M = NMCD                                                       495000
     NM = 0                                                         496000
     DO 3900 KC = 1,M                                               497000
     NM = NM + 1                                                    498000
     READ(4,3010) KST,KCTY,KMCD,KMOD,(YP(1,NM,J),J=1,10)            499000
3010 FORMAT(1X,I1,1X,I2,I3,I1,2X,5F6.0,6X,5F6.0)                    500000
     NM = NM - 1                                                    501000
     IF(NITER.EQ.3.AND.KMOD.NE.3) GO TO 3900                       502000
     IF(NITER.EQ.4.AND.KMOD.NE.4) GO TO 3900                       503000
     NM = NM + 1                                                    504000
     NN(NM,2) = 100000 * KST + 1000 * KCTY + KMCD                   505000
     MSTC = 100 * KST + KCTY                                        506000
3020 IF (MSTC - NMCTY(NCT,3)) 3030,3050,3040                        507000
3030 WRITE(6,2655) NN(NM,2)                                         508000
     CALL EXIT                                                      509000
3040 NCT = NCT + 1                                                  510000
     IF (NCT.GT.NCTY) GO TO 3030                                    511000
     GO TO 3020                                                     512000
3050 NN(NM,1) = NCT                                                 513000
     IF (NITER- 4) 3100,3200,3300                                   514000
C    MCD MODEL 3                                                    514500
3100 ND = 10                                                        515000
3110 IF(YP(1,NM,ND).NE.0) GO TO 3130                                516000
     ND = ND - 1                                                    517000
     IF (ND.NE.0) GO TO 3110                                        518000
     WRITE (6,3120) NN(NM,2)                                        519000
3120 FORMAT(' NO DATA THIS MCD ',I6)                               520000
     NM = NM - 1                                                    521000
     GO TO 3900                                                     522000
3130 GO TO 3400                                                     523000
C    MCD MODEL 4                                                    523500
3200 ND = 10                                                        524000
3210 IF (YP(1,NM,ND).NE.0) GO TO 3240                               525000
     ND = ND - 1                                                    526000
     IF(ND.NE.0) GO TO 3210                                         527000
3220 WRITE(6,3230) NN(NM,2)                                         528000
3230 FORMAT(' BAD DATA THIS MCD ',I6)                              529000
     NM = NM - 1                                                    530000
     GO TO 3900                                                     531000
3240 NX = ND - 1                                                    532000
3250 IF(YP(1,NM,NX).NE.0)  GO TO 3280                               533000
     NX = NX - 1                                                    534000
     IF(NX.EQ.0) GO TO 3220                                         535000
     GO TO 3250                                                     536000
3280 NZ = ND - NX                                                   537000
     IF (NZ.EQ.1) GO TO 3220                                        538000
     ROOT = 1. / FLOAT (NZ)                                         539000
     XRIG = (YP(1,NM,ND) / YP(1,NM,NX)) ** ROOT                     540000
     NLST = ND - 2                                                  543000
     DO 3290 J = NX,NLST                                            544000
3290 YP(1,NM, J+1) = XRIG * YP(1,NM, J)                             545000
     GO TO 3400                                                     546000
C    MCD MODEL 5                                                    546500
3300 ND = 5                                                         547000
3400 NN(NM,3) = ND                                                  548000
     NN(NM,4) = KMOD                                                549000
3900 CONTINUE                                                       550000
```

```
      REWIND 4                                                    551000
4000  KC = 0                                                      552000
      KM = 1                                                      553000
4010  KC = KC + 1                                                 554000
      KSTC = KM                                                   555000
      DO 4030 J = 1,10                                            556000
4030  XNATN (J) = 0.0                                             557000
4035  IF(KC.GT.NCTY) GO TO 4200                                   558000
      IF(NMCTY(KC,3).LT.(NN(KM,2) / 1000)) GO TO 4200            559000
      IF(NMCTY(KC,3).EQ.(NN(KM,2) / 1000)) GO TO 4050            560000
      WRITE(6,4040) NMCTY(KC,3),NN(KM,2)                          561000
4040  FORMAT(' CTY / MCD PROBLEM',2I7)                            562000
      CALL EXIT                                                   563000
4050  XRIG = 0.0                                                  564000
      CMRIG(KM) = 99999.9                                         564500
      XD   = 0.0                                                  565000
      ND = NN(KM,3)                                               566000
      IF(ND.EQ.10) GO TO 4100                                     567000
      DO 4070 J = 2,ND                                            568000
      IF (YP(1,KM,J-1).EQ.0.0.OR.YP(1,KM,J).EQ.0.0)   GO TO 4070  569000
      YRIG = YP(1,KM,J) / YP(1,KM,J-1)                            570000
      IF (YRIG.GT.RIGMAX) YRIG = RIGMAX                           571000
      IF (YRIG.LT.RIGMIN) YRIG = RIGMIN                           572000
      XRIG = XRIG + YRIG                                          573000
      XD = XD + 1.0                                               574000
4070  CONTINUE                                                    575000
      IF(XD.GT.0) XRIG = XRIG / XD                                576000
      CMRIG(KM) = XRIG                                            577000
      NDONE = ND + 1                                              578000
      DO 4080 MQ = NDONE,10                                       579000
4080  YP(1,KM,MQ) = XRIG * YP(1,KM,MQ-1)                          580000
4100  DO 4110 MQ = 6,10                                           581000
4110  XNATN (MQ) = XNATN (MQ) + YP(1,KM,MQ)                       582000
      DO 4120 MQ = 1,10                                           583000
4120  YP(2,KM,MQ) = YP(1,KM,MQ)                                   584000
      KM = KM + 1                                                 585000
      IF(KM.GT.NM)    GO TO 4200                                  586000
      GO TO 4035                                                  587000
4200  KLST = KM - 1                                               588000
      IF (KSTC.EQ.KM) GOTO 4240                                   589000
      WRITE (6,4210) NITER,KYRS                                   590000
4210  FORMAT('1',40X,' MCD PROJECTIONS, MCD MODEL', I2,/,         591000
     1 '      MCD   R-BAR',10I10)                                 592000
      DO 4230 KX = KSTC,KLST                                      593000
      DO 4230 KS = 1,2                                            594000
      DO 4220 KT = 6,10                                           595000
      YP(KS,KX,KT) = HM(KS,KC,KT) * (YP(KS,KX,KT) / XNATN (KT))   596000
      NTS (KT-5) = YP(KS,KX,KT-5)                                 597000
4220  NTS (KT)    = YP(KS,KX,KT)                                  598000
4230  WRITE(6,4235) NN(KX,2), CMRIG(KX),NTS                       599000
4235  FORMAT(I8,F8.5,10I10)                                       600000
4240  IF (KC.GT.NCTY) GO TO 530                                   601000
      IF (KM.GT.NM)    GO TO 530                                  602000
      GO TO 4010                                                  603000
      END                                                         604000
      SUBROUTINE CALC (KK,KF,KT)                                  605000
      DIMENSION YP(2,700,10)                                      606000
      DIMENSION TP(187,11), FP(700,10),   XP(700,5,2), NP(187)    607000
```

```
      COMMON PK, TP, FP, XP, K, NP,                                  608000
    1        NITER, ZP(187,11),NMOD,YP                               609000
      DO 1000 L = KF,KT                                              610000
      IF(NP(L).EQ.KK) GO TO 1006                                     611000
1000  CONTINUE                                                       612000
      WRITE (6,1005) KK                                              613000
1005  FORMAT(I5,' BAD RING OR SECTOR')                              614000
      GO TO 1100                                                     615000
1006  IF(NITER.EQ.1.OR.NITER.EQ.2) GO TO 1008                        616000
      IF(NITER.EQ.5) TP(L,1) = TP(L,1) + PK * YP(1,K,5)              617000
      IF(NITER.NE.NMOD) GO TO 1200                                   618000
      ZP(L,1)= ZP(L,1) + PK * YP (1,K,5)                             619000
1200  DO 1007 N = 1,2                                                620000
      DO 1007 NN = 1,5                                               621000
      NS = 2 * NN + N - 1                                            622000
      IF(NITER.EQ.5) TP(L,NS) = TP(L,NS) + PK * YP(N,K,NN+5)         623000
1007  IF(NITER.EQ.NMOD)ZP(L,NS) = ZP(L,NS) + PK * YP(N,K,NN+5)       624000
      GO TO 1100                                                     625000
1008  TP(L,1) = TP(L,1) + PK * FP(K,3)                               626000
      DO 1010 N = 1,2                                                627000
      DO 1010 NN = 1,5                                               628000
      NS = 2 * NN + N - 1                                            629000
1010  TP(L,NS) = TP(L,NS) + PK * XP(K,NN,N)                          630000
1100  RETURN                                                         631000
      END                                                            632000
//GO.FT04F001 DD UNIT=S2314,DSN=&&MCD,DISP=(NEW,PASS),
//     SPACE=(CYL,(2,1)),DCB=(LRECL=80,BLKSIZE=400,RECFM=FB)
//GO.FT03F001 DD UNIT=S2314,DSN=&&PIE,DISP=(NEW,PASS),
//     SPACE=(CYL,(2,1)),DCB=(LRECL=80,BLKSIZE=400,RECFM=FB)
//GO.S*SIN DD *
1990205040       11
NO      1 73921574 79298741 90795479107593905121941179140279000161804000
NO        21830670002C9848000238298000
S1     H   700000   740000   760000   800000   810000   850000   900000
S1     M   700000   740000   760000   800000   810000   820000   850000
S2     H   940200 1051800 1333300 2052017 2181850 2220000 2351000
S2     M   940200 1051800 1333300 2052017 2181850 2120000 2150000
C1001      207200   208850   226900   245400   290900   330000   370000
C1 02                69950    83050   121430   146720   157000   169000
C1 03      434200   461200   450050   433170   372370   383000   406000
C2 01      343000   465500   763700 1514717 1650000
C2 02      597200   586300   569600   537300   531850
M1001  1521   3900   4000   5100   8200  11800  16.80
M1  1  25111467001472001587001567001461 00 15.90
M1  1  3521    900   1350   1700   3400   5700  19.80
M1  1  4521  20000  19000  22000  23000  23000   3.80
M1  1  5521   9500   9000   8300  16400  25000  48.00
M1  1  6521   7000   9200  11700  18400  22600  12.50
M1  1  7531   1000   1300   2200   3400   4500  28.50
M1  1  8531    700    800    700    400    200   4.00
M1  1  9511  10000  10500  11000  11500  50000   6.00
M1  1 10531   7500   6500   5500   4000   2000100.00
M1002  1411  10000  12000  15000  31000  41000  37.30        96100
M1  2  2431    400    350    300    330    320   0.30          570
M1  2  3421   3900   4400   4050   5800   8800  19.40        27000
M1  2  4411   5900   5700   6600  10500  10700   1.90        13300
M1  2  5421  23400  31000  38000  40000  42000  23.00        85000
M1  2  6411   2800   2500   3100   5000   7500   1.50        16000
```

M1	2	7421	5500	7250	8800	20000	25300	55.00		52000	
M1	2	8431	1300	1150	1200	1100	1200	2.30		5500	
M1	2	9411	3800	3800	4000	5100	7000	1.50		15500	
M1	2	10421	1600	1800	2000	2600	2900	2.70		6500	
M2	01	1311	11400	12400	15100	23817	26500	6.60	29500	29800	29900
M2	1	2311	187000	260000	440000	740000	770000	109.49	790000	810000	813000
M2	1	3311	62000	84000	143000	219000	238000	43.00	245000	247500	249000
M2	1	4311	300	10000	16000	26000	29000	2.10	36000	38000	39000
M2	1	5311	37000	43000	67000	290000	339000	73.70	352000	362000	365900
M2	1	6311	19000	24000	46000	142000	187000	51.00	250000	269000	277000
M2	1	7311	4300	5600	8000	10700	12000	1.00	13000	13500	14000
M2	1	8311	7200	11200	14500	23900	29000	5.30	33000	36000	39000
M2	1	9331	11700	12000	11100	13300	17000	52.70	23000	28000	32000
M2	1	10321	3100	3300	3000	2600	2500	0.50	2200	2300	2400
M2	02	1411	76000	80000	77000	74000	73000	4.30	80000		85000
M2	2	2411	2000	2500	2200	1900	1950	0.10	2200		2500
M2	2	3411	5700	5600	5500	5100	5800	0.20	6200		6500
M2	2	4411	12500	13700	13500	11700	11800	1.20	12000		14000
M2	2	5411	59000	54000	50700	48400	45400	1.30	40000		38000
M2	2	6411	320000	310000	299000	276000	261000	13.50	260000		332000
M2	2	7411	47000	44000	41600	42400	47800	5.10	52000		60000
M2	2	8421	6000	7500	9800	12100	13200	6.10	16000		25000
M2	2	9411	53000	54000	55500	52200	58500	1.40	59000		60000
M2	2	10411	16000	15000	14800	13500	13400	0.70	15000		20000

M2	01	1	1002035001003035002003020002002201000
M2	1	2	2016025002001025002015010001016015000301000051001010951015006 00
M2	1	2	2002004000401001000416000500516001500501001 00
M2	1	3	1002030001001020001016000502001001002002040000200300600050100150
M2	1	3	050200100
M2	1	4	200310000
M2	1	5	2004025002003010002005010001003005001004020001005020001006005 00
M2	1	5	050400300050500200
M2	1	6	011500063011600063010100063010200006301030006301040006301050000 63
M2	1	6	01060006302150012502160012502010012502020010125020300125020400012 5
M2	1	6	02050012502060012503150001403160020003010021003020021403030021 4
M2	1	6	030400214030500214030600214040100004020040004030040004040040 0
M2	1	6	040500400040600400050200300005030050005040030005050040005060050 0
M2	1	6	100601300100500400200600300100300800100400019 8
M2	1	7	100310000
M2	1	8	100306000200304000
M2	1	9	1014024001010502400201401300201501300051400400051500400051600200
M2	1	9	041300100041400300041500300041600300031300100031400200031500200
M2	1	9	031600100
M2	1	10	100310000
M2	2	1	200610000
M2	2	2	200510000
M2	2	3	200510000
M2	2	4	200610000
M2	2	5	200610000
M2	2	6	200505000200605000
M2	2	7	20050800020062000
M2	2	8	200510000
M2	2	9	200610000
M2	2	10	200610000
M1	01	1	010700150010800150010900150011000150011100150011200150011300050
M1	01	1	011400050020700200020800040002090050002100050002110040003090050 0
M1	01	1	031000700031100400040900500041000800041100300050900300051000900
M1	01	1	051100400010090020010100160010110040 0

```
M1  01   2    1010050001011010002010004000
M1  01   3    0311003000312004000313003000411004000412005000413001000511100600
M1  01   3    0512004001011045001012005002011013002010002001010000500
M1  01   4    0113005001140050002120150002130150002140150002110050031302000
M1  01   4    0314015000312005000500
M1  01   5    1010003002080100020009050000201003700
M1  01   6    201005000201105000
M1  01   7    2009010001007005001008025001009040001010010000508050005090030000
M1  01   7    040800200
M1  01   8    0407020000408020000307025000308025000207005000208020003090300
M1  01   9    100705000507030000508010004070100
M1  01  10    200703000200803500100701300100801000200901000100900200
M1  02   1    1011005001012010002011015002012030002013040000
M1  02   2    201210000
M1  02   3    2011020002012070002013010000
M1  02   4    201110000
M1  02   5    2011050002012050000
M1  02   6    201210000
M1  02   7    2013015002014015001012025001013025001014010000513006000413002000
M1  02   7    051200200
M1  02   8    201210000
M1  02   9    201210000
M1  02  10    201110000
//
```

Chapter 8
The Population Program:
Output, The Sample
Problem Printout

This chapter consists of the printout generated by the sample problem data listed in Chapter 7 run on the IBM System 360/67, at Rutgers University. We urge any reader attempting to use this program in another machine system to use the sample problem of Chapter 7 for initial validation, rather than attempting to alter both system and data in one step. This chapter will serve as a check of results. Given successful system adaptation, the user can then change the data.

STATE PROJECTIONS

STATE	R-BAR	1930	1940	1950	1960	1970	1980	1990	2000	2010	2020
1	1.04292	700000	740000	760000	800000	810000	850000	900000	931325	976364	1013963
1	1.03304	700000	740000	760000	800000	810000	820000	850000	871223	904676	930588
2	1.17102	940200	1051800	1333300	2052017	2181850	2220000	2351000	2731645	3215494	3749481
2	1.15590	940200	1051800	1333300	2052017	2181850	2120000	2150000	2465774	2864976	3297539
3	1.14038	72281374	77506941	88702179	104741888	118949329	137209000	158553000	179404029	205656140	233534554
3	1.14068	72281374	77506941	88702179	104741888	118949329	137339000	158804000	179730001	206078347	234069871
NATION		73921574	79298741	90795479	107593905	121941179	140279000	161804000	183066999	209847999	238297999
NATION		73921574	79298741	90795479	107593905	121941179	140279000	161804000	183066999	209848000	238297999

~~~~~~

COUNTY PROJECTIONS

COUNTY	R-BAR	1930	1940	1950	1960	1970	1980	1990	2000	2010	2020
101	1.10283	207200	208850	226900	245400	290900	322413	352380	374954	402058	424789
101	1.10283	207200	208850	226900	245400	290900	311034	332804	350757	372537	389860
102	1.20083	0	69950	83050	121430	146720	153390	160952	186483	217733	250487
102	1.20083	0	69950	83050	121430	146720	147977	152010	174448	201747	229891
103	0.99146	434200	461200	450050	433170	372370	374195	386666	369887	356571	338686
103	0.99146	434200	461200	450050	433170	372370	360988	365185	346017	330391	310837
1	1.04292	700000	740000	760000	800000	810000	850000	900000	931325	976364	1013963
1	1.03304	700000	740000	760000	800000	810000	820000	850000	871223	904676	930588

~~~~~~

COUNTY PROJECTIONS

COUNTY	R-BAR	1930	1940	1950	1960	1970	1980	1990	2000	2010	2020
201	1.36161	343000	465500	763700	1514717	1650000	1804868	2019541	2445268	2967503	3538474
201	1.36161	343000	465500	763700	1514717	1650000	1723567	1846880	2207271	2644017	3111966
202	0.97160	597200	586300	569600	537300	531850	415131	331458	286376	247991	211007
202	0.97160	597200	586300	569600	537300	531850	396432	303119	258503	220958	185573
2	1.17102	940200	1051800	1333300	2052017	2181850	2220000	2351000	2731645	3215494	3749481
2	1.15590	940200	1051800	1333300	2052017	2181850	2120000	2150000	2465774	2864976	3297539

MCD MODEL 1
DENSITIES - 1950 - 2020 AS BELOW

101001	303.57	488.10	702.38	0.0	952.79	1228.10	1518.51	1813.42	2103.55
101002	9981.13	9855.34	9188.68	0.0	10255.71	11147.54	11885.82	12486.76	12969.54
101003	85.86	171.72	287.88	0.0	451.94	658.23	901.42	1172.48	1460.78
101004	5789.47	6052.63	6052.63	0.0	5769.73	5537.01	5349.64	5197.84	5074.20
101005	172.92	341.67	520.83	0.0	741.99	996.38	1274.91	1566.75	1861.47
101006	936.00	1472.00	1808.00	0.0	2100.70	2378.80	2639.42	2879.14	3096.22
101007	77.19	119.30	157.89	0.0	190.03	221.08	250.36	277.29	301.57
101008	175.00	100.00	50.00	0.0	73.88	101.73	132.31	164.20	196.08
101009	1833.33	1916.67	8333.33	0.0	9513.27	10521.52	11369.04	12067.07	12632.97
101010	55.00	40.00	20.00	0.0	34.80	54.81	79.60	108.16	139.14
102001	402.14	831.10	1099.20	0.0	2003.17	3174.66	4523.76	5940.04	7324.29
102002	1000.00	1100.00	1066.67	0.0	912.99	802.78	722.26	662.19	616.59
102003	208.76	298.97	453.61	0.0	661.02	904.60	1175.94	1464.38	1759.21
102004	3473.68	5526.32	5631.58	0.0	7037.81	8344.67	9512.62	10520.96	11368.62
102005	1652.17	1739.13	1826.09	0.0	2118.26	2395.41	2654.82	2893.18	3108.85
102006	2066.67	3333.33	5000.00	0.0	6422.52	7777.71	9011.52	10092.05	11010.48
102007	160.00	363.64	460.00	0.0	668.79	913.50	1185.61	1474.44	1769.30
102008	521.74	478.26	521.74	0.0	507.34	495.39	485.79	478.04	471.77
102009	2666.67	3400.00	4666.66	0.0	6090.60	7466.68	8733.06	9851.35	10807.94
102010	740.74	962.96	1074.07	0.0	1359.08	1652.79	1946.57	2231.95	2502.46
201001	2287.88	3608.64	4015.15	0.0	5425.44	6831.23	8155.62	9346.45	10379.33
201002	4018.63	6758.61	7032.61	0.0	8349.20	9516.61	10524.33	11371.41	12069.03
201003	3325.58	5093.02	5534.88	0.0	6944.69	8259.63	9437.96	10457.39	11315.77
201004	7619.05	12380.95	13809.53	0.0	14029.41	14185.13	14306.00	14399.74	14472.21
201005	909.09	3934.87	4599.73	0.0	6023.31	7403.14	8675.85	9801.68	10765.98
201006	901.96	2784.31	3666.67	0.0	5059.52	6474.04	7825.63	9054.21	10128.82
201007	8000.00	10700.00	12000.00	0.0	12592.91	13054.26	13420.52	13709.21	13935.45
201008	2735.85	4509.43	5471.70	0.0	6883.62	8203.72	9388.78	10415.47	11280.84
201009	210.63	252.37	322.58	0.0	341.77	358.09	372.08	383.99	394.05
201010	6000.00	5200.00	5000.00	0.0	4917.82	4844.59	4784.20	4734.29	4692.94
202001	17906.98	17209.30	16976.75	0.0	16444.05	16027.94	15715.03	15478.55	15299.11
202002	22000.01	19000.00	19500.00	0.0	18293.33	17397.00	16737.59	16247.50	15880.41
202003	27500.00	25500.00	29000.00	0.0	24823.22	22000.00	20049.64	18667.89	17670.32
202004	11250.00	9750.00	9833.33	0.0	10804.73	11603.74	12258.17	12786.55	13208.35
202005	39000.02	37230.79	34923.09	0.0	28637.55	24556.97	21818.61	19922.15	18576.54
202006	22148.14	20444.44	19333.33	0.0	18172.96	17308.91	16672.36	16198.80	15843.78
202007	8156.86	8313.72	9372.55	0.0	10413.17	11278.93	11993.42	12573.63	13038.87
202008	1606.56	1983.61	2163.93	0.0	2441.33	2697.30	2931.84	3143.56	3332.27
202009	39642.87	37285.72	41785.72	0.0	32874.63	27306.23	23674.07	21212.80	19495.39
202010	21142.86	19285.71	19142.86	0.0	18035.10	17207.83	16597.44	16142.77	15801.58

MCD MODEL 1: PRELIMINARY PROJECTIONS

MCD	1950	1960	1970A	1970E	1980	1990	2000	2010	2020
101001	5100	8200	11800	0	16006	20632	25510	30465	35339
101002	158700	156700	146100	0	163065	177245	188984	198539	206215
101003	1700	3400	5700	0	8948	13033	17848	23215	28923
101004	22000	23000	23000	0	21925	21040	20328	19751	19281
101005	8300	16400	25000	0	35615	47826	61195	75204	89350
101006	11700	18400	22600	0	26258	29734	32992	35989	38702
101007	2200	3400	4500	0	5415	6300	7135	7902	8594
101008	700	400	200	0	295	406	529	656	784
101009	11000	11500	50000	0	57079	63129	68214	72402	75797
101010	5500	4000	2000	0	3479	5480	7959	10815	13914
102001	15000	31000	41000	0	74718	118414	168736	221563	273196
102002	300	330	320	0	273	240	216	198	184
102003	4050	5800	8800	0	12823	17549	22813	28409	34128
102004	6600	10500	10700	0	13371	15854	18073	19989	21600
102005	38000	40000	42000	0	48719	55094	61060	66543	71503
102006	3100	5000	7500	0	9633	11666	13517	15138	16515
102007	8800	20000	25300	0	36783	50242	65208	81094	97311
102008	1200	1100	1200	0	1166	1139	1117	1099	1085
102009	4000	5100	7000	0	9135	11200	13099	14777	16211
102010	2000	2600	2900	0	3669	4462	5255	6026	6756
201001	15100	23817	26500	0	35807	45086	53827	61686	68503
201002	440000	740000	770000	0	914154	1041973	1152309	1245056	1321438
201003	143000	219000	238000	0	298621	355164	405832	449668	486578
201004	16000	26000	29000	0	29461	29788	30042	30239	30391
201005	67000	290000	339000	0	443918	545611	639410	722384	793453
201006	46000	142000	187000	0	258035	330175	399107	461764	516570
201007	8000	10700	12000	0	12592	13054	13420	13709	13935
201008	14500	23900	29000	0	36483	43479	49760	55202	59788
201009	11100	13300	17000	0	18011	18871	19608	20236	20766
201010	3000	2600	2500	0	2458	2422	2392	2367	2346
202001	77000	74000	73000	0	70709	68920	67574	66557	65786
202002	2200	1900	1950	0	1829	1739	1673	1624	1588
202003	5500	5100	5800	0	4964	4400	4009	3733	3534
202004	13500	11700	11800	0	12965	13924	14709	15343	15850
202005	50700	48400	45400	0	37228	31924	28364	25898	24149
202006	299000	276000	261000	0	245335	233670	225076	218683	213891
202007	41600	42400	47800	0	53107	57522	61166	64125	66498
202008	9800	12100	13200	0	14892	16453	17884	19175	20326
202009	55500	52200	58500	0	46024	38228	33143	29697	27293
202010	14800	13500	13400	0	12624	12045	11618	11299	11061

MCD MODEL 1: SUM OF PRELIMINARY PROJECTIONS

NO	1950	1960	1970A	1970E	1980	1990	2000	2010	2020
101	226900	245400	290900	0	338091	384829	430698	474942	516904
102	83050	121430	146720	0	210297	285864	369099	454838	538494
103	0	0	0	0	0	0	0	0	0
201	763700	1491317	1650000	0	2049541	2425624	2765707	3062311	3313768
202	569600	537300	531850	0	499681	478828	465221	456141	449978

MCD MODEL 1: COUNTY INCREMENTS

COUNTY	1980H	1980M	1990H	1990M	2000H	2000M	2010H	2010M	2020H	2020M
101	-15677.	-27057.	-32449.	-52026.	-55744.	-79941.	-72885.	-102405.	-92116.	-127045.
102	-56907.	-62320.	-124912.	-133854.	-182616.	-194650.	-237105.	-253092.	-288007.	-308603.
103	374195.	360989.	386667.	365185.	369888.	346017.	356572.	330391.	338687.	310838.
201	-244673.	-325974.	-406083.	-578744.	-320439.	-558436.	-94808.	-418294.	224706.	-201802.
202	-84549.	-103249.	-147371.	-175709.	-178845.	-206718.	-208150.	-235183.	-238971.	-264405.

MCD MODEL 1: FINAL MCD PROJECTIONS

MCD	1980H	1980M	1990H	1990M	2000H	2000M	2010H	2010M	2020H	2020M
101001	15264	14725	18892	17842	22209	20775	25790	23896	29041	26653
101002	155504	150016	162300	153283	164524	153907	168071	155731	169466	155532
101003	8533	8232	11934	11271	15538	14535	19652	18209	23769	21814
101004	20908	20170	19266	18196	17697	16555	16720	15493	15845	14542
101005	33964	32765	43793	41360	53275	49837	63663	58988	73427	67389
101006	25041	24157	27227	25715	28722	26868	30466	28229	31805	29190
101007	5164	4982	5769	5449	6211	5810	6690	6198	7063	6482
101008	281	271	372	351	460	431	556	515	644	591
101009	54432	52511	57806	54594	59385	55553	61291	56791	62290	57168
101010	3318	3201	5018	4739	6929	6482	9155	8483	11434	10494
102001	54499	52576	66671	62967	85252	79750	106063	98276	127080	116631
102002	199	192	135	128	128	102	95	88	86	78
102003	9353	9023	9880	9331	11526	10782	13599	12601	15875	14570
102004	9753	9409	8926	8430	9131	8542	9569	8866	10047	9221
102005	35536	34282	31020	29296	30850	28859	31854	29515	33260	30525
102006	7026	6778	6568	6203	6829	6388	7246	6714	7682	7050
102007	26830	25883	28288	26716	32945	30819	38820	35969	45265	41543
102008	851	821	641	605	564	528	526	487	504	463
102009	6663	6428	6306	5955	6618	6191	7073	6554	7541	6921
102010	2676	2582	2512	2372	2655	2484	2884	2673	3142	2884
201001	31533	30112	37538	34328	47590	42958	59776	53260	73148	64331
201002	805023	768760	867533	793363	1018800	919641	1206509	1074988	1411044	1240965
201003	262972	251126	295704	270423	358811	323889	435746	388246	519573	456946
201004	25944	24775	24801	22681	26561	23976	29303	26108	32452	28540
201005	390923	373314	454268	415431	565327	510304	700019	623710	847257	745133
201006	227231	216995	274899	251397	352865	318521	447468	398690	551598	485111
201007	11089	10590	10868	9939	11865	10710	13284	11836	14880	13086
201008	32127	30680	36200	33105	43995	39713	53492	47661	63842	56147
201009	15861	15146	15712	14368	17336	15649	19609	17471	22174	19501
201010	2165	2067	2016	1844	2114	1909	2293	2043	2505	2203
202001	58744	56098	47708	43629	41596	37548	36185	32241	30848	27130
202002	1519	1451	1204	1101	1030	930	883	787	744	654
202003	4124	3938	3045	2785	2468	2228	2029	1808	1657	1457
202004	10771	10286	9638	8814	9054	8173	8342	7432	7432	6536
202005	30929	29536	22098	20209	17460	15760	14080	12545	11324	9959
202006	203822	194641	161752	147923	138550	125065	118892	105932	100299	88209
202007	44121	42133	39818	36414	37652	33987	34863	31062	31182	27424
202008	12372	11814	11359	10415	11008	9937	10425	9288	9531	8382
202009	38236	36514	26462	24200	20402	18416	16145	14385	12798	11256
202010	10488	10015	8338	7625	7151	6455	6143	5473	5186	4561

MCD MODEL 1: FINAL COUNTY PROJECTIONS

COUNTY	1980H	1980M	1990H	1990M	2000H	2000M	2010H	2010M	2020H	2020M
101	322413	311034	352380	332804	374954	350757	402058	372537	424789	389860
102	153390	147976	160952	152010	186483	174448	217733	201747	250487	229890
103	0	0	0	0	0	0	0	0	0	0
201	1804868	1723566	2019539	1846880	2445265	2207270	2967499	2644013	3538473	3111963
202	415131	396432	331458	303119	286376	258503	247991	220958	211007	185573

ALLOCATIONS: MCD MODEL 1

ZONE	1970A	1980H	1980M	1990H	1990M	2000H	2000M	2010H	2010M	2020H	2020M
101	1178	1431	1367	1731	1583	2223	2006	2819	2511	3475	3056
102	1178	1431	1367	1731	1583	2223	2006	2819	2511	3475	3056
103	1178	1431	1367	1731	1583	2223	2006	2819	2511	3475	3056
104	1178	1431	1367	1731	1583	2223	2006	2819	2511	3475	3056
105	1178	1431	1367	1731	1583	2223	2006	2819	2511	3475	3056
106	1178	1431	1367	1731	1583	2223	2006	2819	2511	3475	3056
107	176	228	220	283	267	333	311	386	358	435	399
108	176	228	220	283	267	333	311	386	358	435	399
109	176	228	220	283	267	333	311	386	358	435	399
110	176	228	220	283	267	333	311	386	358	435	399
111	176	228	220	283	267	333	311	386	358	435	399
112	176	228	220	283	267	333	311	386	358	435	399
113	1208	1121	1082	1057	999	995	931	964	894	937	860
114	1208	1121	1082	1057	999	995	931	964	894	937	860
115	1178	1431	1367	1731	1583	2223	2006	2819	2511	3475	3056
116	1178	1431	1367	1731	1583	2223	2006	2819	2511	3475	3056
201	2337	2840	2712	3436	3142	4410	3981	5593	4983	6894	6063
202	2337	2840	2712	3436	3142	4410	3981	5593	4983	6894	6063
203	2337	2840	2712	3436	3142	4410	3981	5593	4983	6894	6063
204	2337	2840	2712	3436	3142	4410	3981	5593	4983	6894	6063
205	2337	2840	2712	3436	3142	4410	3981	5593	4983	6894	6063
206	2337	2840	2712	3436	3142	4410	3981	5593	4983	6894	6063
207	245	319	308	396	374	467	437	543	503	613	562
208	475	616	594	763	720	897	839	1042	966	1174	1077
209	589	763	736	944	892	1110	1038	1289	1194	1452	1332
210	589	763	736	944	892	1110	1038	1289	1194	1452	1332
211	1621	1656	1597	1719	1623	1773	1658	1867	1730	1953	1793
212	3449	3136	3025	2889	2729	2654	2483	2508	2323	2376	2181
213	3449	3136	3025	2889	2729	2654	2483	2508	2323	2376	2181
214	3449	3136	3025	2889	2729	2654	2483	2508	2323	2376	2181
215	2337	2840	2712	3436	3142	4410	3981	5593	4983	6894	6063
216	2337	2840	2712	3436	3142	4410	3981	5593	4983	6894	6063
301	4311	5174	4941	6206	5676	7919	7148	10000	8909	12289	10807
302	4001	4862	4643	5882	5379	7551	6816	9575	8531	11804	10381
303	4001	4862	4643	5882	5379	7551	6816	9575	8531	11804	10381
304	4001	4862	4643	5882	5379	7551	6816	9575	8531	11804	10381
305	4001	4862	4643	5882	5379	7551	6816	9575	8531	11804	10381
306	4001	4862	4643	5882	5379	7551	6816	9575	8531	11804	10381
307	50	70	67	93	87	115	107	139	128	161	147
308	50	70	67	93	87	115	107	139	128	161	147
309	595	771	744	955	902	1124	1051	1306	1210	1471	1350
310	825	1068	1030	1322	1249	1554	1454	1805	1672	2032	1865
311	642	866	836	1113	1051	1354	1267	1621	1502	1874	1720
312	1377	1386	1337	1440	1360	1506	1409	1622	1503	1743	1599
313	4940	4596	4432	4368	4121	4179	3903	4129	3819	4103	3758
314	3789	3453	3328	3204	3016	3001	2796	2900	2673	2820	2571
315	601	635	606	699	639	840	758	1018	907	1215	1069
316	3909	4703	4491	5655	5171	7230	6526	9145	8148	11253	9897
401	7774	8141	7774	8785	8034	10329	9323	12244	10909	14331	12603
402	7479	9089	8679	10995	10055	14114	12740	17898	15947	22063	19404

ALLOCATIONS: MCD MODEL 1

ZONE	1970A	1980H	1980M	1990H	1990M	2000H	2000M	2010H	2010M	2020H	2020M
403	7479	9089	8679	10995	10055	14114	12740	17898	15947	22063	19404
404	7479	9089	8679	10995	10055	14114	12740	17898	15947	22063	19404
405	7479	9089	8679	10995	10055	14114	12740	17898	15947	22063	19404
406	7479	9089	8679	10995	10055	14114	12740	17898	15947	22063	19404
407	5039	5499	5305	5855	5529	6030	5641	6240	5782	6357	5835
408	129	159	154	189	179	216	202	245	227	270	247
409	589	763	736	944	892	1110	1038	1289	1194	1452	1332
410	943	1221	1178	1511	1427	1776	1662	2063	1911	2323	2132
411	581	799	771	1044	986	1287	1204	1559	1445	1822	1672
412	284	426	411	596	563	776	726	982	910	1188	1090
413	732	780	751	842	790	987	918	1169	1076	1364	1244
414	509	475	454	471	431	520	469	588	524	665	585
415	509	475	454	471	431	520	469	588	524	665	585
416	4359	4500	4298	4809	4397	5614	5067	6620	5899	7720	6789
501	11259	11994	11454	13110	11989	15570	14054	18601	16573	21904	19263
502	7989	9446	9021	11204	10246	14174	12794	17781	15843	21743	19122
503	9349	11361	10849	13744	12569	17643	15926	22373	19934	27579	24255
504	15779	18544	17709	21875	20004	27545	24864	34424	30672	41965	36907
505	14259	16907	16146	20081	18364	25421	22946	31899	28421	39009	34307
506	9349	11361	10849	13744	12569	17643	15926	22373	19934	27579	24255
507	14999	16329	15753	17341	16378	17815	16665	18387	17037	18687	17150
508	5224	5701	5500	6069	5731	6249	5845	6463	5989	6582	6040
509	486	612	591	739	698	852	797	974	902	1083	994
510	1061	1373	1325	1700	1605	1998	1869	2321	2150	2613	2398
511	813	1122	1082	1471	1389	1820	1703	2210	2048	2587	2375
512	733	877	846	1043	985	1280	1197	1562	1447	1856	1703
513	1517	1609	1552	1697	1603	1976	1849	2329	2158	2715	2492
514	679	634	605	628	574	693	625	784	698	886	780
515	679	634	605	628	574	693	625	784	698	886	780
516	11889	12392	11834	13327	12187	15628	14107	18489	16474	21609	19004
1001	131914	140744	134404	154135	140957	183321	165478	219261	195360	258423	227274
1002	80674	89928	85877	101849	93142	124300	112202	151645	135114	181473	159600
1003	73084	81292	77631	92449	84545	113529	102480	139394	124199	167784	147560
1004	71502	82683	78959	96296	88063	120052	108367	148863	132636	180373	158631
1005	75279	87273	83342	101849	93142	127180	114801	157902	140689	191515	168431
1006	41259	49086	46875	58450	53453	74138	66923	93171	83015	114070	100321
1007	25484	27906	26921	29843	28185	30904	28909	32170	29808	33984	30272
1008	1324	1623	1565	1944	1836	2245	2100	2588	2398	2909	2670
1009	2075	2437	2351	2786	2631	3067	2869	3374	3127	3634	3335
1010	76422	82156	79256	86660	81845	88812	83080	91723	84989	93477	85791
1011	19696	22726	21924	25689	24262	28595	26750	31985	29637	35158	32267
1012	10709	12584	12139	14335	13539	17538	16406	21294	19730	25212	23139
1013	6325	6707	6470	7072	6679	8236	7704	9705	8992	11316	10385
1014	6609	6489	6223	6599	6120	7455	6837	8588	7790	9848	8834
1015	50279	52108	49760	55822	51050	65288	58934	77096	68692	89984	79138
1016	116689	122068	116569	131608	120356	154614	139565	183155	163189	214254	188429
2001	194879	203685	194701	219840	201044	258288	233149	305984	272629	357956	314810
2002	128649	140543	134212	156737	143336	189035	170637	228536	203623	271585	238850
2003	94079	99973	95469	109958	100557	131739	118917	158802	141491	188519	165796
2004	84750	97730	93328	113567	103857	141331	127576	175004	155927	211814	186283

ALLOCATIONS: MCD MODEL 1

ZONE	1970A	1980H	1980M	1990H	1990M	2000H	2000M	2010H	2010M	2020H	2020M
2005	223589	194317	185564	173797	158938	170437	153848	170677	152071	171755	151052
2006	347769	266723	254709	211334	193265	183057	165240	160740	143218	140525	123587
2007	599	995	960	1505	1421	2078	1944	2746	2545	3430	3148
2008	3199	4557	4397	6135	5794	7752	7252	9570	8868	11344	1041,2
2009	13149	17830	17201	22975	21699	27951	26147	33416	30962	38563	35392
2010	79103	87459	84372	94976	89699	100193	93727	106410	98597	111333	102178
2011	54550	53873	51972	54091	51086	58686	54899	64798	60041	71051	65208
2012	55479	554C7	53451	56080	52964	63190	59113	72208	66906	81681	74965
2013	21074	26759	25815	31900	30127	40195	37601	49608	45966	59209	54341
2014	6004	6086	5851	6285	5875	7195	6657	8372	7666	9672	8766
2015	79209	82564	78845	88795	81204	104133	93998	123200	109770	143987	126631
2016	192500	201255	192190	216883	198340	254700	229910	301627	268747	352761	310241
3001	0	0	0	0	0	0	0	0	0	0	0
3002	0	0	0	0	0	0	0	0	0	0	0
3003	0	0	0	0	0	0	0	0	0	0	0
3004	0	0	0	0	0	0	0	0	0	0	0
3005	0	0	0	0	0	0	0	0	0	0	0
3006	0	0	0	0	0	0	0	0	0	0	0
3007	0	0	0	0	0	0	0	0	0	0	0
3008	0	0	0	0	0	0	0	0	0	0	0
3009	0	0	0	0	0	0	0	0	0	0	0
3010	0	0	0	0	0	0	0	0	0	0	0
3011	0	0	0	0	0	0	0	0	0	0	0
3012	0	0	0	0	0	0	0	0	0	0	0
3013	0	0	0	0	0	0	0	0	0	0	0
3014	0	0	0	0	0	0	0	0	0	0	0
3015	0	0	0	0	0	0	0	0	0	0	0
3016	0	0	0	0	0	0	0	0	0	0	0
4001	0	0	0	0	0	0	0	0	0	0	0
4002	0	0	0	0	0	0	0	0	0	0	0
4003	0	0	0	0	0	0	0	0	0	0	0
4004	0	0	0	0	0	0	0	0	0	0	0
4005	0	0	0	0	0	0	0	0	0	0	0
4006	0	0	0	0	0	0	0	0	0	0	0
4007	0	0	0	0	0	0	0	0	0	0	0
4008	0	0	0	0	0	0	0	0	0	0	0
4009	0	0	0	0	0	0	0	0	0	0	0
4010	0	0	0	0	0	0	0	0	0	0	0
4011	0	0	0	0	0	0	0	0	0	0	0
4012	0	0	0	0	0	0	0	0	0	0	0
4013	0	0	0	0	0	0	0	0	0	0	0
4014	0	0	0	0	0	0	0	0	0	0	0
4015	0	0	0	0	0	0	0	0	0	0	0
4016	0	0	0	0	0	0	0	0	0	0	0
5001	0	0	0	0	0	0	0	0	0	0	0
5002	0	0	0	0	0	0	0	0	0	0	0
5003	0	0	0	0	0	0	0	0	0	0	0
5004	0	0	0	0	0	0	0	0	0	0	0
5005	0	0	0	0	0	0	0	0	0	0	0
5006	0	0	0	0	0	0	0	0	0	0	0

ZONE	1970A	1980H	1980M	1990H	1990M	2000H	2000M	2010H	2010M	2020H	2020M
5007	0	0	0	0	0	0	0	0	0	0	0
5008	0	0	0	0	0	0	0	0	0	0	0
5009	0	0	0	0	0	0	0	0	0	0	0
5010	0	0	0	0	0	0	0	0	0	0	0
5011	0	0	0	0	0	0	0	0	0	0	0
5012	0	0	0	0	0	0	0	0	0	0	0
5013	0	0	0	0	0	0	0	0	0	0	0
5014	0	0	0	0	0	0	0	0	0	0	0
5015	0	0	0	0	0	0	0	0	0	0	0
5016	0	0	0	0	0	0	0	0	0	0	0

ALLOCATIONS: MCD MODEL 1

SUMMARY BY RINGS (OR ROWS)

	1970A	1980H	1980M	1990H	1990M	2000H	2000M	2010H	2010M	2020H	2020M
1	12904	15069	14426	17670	16274	21775	19786	26803	24032	32289	28569
2	32573	36249	34748	40927	37830	48609	44315	58304	52430	68936	61154
3	41106	47110	45103	54566	50264	66698	60614	81705	73264	98147	86842
4	58858	68690	65688	80500	73942	99742	90428	123084	110142	148480	131140
5	106091	120906	115729	138408	127475	167006	151801	201760	180985	239290	211831
10	789336	867815	830273	967394	889811	1149270	1043412	1371908	1229357	1612405	1426070
20	1578575	1539945	1473026	1564846	1439199	1739944	1580601	1971684	1769011	2225165	1971643
30	0	0	0	0	0	0	0	0	0	0	0
40	0	0	0	0	0	0	0	0	0	0	0
50	0	0	0	0	0	0	0	0	0	0	0

ALLOCATIONS: MCD MODEL 1

SUMMARY BY SECTORS (OR COLUMNS)

	1970A	1980H	1980M	1990H	1990M	2000H	2000M	2010H	2010M	2020H	2020M
1	353666	374211	357355	407246	372429	482061	435142	574504	511877	675274	593880
2	232311	258141	246513	291837	266886	355809	321178	433850	386556	519041	456479
3	191511	210851	201353	238199	217835	291212	262868	356457	317599	428121	376518
4	187029	217183	207400	253785	232088	317229	286353	394180	351210	478391	420728
5	328126	316722	302455	317775	290607	351338	317142	396365	353157	446517	392696
6	413377	345395	329837	305576	279451	303139	273635	312172	278142	326414	287069
7	46597	51349	49537	55319	52246	57744	54018	60614	56164	62669	57516
8	10582	12957	12500	15478	14618	17810	16660	20436	18935	22877	20996
9	17667	23407	22581	29629	27983	35550	33255	42037	38951	48092	44138
10	159125	174271	168120	187398	176987	195779	183145	206000	190874	213668	196099
11	78085	81273	78404	85413	80668	93851	87794	104430	96763	114883	105437
12	72213	74047	71434	76669	72410	87280	81648	100564	93180	114494	105080
13	39250	44711	43130	49827	47050	59225	55392	70414	65230	82025	75263
14	22253	21397	20571	21137	19746	22516	20801	24706	22571	27207	24580
15	134796	140689	134352	151585	138625	178110	160775	211100	188088	247109	217324
16	332865	349192	333462	377450	345180	444421	401165	527450	469953	617968	543482

~~~~~~

ALLOCATIONS: MCD MODEL 1

TOTALS

	1970A	1980H	1980M	1990H	1990M	2000H	2000M	2010H	2010M	2020H	2020M
9999	2619327	2695710	2578917	2864229	2634710	3292989	2990880	3835198	3439148	4424652	3917195

~~~~~~

MCD MODEL 1: CHECK OF ALLOCATION SHARES

MCD									
101001	303.57	488.10	702.38	683.12	929.83	1203.31	1492.82	1787.74	2078.61
101002	9981.13	9855.34	9188.68	11706.57	12341.65	12853.46	13261.50	13584.07	13837.50
101003	85.86	171.72	287.88	282.48	444.34	648.95	890.78	1160.91	1448.71
101004	5789.47	6052.63	6052.63	5367.55	5212.39	5088.08	4982.82	4898.09	4828.34
101005	172.92	341.67	520.83	460.88	669.10	913.85	1185.98	1474.83	1769.70
101006	936.00	1472.00	1808.00	1501.17	1796.10	2086.74	2365.57	2627.14	2867.93
101007	77.19	119.30	157.89	136.38	168.34	200.14	230.70	259.27	285.38
101008	175.00	100.00	50.00	236.98	265.06	290.60	313.41	333.50	350.95
101009	1833.33	1916.67	8333.33	4296.47	5709.14	7104.34	8405.27	9565.70	10566.07
101010	55.00	40.00	20.00	108.49	139.49	171.49	203.20	233.60	261.95
102001	402.14	831.10	1099.20	1751.41	2863.08	4178.26	5587.95	6988.04	8299.24
102002	1000.00	1100.00	1066.67	768.56	696.87	643.00	601.87	570.06	545.18
102003	208.76	298.97	453.61	525.77	747.01	1002.02	1280.94	1572.95	1867.62
102004	3473.68	5526.32	5631.58	6270.26	7635.49	8884.54	9982.51	10918.40	11697.50
102005	1652.17	1739.13	1826.09	2233.51	2503.92	2755.02	2984.20	3190.43	3373.78
102006	2066.67	3333.33	5000.00	4611.98	6028.93	7408.44	8680.66	9805.84	10769.49
102007	160.00	363.64	460.00	436.53	639.40	879.81	1140.93	1436.20	1730.86
102008	521.74	478.26	521.74	495.39	485.79	478.04	471.77	466.67	462.53
102009	2666.67	3400.00	4666.66	5362.50	6770.19	8099.53	9296.98	10337.02	11215.44
102010	740.74	962.96	1074.07	1274.63	1566.46	1861.18	2149.78	2425.19	2682.39
201001	2287.88	3608.64	4015.15	4897.91	6314.38	7676.78	8921.47	10014.38	10945.23
201002	4018.63	6758.61	7032.61	6834.73	8158.84	9349.28	10381.74	11252.73	11972.00
201003	3325.58	5093.02	5534.88	6110.72	7485.63	8750.11	9866.16	10820.41	11616.64
201004	7619.05	12380.95	13809.53	9978.32	10914.88	11694.59	12331.98	12845.68	13255.30
201005	909.09	3934.87	4599.73	2837.37	4149.36	5558.21	6959.43	8273.09	9449.80
201006	901.96	2784.31	3666.67	2824.19	4134.53	5542.91	6944.70	8259.63	9437.96
201007	8000.00	10700.00	12000.00	10270.48	11159.86	11895.96	12494.96	12976.06	13358.66
201008	8000.00	10000.00	12000.00	5444.36	6849.53	8172.43	9361.26	10391.97	11261.26
201009	2735.85	4509.43	5471.70	5503.30	5322.39	5175.69	5056.12	4956.27	4877.89
201010	210.63	252.37	322.58	268.55	293.74	316.20	335.93	353.05	367.78
202001	6000.00	5200.00	5200.00	16976.75	16541.76	16101.06	15770.18	15520.35	15330.83
202002	17906.58	17209.30	16976.75	16541.76	16101.06	15770.18	15520.35	15330.83	15186.69
202003	22000.01	19000.00	19500.00	18683.72	17681.79	16947.95	16404.35	15998.11	15692.86
202004	27500.00	29000.00	29000.00	21319.96	19571.06	18324.20	17419.56	16744.27	16259.95
202005	11250.00	9750.00	9833.33	12565.29	13032.20	13403.09	13695.52	13924.71	14103.63
202006	39000.02	37230.79	34923.09	26214.33	22942.59	20706.87	19136.77	18010.64	17189.86
202007	22148.14	20444.44	19333.33	18758.04	17735.88	16987.83	16434.03	16020.38	15709.36
202008	8156.86	8313.72	9372.55	10389.16	11258.88	11987.05	12560.43	13028.31	13399.99
202009	1606.56	1983.61	2163.93	2190.21	2463.27	2717.06	2950.24	3160.04	3346.89
202010	39642.87	37285.72	41785.72	26669.09	23113.84	20825.56	19221.13	18071.69	17234.64
202011	21142.86	19285.71	19142.86	18249.63	17364.98	16713.93	16229.85	15867.09	15593.59

MCD MODEL 2: PRELIMINARY PROJECTIONS

MCD	1950	1960	1970A	1970E	1980	1990	2000	2010	2020
101001	5100	8200	11800	11476	15621	20215	25079	30034	34920
101002	158700	156700	146100	186134	196232	204370	210857	215986	220016
101003	1700	3400	5700	5593	8797	12849	17637	22985	28684
101004	22000	23000	23000	20396	19807	19327	18934	18612	18347
101005	8300	16400	25000	22122	32116	43864	56927	70792	84945
101006	11700	18400	22600	18764	22451	26084	29569	32839	35849
101007	2200	3400	4500	3886	4797	5703	6574	7389	8133
101008	700	400	200	947	1060	1162	1253	1333	1403
101009	11000	11500	50000	25778	34254	42626	50431	57394	63396
101010	5500	4000	2000	10848	13949	17149	20320	23360	26194
102001	15000	31000	41000	65327	106792	155849	208430	260653	309561
102002	300	330	320	230	209	192	180	171	163
102003	4050	5800	8800	10199	14492	19439	24850	30515	36231
102004	6600	10500	10700	11913	14507	16880	18966	20744	22225
102005	38000	40000	42000	51370	57590	63365	68636	73380	77596
102006	3100	5000	7500	6917	9043	11112	13020	14708	16154
102007	8800	20000	25300	24009	35167	48389	63191	78991	95197
102008	1200	1100	1200	1139	1117	1099	1085	1073	1063
102009	4000	5100	7000	8043	10155	12149	13945	15505	16823
102010	2000	2600	2900	3441	4229	5025	5804	6548	7242
201001	15100	23817	26500	32326	41674	50666	58881	66094	72238
201002	440000	740000	770000	748334	893311	1023653	1136697	1232061	1310815
201003	143000	219000	238000	262761	321882	376255	424244	465277	499515
201004	16000	26000	29000	20954	22921	24558	25897	26975	27836
201005	67000	290000	339000	209114	305808	409640	512910	609727	696450
201006	46000	142000	187000	144033	210861	282688	354179	421241	481336
201007	8000	10700	12000	10270	11159	11895	12494	12976	13358
201008	14500	23900	29000	28855	36302	43313	49614	55077	59684
201009	11100	13300	17000	14152	15480	16663	17703	18605	19381
201010	3000	2600	2500	2751	2661	2587	2528	2479	2438
202001	77000	74000	73000	71129	69234	67811	66737	65922	65302
202002	2200	1900	1950	1868	1768	1694	1640	1599	1569
202003	5500	5100	5800	4263	3914	3664	3483	3350	3251
202004	13500	11700	11800	15078	15638	16083	16434	16709	16924
202005	50700	48400	45400	34078	29825	26918	24877	23413	22346
202006	299000	276000	261000	253233	239434	229335	221859	216275	212076
202007	41600	42400	47800	52984	57420	61082	64058	66444	68339
202008	9800	12100	13200	13360	15025	16577	17996	19276	20416
202009	55500	52200	58500	37056	32359	29155	26909	25300	24128
202010	14800	13500	13400	12774	12155	11699	11360	11106	10915

MCD MODEL 2: SUM OF PRELIMINARY PROJECTIONS

NO	1950	1960	1970A	1970E	1980	1990	2000	2010	2020
101	226900	245400	290900	305949	349088	393352	437586	480728	521892
102	83050	121430	146720	182593	253303	333502	418111	502291	582259
103	0	0	0	0	0	0	0	0	0
201	763700	1491317	1650000	1473551	1862060	2241918	2595147	2910512	3183051
202	569600	537300	531850	495828	476776	464025	455358	449399	445271

MCD MODEL 2: COUNTY INCREMENTS

COUNTY	1980H	1980M	1990H	1990M	2000H	2000M	2010H	2010M	2020H	2020M
101	-26675.	-38054.	-40971.	-60548.	-62632.	-86829.	-78670.	-108190.	-97103.	-132032.
102	-99913.	-105327.	-172551.	-181492.	-231628.	-243663.	-284558.	-300545.	-331772.	-352369.
103	374195.	360989.	386667.	365185.	369888.	346017.	356572.	330391.	338687.	310838.
201	-57192.	-138493.	-222377.	-395038.	-149879.	-387876.	56991.	-266495.	355423.	-71085.
202	-61644.	-80344.	-132567.	-160905.	-168982.	-196855.	-201408.	-228441.	-234264.	-259698.

MCD MODEL 2: FINAL MCD PROJECTIONS

MCD	1980H	1980M	1990H	1990M	2000H	2000M	2010H	2010M	2020H	2020M
101001	15621	15621	20215	19654	24334	22947	28219	26375	31744	29407
101002	174715	165536	171321	158663	164558	152899	162905	149642	159969	145243
101003	8797	8797	12849	12492	17113	16138	21597	20185	26075	24155
101004	19807	19807	19327	18790	18372	17325	17488	16345	16678	15450
101005	32116	32116	43864	42647	55235	52088	66515	62168	77218	71533
101006	22451	22451	26084	25360	28691	27056	30855	28839	32588	30189
101007	4797	4797	5703	5545	6379	6015	6942	6489	7393	6849
101008	658	486	544	382	468	399	505	423	528	434
101009	34254	34254	42626	41443	48933	46144	53927	50402	57629	53386
101010	9193	7164	9844	7824	10867	9744	13100	11665	14963	13210
102001	56319	54036	68596	64418	87527	81527	108326	100030	128993	118043
102002	157	153	115	109	96	91	87	81	81	75
102003	9544	9234	10190	9669	11935	11220	14130	13158	16545	15263
102004	9742	9432	8851	8398	8965	8419	9344	8683	9794	9008
102005	34119	32888	28410	26711	27463	25487	27974	25639	29061	26316
102006	6829	6636	6625	6327	6987	6612	7485	7017	8000	7429
102007	26557	25805	28851	27554	33911	32092	40200	37686	47149	43782
102008	843	819	655	626	582	551	546	512	526	489
102009	6625	6408	6200	5874	6440	6038	6847	6353	7288	6693
102010	2652	2562	2454	2320	2573	2406	2790	2582	3045	2789
201001	35258	33439	40511	36609	50354	44954	66094	54917	75600	65498
201002	880669	841665	936197	857361	1084556	980311	1238017	1132304	1393485	1294241
201003	292565	278511	319348	290371	380023	331116	465277	402844	522763	468438
201004	22596	21596	22460	20569	24709	22334	29187	24791	37177	27484
201005	301480	288128	376642	343094	489383	442345	644638	560359	858748	6876644
201006	207876	198670	258537	236765	337933	305452	433054	387134	546703	475250
201007	11001	10514	10879	9963	11921	10775	13451	11925	15709	13189
201008	35788	34203	39613	36277	47338	42788	55117	50617	62607	58930
201009	15261	14585	15240	13956	16891	15267	19388	17099	23131	19136
201010	2371	2255	2115	1915	2160	1928	2479	2026	2552	2156
202001	61535	58819	49698	45557	43235	39150	37642	33677	32210	28480
202002	1571	1502	1242	1138	1062	962	913	817	774	684
202003	3478	3325	2685	2462	2257	2043	1913	1711	1604	1418
202004	10621	10007	8509	7527	7368	6362	6263	5258	5069	4102
202005	26508	25338	19728	18084	16116	14594	13369	11961	11022	9746
202006	212807	203416	168078	154073	143729	130149	123496	110487	104606	92493
202007	45849	43597	39582	35852	36314	32993	32756	28759	28524	24620
202008	13194	12605	11989	10976	11498	10397	10846	9687	9909	8743
202009	28760	27491	21368	19587	17433	15785	14446	12925	11901	10523
202010	10803	10326	8574	7860	7360	6664	6342	5674	5384	4760

MCD MODEL 2: FINAL COUNTY PROJECTIONS

COUNTY	1980H	1980M	1990H	1990M	2000H	2000M	2010H	2010M	2020H	2020M
101	322413	311034	352380	332804	374954	350757	402058	372537	424789	389860
102	153390	147977	160952	152010	186483	174448	217733	201747	250487	229890
103	0	0	0	0	0	0	0	0	0	0
201	1804866	1723567	2019543	1846881	2445268	2207272	2967502	2644016	3538475	3111966
202	415131	396432	331458	303120	286376	258503	247991	220958	211007	185573

ALLOCATIONS: MCD MODEL 2

ZONE	1970A	1960H	1980M	1990H	1990M	2000H	2000M	2010H	2010M	2020H	2020M
101	1178	1309	1251	1628	1491	2128	1924	2728	2438	3444	2994
102	1178	1309	1251	1628	1491	2128	1924	2728	2438	3444	2994
103	1178	1309	1251	1628	1491	2128	1924	2728	2438	3444	2994
104	1178	1309	1251	1628	1491	2128	1924	2728	2438	3444	2994
105	1178	1309	1251	1628	1491	2128	1924	2728	2438	3444	2994
106	1178	1309	1251	1628	1491	2128	1924	2728	2438	3444	2994
107	176	234	234	303	294	365	344	423	395	476	441
108	176	234	234	303	294	365	344	423	395	476	441
109	176	234	234	303	294	365	344	423	395	476	441
110	176	234	234	303	294	365	344	423	395	476	441
111	176	234	234	303	294	365	344	423	395	476	441
112	176	234	234	303	294	365	344	423	395	476	441
113	1208	1068	1068	1067	1037	1040	980	1015	949	992	919
114	1208	1068	1068	1067	1037	1040	980	1015	949	992	919
115	1178	1309	1251	1628	1491	2128	1924	2728	2438	3444	2994
116	1178	1309	1251	1628	1491	2128	1924	2728	2438	3444	2994
201	2337	2598	2483	3231	2959	4224	3818	5413	4839	6833	5940
202	2337	2598	2483	3231	2959	4224	3818	5413	4839	6833	5940
203	2337	2598	2483	3231	2959	4224	3818	5413	4839	6833	5940
204	2337	2598	2483	3231	2959	4224	3818	5413	4839	6833	5940
205	2337	2598	2483	3231	2959	4224	3818	5413	4839	6833	5940
206	2337	2598	2483	3231	2959	4224	3818	5413	4839	6833	5940
207	245	345	336	431	412	510	478	589	548	661	609
208	475	638	634	819	793	982	925	1138	1063	1280	1184
209	589	781	781	1010	982	1216	1147	1410	1318	1587	1470
210	589	781	781	1010	982	1216	1147	1410	1318	1587	1470
211	1621	1615	1615	1774	1725	1891	1784	2003	1872	2103	1948
212	3449	2971	2971	2899	2818	2755	2598	2623	2451	2501	2317
213	3449	2971	2971	2899	2818	2755	2598	2623	2451	2501	2317
214	3449	2971	2971	2899	2818	2755	2598	2623	2451	2501	2317
215	2337	2598	2483	3231	2959	4224	3818	5413	4839	6833	5940
216	2337	2598	2483	3231	2959	4224	3818	5413	4839	6833	5940
301	4311	4805	4592	5897	5400	7638	6904	9713	8695	12177	10627
302	4001	4448	4251	5532	5066	7231	6536	9267	8284	11699	10170
303	4001	4448	4251	5532	5066	7231	6536	9267	8284	11699	10170
304	4001	4448	4251	5532	5066	7231	6536	9267	8284	11699	10170
305	4001	4448	4251	5532	5066	7231	6536	9267	8284	11699	10170
306	4001	4448	4251	5532	5066	7231	6536	9267	8284	11699	10170
307	50	164	121	136	95	117	99	126	105	132	108
308	50	164	121	136	95	117	99	126	105	132	108
309	595	800	795	1027	994	1230	1159	1426	1331	1603	1483
310	825	1093	1093	1415	1375	1703	1606	1975	1846	2222	2058
311	642	888	888	1194	1160	1486	1402	1776	1660	2052	1900
312	1377	1342	1342	1480	1439	1603	1511	1738	1624	1876	1738
313	4940	4377	4371	4403	4272	4356	4101	4339	4045	4349	4006
314	3789	3276	3262	3203	3097	3093	2904	3011	2793	2964	2700
315	601	596	569	666	610	810	732	994	883	1228	1048
316	3909	4310	4119	5323	4874	6927	6251	8854	7913	11165	9696
401	7774	8889	8496	9465	8668	10980	9925	12553	11477	14153	13132
402	7479	8315	7946	10341	9470	13517	12218	17322	15485	21868	19010

ALLOCATIONS: MCD MODEL 2

ZONE	1970A	1980H	1980M	1990H	1990M	2000H	2000M	2010H	2010M	2020H	2020M
403	7479	8315	7946	10341	9470	13517	12218	17322	15485	21868	19010
404	7479	8315	7946	10341	9470	13517	12218	17322	15485	21868	19010
405	7479	8315	7946	10341	9470	13517	12218	17322	15485	21868	19010
406	7479	8315	7946	10341	9470	13517	12218	17322	15485	21868	19010
407	5039	3557	3522	4371	4220	4987	4694	5493	5124	5868	5425
408	129	227	193	223	187	221	200	239	214	253	223
409	589	781	781	1010	982	1216	1147	1410	1318	1587	1470
410	943	1249	1249	1617	1572	1946	1835	2257	2110	2539	2352
411	581	820	820	1120	1089	1414	1333	1710	1598	1995	1848
412	284	439	439	642	624	855	806	1079	1009	1303	1207
413	732	771	749	857	815	1018	955	1213	1126	1435	1308
414	509	457	437	457	418	506	458	581	512	693	574
415	509	457	437	457	418	506	458	581	512	693	574
416	4359	4861	4645	5138	4705	5929	5359	6771	6174	7661	7045
501	11269	13195	12594	14152	12929	16545	14919	19359	17365	21776	19968
502	7989	9161	8745	10949	10006	13938	12574	17644	15642	21628	18991
503	9349	10393	9933	12926	11838	16896	15272	21652	19356	27335	23762
504	15779	15280	14603	18995	17395	24819	22433	32354	28424	42163	34886
505	14259	14344	13709	17834	16332	23304	21064	30230	26692	39043	32762
506	9349	10393	9933	12926	11838	16896	15272	21652	19356	27335	23762
507	14999	10276	10276	12787	12432	14679	13843	16521	15120	17288	16016
508	5224	3665	3665	4547	4421	5212	4915	5739	5364	6132	5681
509	488	612	612	777	756	921	868	1054	985	1174	1087
510	1061	1405	1405	1819	1768	2190	2065	2539	2373	2856	2646
511	813	1152	1152	1579	1535	2000	1886	2424	2266	2834	2625
512	733	883	868	1091	1050	1362	1287	1667	1561	1986	1841
513	1517	1593	1548	1731	1653	2034	1925	2412	2261	2828	2626
514	679	610	583	609	558	675	610	775	683	925	765
515	679	610	583	609	558	675	610	775	683	925	765
516	11889	13515	12916	14347	13139	16606	15010	18958	17326	21364	19796
1001	131914	154946	147864	166383	151955	154763	175567	228618	204556	257139	235407
1002	80674	100110	95257	109983	95924	131631	118069	162716	140074	183289	163456
1003	73084	78891	75296	90356	82555	111613	100605	139050	122532	169960	146031
1004	71502	64412	61559	80047	73306	104567	94516	137662	119737	182574	146938
1005	75279	68611	65572	85269	78089	111393	100687	145409	127557	193617	156538
1006	41259	42097	40233	52341	47934	68400	61826	88568	78345	114008	96164
1007	25484	18562	18298	22877	22015	26198	24639	29013	27042	31129	28753
1008	1324	2118	1915	2410	2168	2681	2478	3045	2788	3344	3033
1009	2075	2415	2374	2882	2767	3255	3060	3603	3356	3891	3591
1011	76422	91740	87150	91423	84935	89323	83092	89737	82564	89423	81365
1012	19696	24871	23839	27152	25495	29506	27546	32554	30104	35450	32272
1013	10709	12711	12294	14715	13955	18086	16982	21962	20434	25990	23957
1014	6325	6639	6451	7212	6888	8477	8023	10050	9421	11787	10945
1015	6609	6318	6081	6542	6105	7445	6873	8673	7872	10266	8971
1016	50279	56502	54000	59829	54791	69127	62482	78934	72042	89160	82247
2001	116689	133563	127642	142026	130055	164583	148752	188028	171859	211636	196678
2002	194879	223092	213201	237242	217243	274939	248489	314157	287104	353598	328624
2003	128649	155778	148415	169938	154103	200627	180154	242241	211921	272404	245694
2004	94079	91666	87488	103033	94133	125455	113142	156914	136228	194580	161026
	84750	75370	72032	93660	85773	122345	110586	161359	140089	214687	171911

ALLOCATIONS: MCD MODEL 2

ZONE	1970A	1980H	1980M	1990H	1990M	2000H	2000M	2010H	2010M	2020H	2020M
2005	223589	191476	182832	169086	154605	164673	148627	166170	146503	173285	145553
2006	347769	260039	248372	207591	189927	180779	163274	159356	142105	139997	123041
2007	599	2758	2149	2953	2347	3260	2923	3930	3499	4488	3963
2008	3199	6429	5719	7831	7003	9327	8619	11236	10299	12959	11776
2009	13149	17457	17254	23487	22660	29342	27620	35262	32899	40845	37772
2010	79103	93170	89499	98057	92174	100948	94282	105632	97682	109374	100142
2011	54550	52180	50760	52551	49975	57356	53668	63432	58766	69712	63949
2012	55479	55092	53136	55514	52388	62451	58351	71342	66005	80708	73943
2013	21074	27465	26409	32785	30867	41291	38547	50773	46981	60324	55311
2014	6004	5967	5766	6308	5947	7282	6798	8550	7875	10079	9055
2015	79209	90050	86062	95600	87550	110651	100015	126322	115453	142355	131911
2016	192500	220167	210416	234049	214340	271139	245077	309504	283076	348371	323560
3001	0	0	0	0	0	0	0	0	0	0	0
3002	0	0	0	0	0	0	0	0	0	0	0
3003	0	0	0	0	0	0	0	0	0	0	0
3004	0	0	0	0	0	0	0	0	0	0	0
3005	0	0	0	0	0	0	0	0	0	0	0
3006	0	0	0	0	0	0	0	0	0	0	0
3007	0	0	0	0	0	0	0	0	0	0	0
3008	0	0	0	0	0	0	0	0	0	0	0
3009	0	0	0	0	0	0	0	0	0	0	0
3010	0	0	0	0	0	0	0	0	0	0	0
3011	0	0	0	0	0	0	0	0	0	0	0
3012	0	0	0	0	0	0	0	0	0	0	0
3013	0	0	0	0	0	0	0	0	0	0	0
3014	0	0	0	0	0	0	0	0	0	0	0
3015	0	0	0	0	0	0	0	0	0	0	0
3016	0	0	0	0	0	0	0	0	0	0	0
4001	0	0	0	0	0	0	0	0	0	0	0
4002	0	0	0	0	0	0	0	0	0	0	0
4003	0	0	0	0	0	0	0	0	0	0	0
4004	0	0	0	0	0	0	0	0	0	0	0
4005	0	0	0	0	0	0	0	0	0	0	0
4006	0	0	0	0	0	0	0	0	0	0	0
4007	0	0	0	0	0	0	0	0	0	0	0
4008	0	0	0	0	0	0	0	0	0	0	0
4009	0	0	0	0	0	0	0	0	0	0	0
4010	0	0	0	0	0	0	0	0	0	0	0
4011	0	0	0	0	0	0	0	0	0	0	0
4012	0	0	0	0	0	0	0	0	0	0	0
4013	0	0	0	0	0	0	0	0	0	0	0
4014	0	0	0	0	0	0	0	0	0	0	0
4015	0	0	0	0	0	0	0	0	0	0	0
4016	0	0	0	0	0	0	0	0	0	0	0
5001	0	0	0	0	0	0	0	0	0	0	0
5002	0	0	0	0	0	0	0	0	0	0	0
5003	0	0	0	0	0	0	0	0	0	0	0
5004	0	0	0	0	0	0	0	0	0	0	0
5005	0	0	0	0	0	0	0	0	0	0	0
5006	0	0	0	0	0	0	0	0	0	0	0

ALLOCATIONS: MCD MODEL 2

ZONE	1970A	1980H	1980M	1990H	1990M	2000H	2000M	2010H	2010M	2020H	2020M
5007	0	0	0	0	0	0	0	0	0	0	0
5008	0	0	0	0	0	0	0	0	0	0	0
5009	0	0	0	0	0	0	0	0	0	0	0
5010	0	0	0	0	0	0	0	0	0	0	0
5011	0	0	0	0	0	0	0	0	0	0	0
5012	0	0	0	0	0	0	0	0	0	0	0
5013	0	0	0	0	0	0	0	0	0	0	0
5014	0	0	0	0	0	0	0	0	0	0	0
5015	0	0	0	0	0	0	0	0	0	0	0
5016	0	0	0	0	0	0	0	0	0	0	0

ALLOCATIONS: MCD MODEL 2

SUMMARY BY RINGS (OR ROWS)

	1970A	1980H	1980M	1990H	1990M	2000H	2000M	2010H	2010M	2020H	2020M
1	12904	14019	13555	16984	15777	21302	19422	26396	23783	32396	28438
2	32573	33861	32928	39598	37029	47879	43825	57728	52190	69395	61162
3	41106	44063	42537	52547	48751	65244	59467	80418	72431	98399	86328
4	58858	64089	61508	77068	71056	97170	88265	120505	108607	147525	130212
5	106091	107095	103132	127685	118215	158760	144561	195420	175466	237598	207938
10	789336	864511	825832	961456	882943	1141045	1035262	1368618	1220280	1611653	1416339
20	1578575	1568142	1499499	1588979	1461025	1761648	1600156	1986165	1786468	2227750	1986839
30	0	0	0	0	0	0	0	0	0	0	0
40	0	0	0	0	0	0	0	0	0	0	0
50	0	0	0	0	0	0	0	0	0	0	0

ALLOCATIONS: MCD MODEL 2

SUMMARY BY SECTORS (OR COLUMNS)

	1970A	1980H	1980M	1990H	1990M	2000H	2000M	2010H	2010M	2020H	2020M
1	353666	408837	390484	438001	400648	511221	461548	592542	536477	669123	616315
2	232311	281722	268350	310906	283023	373098	335295	457332	398686	521167	462208
3	191511	197623	188651	227051	207515	281067	253576	352348	309166	434721	368935
4	187029	171734	164128	213438	195464	278835	252034	366107	319299	483270	391851
5	328126	291104	278047	292925	268015	326474	294876	377542	331800	449791	372970
6	413377	329202	314473	314594	268688	293179	264870	304308	270855	325187	281083
7	46597	35898	34940	43861	41819	50118	47023	55755	51838	60045	55317
8	10582	13478	12484	16272	14965	18907	17582	21950	20232	24578	22449
9	17667	23082	22834	30499	29438	37549	35347	44592	41606	51164	47317
10	159125	189675	181414	195646	183104	197693	184374	203977	188291	208479	190477
11	78085	81763	79311	85676	81277	94021	87965	104325	96663	114624	105187
12	72213	73674	71287	76645	72571	87480	81882	100838	93481	114843	105448
13	39250	44887	43569	50957	48353	60974	57133	72428	67237	84219	77435
14	22253	26670	20171	21088	19983	22799	21224	25231	23140	28424	25303
15	134796	152126	145388	162024	148380	188124	170042	215748	196854	244640	225481
16	332865	380324	363475	405744	371567	471538	426203	540259	493628	610477	565511

ALLOCATIONS: MCD MODEL 2

TOTALS

	1970A	1980H	1980M	1990H	1990M	2000H	2000M	2010H	2010M	2020H	2020M
9999	2619327	2695707	2577916	2864243	2634716	3292983	2990889	3835201	3439154	4424659	3917211

MCD MODEL 2: CHECK OF ALLOCATION SHARES

MCD PROJECTIONS, MCD MODEL 3

MCD	R-BAR	1930	1940	1950	1960	1970	1980	1990	2000	2010	2020
201001	1.14926	11400	12400	15100	23817	26500	30018	32777	39282	44850	50276
201001	1.14926	11400	12400	15100	23817	26500	28666	29974	35659	39961	44216
201002	1.21227	187000	260000	440000	740000	770000	803882	890925	1068129	1286380	1521055
201002	1.21227	187000	260000	440000	740000	770000	767570	814755	964168	1146152	1337715
201003	1.21247	62000	84000	143000	219000	238000	249305	272227	327139	394047	466008
201003	1.21247	62000	84000	143000	219000	238000	238075	248953	295298	351092	409938
201004	1.27695	300	10000	16000	26000	29000	36632	41796	51238	65000	80959
201004	1.27695	300	10000	16000	26000	29000	34982	38223	46251	57914	71200
201005	1.20124	37000	43000	67000	290000	339000	358185	398166	480724	573679	672161
201005	1.20124	37000	43000	67000	290000	339000	342050	364125	433935	511143	591142
201006	1.28896	19000	24000	46000	142000	187000	254393	295875	363926	466011	585882
201006	1.28896	19000	24000	46000	142000	187000	242933	270579	328505	415211	515263
201007	1.19267	4300	5600	8000	10700	12000	13228	14848	18393	21793	25352
201007	1.19267	4300	5600	8000	10700	12000	12632	13579	16603	19417	22296
201008	1.26003	7200	11200	14500	23900	29000	33579	39596	51238	64139	78827
201008	1.26003	7200	11200	14500	23900	29000	32067	36211	46251	57147	69326
201009	1.16289	11700	12000	11100	13300	17000	23404	30797	42042	48569	55091
201009	1.16289	11700	12000	11100	13300	17000	22349	28168	37950	43275	48450
201010	0.96725	3100	3300	3000	2600	2500	2238	2529	3153	3029	2858
201010	0.96725	3100	3300	3000	2600	2500	2137	2313	2846	2699	2513

MCD PROJECTIONS, MCD MODEL 4

MCD	R-BAR	1930	1940	1950	1960	1970	1980	1990	2000	2010	2020
102001	1.37876	10000	12000	15000	31000	41000	44815	48721	59226	72359	86886
102001	1.37876	10000	12000	15000	31000	41000	43234	46014	55404	67046	79742
102002	1.07852	400	350	300	330	320	304	288	274	262	246
102002	1.07852	400	350	300	330	320	294	272	257	243	226
102003	1.33013	3900	4400	4050	5800	8800	11005	13688	16053	18920	21918
102003	1.33013	3900	4400	4050	5800	8800	10616	12928	15017	17531	20115
102004	1.14547	5900	5700	6600	10500	10700	8517	6742	6809	6912	6895
102004	1.14547	5900	5700	6600	10500	10700	8216	6368	6370	6404	6328
102005	1.24974	23400	31000	38000	40000	42000	42659	43093	47483	52583	57231
102005	1.24974	23400	31000	38000	40000	42000	41153	40699	44418	48722	52525
102006	1.34234	2800	2500	3100	5000	7500	7821	8111	9600	11819	13349
102006	1.34234	2800	2500	3100	5000	7500	7545	7661	8980	10580	12251
102007	1.36071	5500	7250	8800	20000	25300	25896	26363	31627	38135	45192
102007	1.36071	5500	7250	8800	20000	25300	24982	24898	29586	35335	41476
102008	1.15554	1300	1150	1200	1100	1200	1834	2788	2841	2910	2930
102008	1.15554	1300	1150	1200	1100	1200	1769	2633	2658	2697	2689
102009	1.27938	3800	3800	4000	5100	7000	7436	7858	8864	10049	11196
102009	1.27938	3800	3800	4000	5100	7000	7174	7421	8292	9311	10276
102010	1.27429	1600	1800	2000	2600	2900	3099	3295	3702	4180	4639
102010	1.27429	1600	1800	2000	2600	2900	2990	3112	3463	3873	4258

MCD PROJECTIONS, MCD MODEL 4

MCD	R-BAR	1930	1940	1950	1960	1970	1980	1990	2000	2010	2020
202001	1.01716	76000	80000	77000	74000	73000	61228	46359	37856	32720	27730
202601	1.01716	76000	80000	77000	74000	73000	58470	42395	34172	29154	24388
202002	1.04002	2000	2500	2200	1900	1950	1683	1318	1113	984	852
202002	1.04002	2000	2500	2200	1900	1950	1607	1205	1005	876	749
202003	1.02084	5700	5600	5500	5100	5800	4745	3568	2894	2511	2135
202003	1.02084	5700	5600	5500	5100	5800	4531	3263	2613	2237	1878
202004	1.01912	12500	13700	13500	11700	11800	8770	6663	5628	4811	4032
202004	1.01912	12500	13700	13500	11700	11800	9184	7286	6235	5390	4585
202005	0.93960	59000	54000	50700	48400	45400	30614	21918	16924	13512	10578
202005	0.93960	59000	54000	50700	48400	45400	29235	20044	15277	12039	9303
202006	1.00831	320000	310000	299000	276000	261000	198993	165173	147864	126693	106437
202006	1.00831	320000	310000	299000	276000	261000	190030	151051	133473	112882	93608
202007	1.03777	47000	44000	41600	42400	47800	39798	31402	26722	23565	20376
202007	1.03777	47000	44000	41600	42400	47800	38006	28717	24121	20996	17920
202008	1.22777	6000	7500	9800	12100	13200	12245	11243	11134	11616	11883
202008	1.22777	6000	7500	9800	12100	13200	11694	10282	10050	10350	10451
202009	1.01904	53000	54000	55500	52200	58500	45156	33449	26722	23140	19647
202009	1.01904	53000	54000	55500	52200	58500	43122	30589	24121	20617	17279
202010	1.03682	16000	15000	14800	13500	13400	11480	9737	8907	7847	6779
202010	1.03682	16000	15000	14800	13500	13400	10963	8904	8040	6992	5962

MCD PROJECTIONS, MCD MODEL 5

MCD	R-BAR	1930	1940	1950	1960	1970	1980	1990	2000	2010	2020
101001	1.30992	3900	4000	5100	8200	11800	15566	19959	24541	29936	35416
101601	1.30992	3900	4000	5100	8200	11800	15017	18850	22957	27738	32504
101002	1.00032	146700	147200	158700	156700	146100	147183	144116	135318	126054	113882
101002	1.00032	146700	147200	158700	156700	146100	141988	136109	126585	116799	104518
101003	1.43981	900	1350	1700	3400	5700	8265	11648	15742	21108	27448
101003	1.43981	900	1350	1700	3400	5700	7973	11001	14726	19558	25191
101004	1.03834	20000	19000	22000	23000	23000	24051	24444	23824	23037	21603
101004	1.03834	20000	19000	22000	23000	23000	23202	23086	22287	21345	19827
101005	1.21740	9500	9000	8300	16400	25000	30650	36524	41737	47317	52025
101005	1.21740	9500	9000	8300	16400	25000	29569	34495	39043	43843	47747
101006	1.32857	7000	9200	11700	18400	22600	30238	39324	49040	60673	72802
101006	1.32857	7000	9200	11700	18400	22600	29171	37139	45875	56218	66815
101007	1.40588	1000	1300	2200	3400	4500	6371	8767	11570	15148	19233
101007	1.40588	1000	1300	2200	3400	4500	6146	8280	10823	14035	17652
101008	0.77232	700	800	700	400	200	155	117	85	61	42
101008	0.77232	700	800	700	400	200	150	111	79	56	39
101009	1.16077	10000	10500	11000	11500	50000	58450	66411	72359	78217	81999
101009	1.16077	10000	10500	11000	11500	50000	56387	62722	67689	72474	75256
101010	0.73502	7500	6500	5500	4000	2000	1480	1065	734	503	333
101010	0.73502	7500	6500	5500	4000	2000	1428	1005	687	466	306

MCD	R-BAR	1930	1940	1950	1960	1970	1980	1990	2000	2010	2020
102001	1.31814	10000	12000	15000	31000	41000	45426	50313	61296	74977	90048
102001	1.31814	10000	12000	15000	31000	41000	43822	47517	57340	69472	82643
102002	0.95046	400	350	300	330	320	255	204	179	158	136
102002	0.95046	400	350	300	330	320	246	192	167	146	125
102003	1.24519	3900	4400	4050	5800	8800	9210	9636	11090	12814	14538
102003	1.24519	3900	4400	4050	5800	8800	8885	9101	10374	11874	13343
102004	1.16076	5900	5700	6600	10500	10700	10439	10182	10923	11766	12444
102004	1.16076	5900	5700	6600	10500	10700	10071	9616	10218	10902	11421
102005	1.16331	23400	31000	38000	40000	42000	41067	40142	43160	46592	49384
102005	1.16331	23400	31000	38000	40000	42000	39618	37912	40375	43171	45323
102006	1.28321	2800	2500	3100	5000	7500	8089	8722	10344	12318	14402
102006	1.28321	2800	2500	3100	5000	7500	7803	8237	9677	11413	13218
102007	1.32424	5500	7250	8800	20000	25300	28160	31334	38351	47128	56363
102007	1.32424	5500	7250	8800	20000	25300	27167	29593	35876	43668	52187
102008	0.98392	1300	1150	1200	1100	1200	992	820	746	681	610
102008	0.98392	1300	1150	1200	1100	1200	957	774	697	631	560
102009	1.17504	3800	3800	4000	5100	7000	6913	6826	7413	8083	8654
102009	1.17504	3800	3800	4000	5100	7000	6669	6446	6935	7490	7942
102010	1.16287	1600	1800	2000	2600	2900	2834	2769	2976	3212	3403
102010	1.16287	1600	1800	2000	2600	2900	2734	2615	2784	2976	3123

MCD	R-BAR	1930	1940	1950	1960	1970	1980	1990	2000	2010	2020
201001	1.22953	11400	12400	15100	23817	26500	26348	26776	29425	32389	35011
201001	1.22953	11400	12400	15100	23817	26500	25161	24487	26561	28858	30791
201002	1.35773	187000	260000	440000	740000	770000	845425	948748	1151295	1399414	1670434
201002	1.35773	187000	260000	440000	740000	770000	807343	867634	1039240	1246865	1469089
201003	1.36040	62000	84000	143000	219000	238000	261827	294404	357958	435959	521413
201003	1.36040	62000	84000	143000	219000	238000	250033	269233	323118	388435	458564
201004	1.40385	300	10000	16000	26000	29000	32922	38200	47930	60239	74348
201004	1.40385	300	10000	16000	26000	29000	31439	34934	43265	53672	65386
201005	1.33278	37000	43000	67000	290000	339000	365368	402487	479440	572058	670300
201005	1.33278	37000	43000	67000	290000	339000	348909	368076	432776	509698	589506
201006	1.39501	19000	24000	46000	142000	187000	210956	243239	303274	378757	464526
201006	1.39501	19000	24000	46000	142000	187000	201453	222443	273757	337469	408535
201007	1.29747	4300	5600	8000	10700	12000	12590	13502	15657	18187	20746
201007	1.29747	4300	5600	8000	10700	12000	12023	12348	14133	16205	18245
201008	1.37701	7200	11200	14500	23900	29000	32292	36754	45233	55763	67507
201008	1.37701	7200	11200	14500	23900	29000	30838	33611	40831	49684	59370
201009	1.10676	11700	12000	11100	13300	17000	15215	13918	13767	13641	13273
201009	1.10676	11700	12000	11100	13300	17000	14529	12728	12427	12154	11673
201010	0.95045	3100	3300	3000	2600	2500	1921	1509	1282	1091	911
201010	0.95045	3100	3300	3000	2600	2500	1834	1380	1157	972	801

MCD PROJECTIONS, MCD MODEL 5

MCD	R-BAR	1930	1940	1950	1960	1970	1980	1990	2000	2010	2020
202001	0.99066	76000	80000	77000	74000	73000	57783	46672	40677	35416	30184
202001	0.99066	76000	80000	77000	74000	73000	55180	42682	36717	31555	26546
202002	1.00499	2000	2500	2200	1900	1950	1565	1283	1134	1001	866
202002	1.00499	2000	2500	2200	1900	1950	1495	1173	1023	892	761
202003	1.00728	5700	5600	5500	5100	5800	4668	3833	3397	3007	2606
202003	1.00728	5700	5600	5500	5100	5800	4457	3505	3066	2679	2292
202004	0.98915	12500	13700	13500	11700	11800	9326	7521	6545	5690	4842
202004	0.98915	12500	13700	13500	11700	11800	8906	6878	5908	5069	4258
202005	0.93670	59000	54000	50700	48400	45400	33979	25950	21384	17604	14186
202005	0.93670	59000	54000	50700	48400	45400	32448	23731	19303	15685	12476
202006	0.95050	320000	310000	299000	276000	261000	198220	153613	128452	107306	87746
202006	0.95050	320000	310000	299000	276000	261000	189291	140480	115950	95609	77169
202007	1.00705	47000	44000	41600	42400	47800	38462	31580	27978	24763	21454
202007	1.00705	47000	44000	41600	42400	47800	36729	28880	25255	22064	18868
202008	1.22057	6000	7500	9800	12100	13200	12873	12811	13756	14757	15495
202008	1.22057	6000	7500	9800	12100	13200	12293	11715	12417	13148	13627
202009	1.02697	53000	54000	55500	52200	58500	48003	40193	36314	32776	28958
202009	1.02697	53000	54000	55500	52200	58500	45840	36757	32779	29203	25467
202010	0.95723	16000	15000	14800	13500	13400	10248	7998	6735	5666	4666
202010	0.95723	16000	15000	14800	13500	13400	9787	7314	6080	5049	4104

ALLOCATIONS: MCD MODEL 5

ZONE	1970A	1980H	1980M	1990H	1990M	2000H	2000M	2010H	2010M	2020H	2020M
101	1178	1329	1269	1532	1401	1910	1724	2386	2126	2926	2573
102	1178	1329	1269	1532	1401	1910	1724	2386	2126	2926	2573
103	1178	1329	1269	1532	1401	1910	1724	2386	2126	2926	2573
104	1178	1329	1269	1532	1401	1910	1724	2386	2126	2926	2573
105	1178	1329	1269	1532	1401	1910	1724	2386	2126	2926	2573
106	1178	1329	1269	1532	1401	1910	1724	2386	2126	2926	2573
107	176	233	225	299	282	368	344	449	416	531	487
108	176	233	225	299	282	368	344	449	416	531	487
109	176	233	225	299	282	368	344	449	416	531	487
110	176	233	225	299	282	368	344	449	416	531	487
111	176	233	225	299	282	368	344	449	416	531	487
112	176	233	225	299	282	368	344	449	416	531	487
113	1208	1280	1235	1322	1248	1313	1229	1301	1205	1257	1153
114	1208	1280	1235	1322	1248	1313	1229	1301	1205	1257	1153
115	1178	1329	1269	1532	1401	1910	1724	2386	2126	2926	2573
116	1178	1329	1269	1532	1401	1910	1724	2386	2126	2926	2573
201	2337	2636	2518	3040	2780	3790	3421	4734	4218	5806	5106
202	2337	2636	2518	3040	2780	3790	3421	4734	4218	5806	5106
203	2337	2636	2518	3040	2780	3790	3421	4734	4218	5806	5106
204	2337	2636	2518	3040	2780	3790	3421	4734	4218	5806	5106
205	2337	2636	2518	3040	2780	3790	3421	4734	4218	5806	5106
206	2337	2636	2518	3040	2780	3790	3421	4734	4218	5806	5106
207	245	319	307	405	382	495	463	601	557	710	652
208	475	625	750	800	756	983	919	1198	1110	1417	1300
209	589	778	750	997	942	1227	1147	1496	1386	1770	1625
210	589	778	750	997	942	1227	1147	1496	1386	1770	1625
211	1621	1825	1760	2020	1908	2172	2032	2349	2176	2496	2291
212	3449	3607	3480	3666	3463	3573	3343	3455	3201	3240	2974
213	3449	3607	3480	3666	3463	3573	3343	3455	3201	3240	2974
214	3449	3607	3480	3666	3463	3573	3343	3455	3201	3240	2974
215	2337	2636	2518	3040	2780	3790	3421	4734	4218	5806	5106
216	2337	2636	2518	3040	2780	3790	3421	4734	4218	5806	5106
301	4311	4852	4634	5582	5105	6944	6268	8653	7710	10590	9313
302	4001	4514	4311	5205	4760	6490	5858	8105	7221	9940	8742
303	4001	4514	4311	5205	4760	6490	5858	8105	7221	9940	8742
304	4001	4514	4311	5205	4760	6490	5858	8105	7221	9940	8742
305	4001	4514	4311	5205	4760	6490	5858	8105	7221	9940	8742
306	4001	4514	4311	5205	4760	6490	5858	8105	7221	9940	8742
307	50	38	37	29	27	21	19	15	14	10	9
308	50	38	37	29	27	21	19	15	14	10	9
309	595	782	755	1001	945	1229	1150	1498	1388	1772	1626
310	825	1089	1051	1397	1319	1717	1607	2095	1941	2479	2275
311	642	870	839	1147	1084	1453	1360	1830	1696	2240	2055
312	1377	1533	1479	1688	1594	1820	1703	1996	1849	2178	1999
313	4940	5210	5024	5377	5074	5374	5023	5377	4977	5276	4837
314	3789	3911	3770	3945	3717	3849	3591	3728	3444	3506	3207
315	601	599	572	618	565	699	631	803	715	915	805
316	3909	4371	4174	5003	4576	6203	5599	7711	6870	9423	8287
401	7774	8538	8154	9584	8765	11634	10501	14145	12603	16890	14854
402	7479	8438	8058	9729	8897	12130	10950	15150	13498	18581	16341

ALLOCATIONS: MCD MODEL 5

ZONE	1970A	1980H	1980M	1990H	1990M	2000H	2000M	2010H	2010M	2020H	2020M
403	7479	8438	8058	9729	8897	12130	10950	15150	13498	18581	16341
404	7479	8438	8058	9729	8897	12130	10950	15150	13498	18581	16341
405	7479	8438	8058	9729	8897	12130	10950	15150	13498	18581	16341
406	7479	8438	8058	9729	8897	12130	10950	15150	13498	18581	16341
407	5039	5876	5668	6664	6294	7252	6784	7833	7258	8208	7533
408	129	158	152	198	187	248	232	315	292	393	360
409	589	778	750	997	942	1227	1147	1496	1386	1770	1625
410	943	1245	1201	1596	1508	1963	1836	2394	2219	2833	2600
411	581	797	769	1064	1005	1365	1277	1742	1614	2160	1982
412	284	413	398	582	550	787	736	1055	977	1372	1259
413	732	798	768	882	829	1062	989	1290	1190	1544	1412
414	509	456	435	417	381	413	372	409	364	398	350
415	509	456	435	417	381	413	372	409	364	398	350
416	4359	4683	4472	5161	4720	6169	5569	7406	6598	8750	7695
501	11269	12381	11823	13903	12714	16882	15239	20533	18295	24525	21569
502	7989	8946	8543	10241	9365	12677	11443	15722	14008	19149	16841
503	9349	10572	10072	12161	11122	15163	13687	18937	16873	23226	20426
504	15779	17289	16510	19371	17715	23481	21196	28524	25415	34044	29941
505	14259	15745	15036	17779	16259	21719	19605	26591	23692	31987	28131
506	9349	10547	10072	12161	11122	15163	13687	18937	16873	23226	20426
507	14999	17535	16916	19923	18816	21701	20306	23465	21742	24599	22576
508	5224	6163	5946	7079	6686	7814	7310	8579	7949	9161	8408
509	488	658	634	861	813	1083	1013	1352	1253	1639	1504
510	1061	1400	1351	1796	1696	2208	2066	2694	2496	3187	2925
511	813	1118	1079	1497	1414	1926	1801	2463	2283	3063	2811
512	733	893	862	1092	1031	1396	1306	1786	1655	2235	2051
513	1517	1689	1630	1880	1775	2301	2152	2827	2620	3411	3131
514	679	608	581	556	509	550	497	545	486	530	466
515	679	608	581	556	509	550	497	545	486	530	466
516	11889	12985	12400	14509	13269	17544	15837	21264	18946	25321	22269
1001	131914	144939	138410	162768	148852	197658	178420	240427	214218	287195	252578
1002	80674	87770	83816	97692	89340	117686	106232	142124	126631	168677	148346
1003	73084	78254	74729	86019	78665	102613	92625	122976	109570	145094	127605
1004	71502	77250	73770	85313	78019	101892	91975	121911	108621	143257	125990
1005	75279	81511	77840	90227	82513	108019	97505	129561	115438	152641	134242
1006	41259	45692	43634	51745	47321	63397	57227	77841	69355	93903	82584
1007	23484	29736	28686	33782	31905	36853	34475	39931	36999	42004	38550
1008	1324	1740	1679	2298	2170	2966	2774	3837	3555	4841	4443
1009	2075	2889	2787	3927	3709	5133	4802	6668	6178	8408	7717
1010	76422	78052	75297	77806	73483	74781	69955	71806	66534	67464	61917
1011	19696	21331	20578	22967	21691	24662	23070	27050	25064	29659	27220
1012	10709	11996	11572	13447	12700	16504	15439	20335	18842	24593	22570
1013	6325	7040	6791	7833	7398	9587	8969	11782	10917	14215	13046
1014	6609	6467	6203	6473	6014	7139	6570	7986	7283	8872	8020
1015	50279	54377	51927	60265	55112	72381	65337	87238	77728	103411	90946
1016	116689	128122	122351	143784	131491	174483	157501	212091	188971	253172	222656
2001	194879	213974	204336	240131	219600	291603	263041	354213	315600	422822	371857
2002	128649	141182	134823	158389	144847	192177	173473	235599	208134	278883	245268
2003	94079	103355	98699	116170	106238	141330	127575	172385	153594	206668	181757
2004	84750	91342	87227	100621	92019	119860	108194	143014	127424	167575	147376

ZONE	1970A	1980H	1980M	1990H	1990M	2000H	2000M	2010H	2010M	2020H	2020M
2005	223589	185524	177167	160247	146547	152841	137965	149436	133146	147034	129312
2006	347769	272472	260199	218756	200053	190577	172028	167123	148905	144937	127467
2007	599	444	428	319	301	220	206	150	139	100	91
2008	3199	3583	3456	4025	3801	4430	4145	4907	4547	5319	4881
2009	13149	16110	15541	19245	18176	22099	20673	25223	23371	27969	25669
2010	79103	85498	82481	91055	85997	94404	88312	98688	91442	101752	93385
2011	54550	58657	56587	63674	60136	73460	68719	85165	78912	96924	88954
2012	55479	56860	54853	58484	55234	66416	62130	76001	70421	85688	78642
2013	21074	23315	22492	25789	24356	31380	29355	38341	35526	46002	42220
2014	6004	6202	5963	6509	6093	7542	6997	8842	8130	10255	9345
2015	79209	86520	82623	96684	88418	116919	105539	141714	126266	168768	148426
2016	192500	211356	201835	237187	216908	287823	259810	349853	311716	417608	367272
3001	0	0	0	0	0	0	0	0	0	0	0
3002	0	0	0	0	0	0	0	0	0	0	0
3003	0	0	0	0	0	0	0	0	0	0	0
3004	0	0	0	0	0	0	0	0	0	0	0
3005	0	0	0	0	0	0	0	0	0	0	0
3006	0	0	0	0	0	0	0	0	0	0	0
3007	0	0	0	0	0	0	0	0	0	0	0
3008	0	0	0	0	0	0	0	0	0	0	0
3009	0	0	0	0	0	0	0	0	0	0	0
3010	0	0	0	0	0	0	0	0	0	0	0
3011	0	0	0	0	0	0	0	0	0	0	0
3012	0	0	0	0	0	0	0	0	0	0	0
3013	0	0	0	0	0	0	0	0	0	0	0
3014	0	0	0	0	0	0	0	0	0	0	0
3015	0	0	0	0	0	0	0	0	0	0	0
3016	0	0	0	0	0	0	0	0	0	0	0
4001	0	0	0	0	0	0	0	0	0	0	0
4002	0	0	0	0	0	0	0	0	0	0	0
4003	0	0	0	0	0	0	0	0	0	0	0
4004	0	0	0	0	0	0	0	0	0	0	0
4005	0	0	0	0	0	0	0	0	0	0	0
4006	0	0	0	0	0	0	0	0	0	0	0
4007	0	0	0	0	0	0	0	0	0	0	0
4008	0	0	0	0	0	0	0	0	0	0	0
4009	0	0	0	0	0	0	0	0	0	0	0
4010	0	0	0	0	0	0	0	0	0	0	0
4011	0	0	0	0	0	0	0	0	0	0	0
4012	0	0	0	0	0	0	0	0	0	0	0
4013	0	0	0	0	0	0	0	0	0	0	0
4014	0	0	0	0	0	0	0	0	0	0	0
4015	0	0	0	0	0	0	0	0	0	0	0
4016	0	0	0	0	0	0	0	0	0	0	0
5001	0	0	0	0	0	0	0	0	0	0	0
5002	0	0	0	0	0	0	0	0	0	0	0
5003	0	0	0	0	0	0	0	0	0	0	0
5004	0	0	0	0	0	0	0	0	0	0	0
5005	0	0	0	0	0	0	0	0	0	0	0
5006	0	0	0	0	0	0	0	0	0	0	0

Population Program: Output

133

ALLOCATIONS: MCD MODEL 5

ZONE	1970A	1980H	1980M	1990H	1990M	2000H	2000M	2010H	2010M	2020H	2020M
5007	0	0	0	0	0	0	0	0	0	0	0
5008	0	0	0	0	0	0	0	0	0	0	0
5009	0	0	0	0	0	0	0	0	0	0	0
5010	0	0	0	0	0	0	0	0	0	0	0
5011	0	0	0	0	0	0	0	0	0	0	0
5012	0	0	0	0	0	0	0	0	0	0	0
5013	0	0	0	0	0	0	0	0	0	0	0
5014	0	0	0	0	0	0	0	0	0	0	0
5015	0	0	0	0	0	0	0	0	0	0	0
5016	0	0	0	0	0	0	0	0	0	0	0

ALLOCATIONS: MCD MODEL 5

SUMMARY BY RINGS (OR ROWS)

	1970A	1980H	1980M	1990H	1990M	2000H	2000M	2010H	2010M	2020H	2020M
1	12904	14593	13975	16699	15404	20121	18321	24386	21916	29114	25823
2	32573	36245	34760	40546	37565	47154	43116	55386	49971	64340	57270
3	41106	45872	43933	51848	47840	61786	56267	74252	66733	88107	78141
4	58858	66393	63499	76216	70055	93191	84572	114250	102365	137624	121731
5	106091	119121	114043	135373	124821	162172	147649	194772	175076	229842	203950
10	789336	857172	820078	946353	870390	1115758	1012883	1323557	1185903	1547396	1368421
20	1578575	1556386	1488698	1597273	1468715	1792868	1628144	2048637	1837255	2328291	2061903
30	0	0	0	0	0	0	0	0	0	0	0
40	0	0	0	0	0	0	0	0	0	0	0
50	0	0	0	0	0	0	0	0	0	0	0

ALLOCATIONS: MCD MODEL 5

SUMMARY BY SECTORS (OR COLUMNS)

	1970A	1980H	1980M	1990H	1990M	2000H	2000M	2010H	2010M	2020H	2020M
1	353666	388653	371145	436542	399220	530224	478617	645093	574772	770756	677853
2	232311	254818	243339	285830	261393	346864	313104	421821	375839	503966	443221
3	191511	209076	199658	233859	213865	283430	255844	344676	307103	412243	362553
4	187029	202800	193665	224814	205594	269556	243321	323826	288526	382132	336072
5	328126	299700	286200	287761	263158	306902	277031	335965	299342	368917	324450
6	413377	345631	330062	302171	276337	293460	264898	294279	262200	299322	263243
7	46597	54182	52270	61424	58011	66919	62600	72447	67128	76165	69902
8	10582	12544	12101	14731	13913	16832	15746	19302	17885	21675	19893
9	17667	22231	21446	27332	25813	32368	30279	38185	35382	43862	40255
10	159125	168298	162358	174949	165230	176671	165270	179625	166437	180019	165216
11	78085	84835	81840	92671	87522	105409	98607	121051	112163	137075	125804
12	72213	75537	72871	79260	74857	90867	85003	105079	97364	119839	109985
13	39250	42941	41423	46751	44146	54593	51061	64375	59639	74949	68776
14	22253	22534	21671	22891	21428	24382	22601	26270	24117	28060	25518
15	134796	146528	139927	163115	149169	196666	177524	237831	211906	282758	248676
16	332865	365485	349022	410218	375146	497926	449463	605447	539448	723009	635861

ALLOCATIONS: MCD MODEL 5

TOTALS

	1970A	1980H	1980M	1990H	1990M	2000H	2000M	2010H	2010M	2020H	2020M
9999	2619327	2695714	2578722	2864238	2634730	3292983	2990878	3835184	3439158	4424661	3917180

MCD MODEL 5: CHECK OF ALLOCATION SHARES

ALLOCATIONS: MCD MODELS 3, 4, 5

ZONE	1970A	1980H	1980M	1990H	1990M	2000H	2000M	2010H	2010M	2020H	2020M
101	1178	1602	1530	1864	1704	2292	2069	2935	2615	3691	3246
102	1178	1602	1530	1864	1704	2292	2069	2935	2615	3691	3246
103	1178	1602	1530	1864	1704	2292	2069	2935	2615	3691	3246
104	1178	1602	1530	1864	1704	2292	2069	2935	2615	3691	3246
105	1178	1602	1530	1864	1704	2292	2069	2935	2615	3691	3246
106	1178	1602	1530	1864	1704	2292	2069	2935	2615	3691	3246
107	176	233	225	299	282	368	344	449	416	531	487
108	176	233	225	299	282	368	344	449	416	531	487
109	176	233	225	299	282	368	344	449	416	531	487
110	176	233	225	299	282	368	344	449	416	531	487
111	176	233	225	299	282	368	344	449	416	531	487
112	176	233	225	299	282	368	344	449	416	531	487
113	1208	1280	1235	1322	1248	1313	1229	1301	1205	1257	1153
114	1208	1280	1235	1322	1248	1313	1229	1301	1205	1257	1153
115	1178	1602	1530	1864	1704	2292	2069	2935	2615	3691	3246
116	1178	1602	1530	1864	1704	2292	2069	2935	2615	3691	3246
201	2337	3179	3036	3698	3382	4549	4106	5825	5190	7323	6440
202	2337	3129	3036	3698	3382	4549	4106	5825	5190	7323	6440
203	2337	3179	3036	3698	3382	4549	4106	5825	5190	7323	6440
204	2337	3179	3036	3698	3382	4549	4106	5825	5190	7323	6440
205	2337	3179	3036	3698	3382	4549	4106	5825	5190	7323	6440
206	2337	3179	3036	3698	3382	4549	4106	5825	5190	7323	6440
207	245	319	307	405	382	495	463	601	557	710	652
208	475	625	603	800	756	983	919	1198	1110	1417	1300
209	589	778	750	997	942	1227	1147	1496	1386	1770	1625
210	589	778	750	997	942	1227	1147	1496	1386	1770	1625
211	1621	1825	1760	2020	1908	2172	2032	2349	2176	2496	2291
212	3449	3607	3480	3666	3463	3573	3343	3455	3201	3240	2974
213	3449	3607	3480	3666	3463	3573	3343	3455	3201	3240	2974
214	3449	3607	3480	3666	3463	3573	3343	3455	3201	3240	2974
215	2337	3179	3036	3698	3382	4549	4106	5825	5190	7323	6440
216	4311	5744	5485	6658	6089	8176	7380	10429	9292	13064	11489
301	4001	5444	5198	6331	5790	7788	7030	9972	8885	12537	11026
302	4001	5444	5198	6331	5790	7788	7030	9972	8885	12537	11026
303	4001	5444	5198	6331	5790	7788	7030	9972	8885	12537	11026
304	4001	5444	5198	6331	5790	7788	7030	9972	8885	12537	11026
305	4001	5444	5198	6331	5790	7788	7030	9972	8885	12537	11026
306	4001	5444	5198	6331	5790	7788	7030	9972	8885	12537	11026
307	50	38	37	29	27	21	19	15	14	10	9
308	50	38	37	29	27	21	19	15	14	10	9
309	595	782	755	1001	945	1229	1150	1498	1388	1772	1626
310	825	1089	1051	1397	1319	1717	1607	2095	1941	2479	2275
311	642	870	839	1147	1084	1453	1360	1830	1696	2240	2055
312	1377	1533	1479	1688	1594	1820	1703	1996	1849	2178	1999
313	4940	5292	5103	5546	5229	5657	5278	5726	5288	5695	5205
314	3789	4075	3927	4282	4026	4414	4102	4427	4067	4342	3943
315	601	824	787	1030	942	1350	1218	1623	1446	1922	1690
316	3909	5321	5082	6225	5693	7698	6949	9805	8736	12268	10789
401	7774	8140	7773	9027	8255	10826	9773	13050	11627	15444	13583
402	7479	10175	9717	11835	10823	14557	13140	18640	16608	23335	20610

ALLOCATIONS: MCD MODELS 3, 4, 5

ZONE	1970A	1980H	1980M	1990H	1990M	2000H	2000M	2010H	2010M	2020H	2020M
403	7479	10175	9717	11835	10823	14557	13140	18640	16608	23435	20610
404	7479	10175	9717	11835	10823	14557	13140	18640	16608	23435	20610
405	7479	10175	9717	11835	10823	14557	13140	18640	16608	23435	20610
406	7479	10175	9717	11835	10823	14557	13140	18640	16608	23435	2061C
407	5039	5876	5668	6664	6294	7252	6744	7633	7258	8208	7533
408	129	158	152	198	187	248	232	315	292	393	360
409	589	778	750	997	942	1227	1147	1496	1386	1770	1625
410	943	1245	1201	1596	1508	1963	1836	2394	2219	2833	2600
411	581	797	769	1064	1005	1365	1277	1742	1614	2160	1982
412	284	413	398	582	550	787	736	1055	977	1372	1259
413	732	834	802	951	889	1210	1118	1459	1335	1729	1565
414	509	702	670	923	844	1261	1138	1457	1298	1652	1453
415	5C9	702	670	923	844	1261	1138	1457	1298	1652	1453
416	4359	4721	4508	5378	4918	6601	5959	788A	7029	9258	8142
501	11265	11778	11247	12992	11881	15588	14071	18774	16727	22200	19524
502	7989	10124	9668	11598	10606	14189	12808	17920	15967	22236	19556
503	9349	12719	12146	14793	13528	18196	16425	23300	20760	29294	25763
504	15779	18377	17549	20821	19041	25339	22873	31190	27790	37741	33192
505	14259	17339	16558	19798	18105	24171	21818	30114	26831	36878	32433
506	9349	12719	12146	14793	13528	18196	16425	23300	20760	29294	25763
507	14999	17535	16916	19923	18816	21707	20306	23465	21742	24599	22576
508	5224	6163	5946	7079	6686	7814	7310	8579	7949	9161	8408
509	488	658	634	861	813	1083	1013	1352	1253	1639	1504
510	1061	1400	1351	1796	1696	2208	2066	2694	2496	3187	2925
511	813	1118	1079	1497	1414	1926	1801	2463	2283	3063	2811
512	733	848	818	993	938	1262	1180	1607	1489	2001	1837
513	1517	1553	1498	1581	1493	1897	1775	2288	2120	2711	2488
514	679	936	893	1231	1126	1681	1518	1942	1731	2203	1938
515	679	936	893	1231	1126	1681	1518	1942	1731	2203	1938
516	11889	12526	11962	13979	12784	16862	15221	20267	18057	23917	21034
1001	131914	137886	131674	152001	139006	182387	164636	219667	195722	259757	228847
1002	80674	85297	81455	93140	85177	111890	101000	13391!	119314	157399	138427
1003	73084	84382	80581	96186	87963	119189	107588	144969	129166	173583	152660
1004	71502	76674	73220	85491	78182	103350	93291	123962	110449	146032	128430
1005	75279	81812	78127	91668	83648	110701	99927	133376	118837	157867	138839
1006	41259	50980	48683	58372	53381	71346	64402	89265	79534	109772	96541
1007	25484	29736	28686	33782	31905	36853	34475	39931	36999	42004	38550
1008	1324	1740	1679	2298	2170	2966	2774	3637	3555	4841	4443
1009	2075	2889	2787	3927	3709	5133	4802	6668	6178	8408	7717
1010	76422	78052	75297	77806	73483	74781	69955	71806	66534	67464	61917
1011	19696	21301	20549	22887	21616	24559	22974	26919	24943	29501	27075
1012	10709	11368	10967	12045	11376	14616	13673	17825	16516	21359	19602
1013	6325	6474	6245	6590	6224	7906	7396	9553	8633	11298	103690
1014	6609	8206	7862	10027	9249	13252	12066	15470	13919	17741	15775
1015	50279	53849	51424	60846	55644	74177	66958	88839	79155	104485	91891
1016	116689	121828	116340	134999	123458	161855	146101	194927	173678	230488	202706
2001	194879	203463	194298	225453	206178	270303	243995	325635	290048	384923	338527
2002	128649	134879	128803	147805	135168	177509	160232	213559	190279	252273	221865
2003	94079	106845	102032	120340	110052	147291	132955	180637	160945	217722	191479
2004	84750	89546	85512	99541	91031	120181	108483	143419	127785	168040	147785

ALLOCATIONS: MCD MODELS 3, 4, 5

ZONE	1970A	1980H	1980M	1990H	1990M	2000H	2000M	2010H	2010M	2020H	2020M
2005	223589	185829	177458	163656	143664	158525	143096	154678	137817	151607	133333
2006	347769	272752	260466	216494	197985	186841	168555	164661	146711	144191	126811
2007	599	444	428	319	301	220	206	150	139	100	91
2008	3199	3583	3456	4025	3801	4430	4145	4907	4547	5319	4881
2009	13149	16110	15541	19245	18176	22099	20673	25223	23371	27969	25669
2010	79103	85498	82481	91055	85997	94404	88312	98688	91442	101752	93385
2011	54550	58063	56014	62807	59318	72914	68209	85103	78854	97537	89516
2012	55479	59875	57761	64792	61193	74327	69530	85886	79579	97748	89710
2013	21074	22911	22102	24811	23433	30039	28101	36656	33872	43725	40129
2014	6004	6927	6652	7958	7396	10209	9371	12034	10926	13940	12519
2015	79209	83430	79672	93096	85136	112278	101350	134952	120240	159267	140070
2016	192500	200970	191917	222731	203688	267032	241042	321595	286538	380263	334428
3001	0	0	0	0	0	0	0	0	0	0	0
3002	0	0	0	0	0	0	0	0	0	0	0
3003	0	0	0	0	0	0	0	0	0	0	0
3004	0	0	0	0	0	0	0	0	0	0	0
3005	0	0	0	0	0	0	0	0	0	0	0
3006	0	0	0	0	0	0	0	0	0	0	0
3007	0	0	0	0	0	0	0	0	0	0	0
3008	0	0	0	0	0	0	0	0	0	0	0
3009	0	0	0	0	0	0	0	0	0	0	0
3010	0	0	0	0	0	0	0	0	0	0	0
3011	0	0	0	0	0	0	0	0	0	0	0
3012	0	0	0	0	0	0	0	0	0	0	0
3013	0	0	0	0	0	0	0	0	0	0	0
3014	0	0	0	0	0	0	0	0	0	0	0
3015	0	0	0	0	0	0	0	0	0	0	0
3016	0	0	0	0	0	0	0	0	0	0	0
4001	0	0	0	0	0	0	0	0	0	0	0
4002	0	0	0	0	0	0	0	0	0	0	0
4003	0	0	0	0	0	0	0	0	0	0	0
4004	0	0	0	0	0	0	0	0	0	0	0
4005	0	0	0	0	0	0	0	0	0	0	0
4006	0	0	0	0	0	0	0	0	0	0	0
4007	0	0	0	0	0	0	0	0	0	0	0
4008	0	0	0	0	0	0	0	0	0	0	0
4009	0	0	0	0	0	0	0	0	0	0	0
4010	0	0	0	0	0	0	0	0	0	0	0
4011	0	0	0	0	0	0	0	0	0	0	0
4012	0	0	0	0	0	0	0	0	0	0	0
4013	0	0	0	0	0	0	0	0	0	0	0
4014	0	0	0	0	0	0	0	0	0	0	0
4015	0	0	0	0	0	0	0	0	0	0	0
4016	0	0	0	0	0	0	0	0	0	0	0
5001	0	0	0	0	0	0	0	0	0	0	0
5002	0	0	0	0	0	0	0	0	0	0	0
5003	0	0	0	0	0	0	0	0	0	0	0
5004	0	0	0	0	0	0	0	0	0	0	0
5005	0	0	0	0	0	0	0	0	0	0	0
5006	0	0	0	0	0	0	0	0	0	0	0

ALLOCATIONS: MCD MODELS 3, 4, 5

ZONE	1970A	1980H	1980M	1990H	1990M	2000H	2000M	2010H	2010M	2020H	2020M
5007	0	0	0	0	0	0	0	0	0	0	0
5008	0	0	0	0	0	0	0	0	0	0	0
5009	0	0	0	0	0	0	0	0	0	0	0
5010	0	0	0	0	0	0	0	0	0	0	0
5011	0	0	0	0	0	0	0	0	0	0	0
5012	0	0	0	0	0	0	0	0	0	0	0
5013	0	0	0	0	0	0	0	0	0	0	0
5014	0	0	0	0	0	0	0	0	0	0	0
5015	0	0	0	0	0	0	0	0	0	0	0
5016	0	0	0	0	0	0	0	0	0	0	0

ALLOCATIONS: MCD MODELS 3, 4, 5

SUMMARY BY RINGS (OR ROWS)

	1970A	1980H	1980M	1990H	1990M	2000H	2000M	2010H	2010M	2020H	2020M
1	12904	16783	16065	19352	17830	23178	21081	28784	25835	35230	31202
2	32573	40589	38908	45810	42379	53219	48591	64111	57745	76476	67943
3	41106	52832	50579	60695	55931	72502	65940	89327	80164	108672	96227
4	58858	75248	71955	87485	80357	106791	96844	133353	119379	163652	144612
5	106091	126736	121312	144975	133590	173807	158133	211203	189691	252334	223695
10	789336	852480	815583	941873	866197	1114965	1012024	1320897	1183329	1541989	1363393
20	1578575	1531116	1464585	1564117	1438505	1748588	1588344	1987564	1783080	2246357	1990184
30	0	0	0	0	0	0	0	0	0	0	0
40	0	0	0	0	0	0	0	0	0	0	0
50	0	0	0	0	0	0	0	0	0	0	0

ALLOCATIONS: MCD MODELS 3, 4, 5

SUMMARY BY SECTORS (OR COLUMNS)

	1970A	1980H	1980M	1990H	1990M	2000H	2000M	2010H	2010M	2020H	2020M
1	353666	371795	355047	411696	376498	494124	446031	596218	531224	706405	621258
2	232311	250704	239410	276273	252653	332775	300386	402765	358860	478896	421173
3	191511	224348	214242	255050	233244	313863	283315	386281	344172	467587	411226
4	187029	204999	195765	229583	209955	278057	250994	335947	299326	398801	350732
5	328126	305383	291627	298651	273118	322585	291188	355542	316785	393341	345930
6	413377	356854	340780	313389	286596	305570	275829	314601	280306	330246	290440
7	46597	84182	52270	61424	58011	66919	62600	72447	67128	76165	69902
8	10582	12544	12101	14731	13913	16832	15746	19302	17885	21675	19893
9	17667	22231	21446	27332	25813	32368	30279	38185	35382	43862	40255
10	159125	168298	162358	174949	165230	176671	165270	179625	164437	180019	165216
11	78085	84210	81238	91725	86629	104760	98000	120858	111984	137530	126221
12	72213	77879	75131	84067	79397	96755	90511	112274	104030	128431	117870
13	39250	41954	40468	44471	41982	51600	48242	60321	55857	69657	63887
14	22253	25735	24722	29413	27354	35707	32769	40088	36350	44378	39758
15	134796	144525	138015	162691	148781	197590	178359	237576	211677	280545	246729
16	332865	350151	334378	388877	355630	466892	421450	563244	501845	667210	586788

ALLOCATIONS: MCD MODELS 3, 4, 5

TOTALS

	1970A	1980H	1980M	1990H	1990M	2000H	2000M	2010H	2010M	2020H	2020M
9999	2619327	2655707	2578916	2864234	2634730	3292994	2990894	3835181	3439160	4424655	3917196

MCD MODELS 3, 4, 5: CHECK OF ALLOCATION SHARES

END OF PROJECTIONS

Part II
Employment Projections

Introduction

This part of the monograph presents a set of projection models accompanied by computer programs whose task is to project employment at the county level for periods of twenty-five years into the future. With the exception of Model 2, *Simple Linear Regression*, they are step-down models, which use national projections as controls on the state and county totals. While the programs were written with reference to national totals, in a more general sense any larger region or state can be employed in analogous fashion as the exogenous component for projections at smaller geographic scales. In addition, the models are not restricted either to the county spatial scale or the twenty-five year temporal framework. They can be modified for other situations.

The first model, *Constant Share*, is based on the assumption that a county's employment will grow at the same rate as that of the encompassing state jurisdiction, and will therefore maintain a constant share of the statewide employment totals. Model 2 is a *Simple Linear Regression* technique which extrapolates historical trends to the future regardless of either state or national patterns of growth. The third model, which for purposes of brevity is entitled *Population/Employment*, modifies Model 1 (constant share) by differential population growth rates, i.e., by ratios of a county's change in population to the change in population experienced by a larger state. Model 4—*OBERS*—comprises trend extrapolations of a county's share of state employment over time. It is more exactly described as a modified double exponential implicit shift share model.

No single employment projection model has been deemed the most effective or accurate. These four were selected as prototypical of various sets of models that can be operationalized at modest cost, require data that are readily available for most jurisdictions, and whose calibration is not overly complex. The broad approaches were isolated and programmed in conjunction with a concurrent study of New Jersey county employment. Hence, the examples within this monograph have been secured from that study.

The following presentation is in a format analogous to Part I. Chapters 9–11 consist of a general discussion of economic models and data considerations. The main emphasis is reduced to four techniques: Constant Share, Simple Linear Regression, Population/Employment, and OBERS. These four models are illustrated using employment data for the State of New Jersey and Middlesex County, New Jersey as examples. Several data sources and the various options available in the computer programming for the four models, including input formats, the overall program, as well as a sample problem data set and the sample problem output, are reviewed.

Chapter 9
An Overview of Employment Projection Models

Before detailing the four programmed models, employment projection techniques will be overviewed. As part of this analysis, the various factors which affect the choice and accuracy of models will be examined.

A Classification of Types of Models

At the risk of oversimplifying, the differences among techniques available for employment projection can be understood by partitioning them into three broad categories: (1) trend extrapolations that are statistical projections of employment as a function of time; (2) market share models that project change in one geographic area as a direct function of exogenously projected changes in another market area of which the former is a part; and (3) models of sectoral interdependence that most commonly see the changes in the exporting sectors of the economy as having a multiplier effect on the non-exporting sector of the economy.

The driving force in models of the first type is time; in the second is the fate of the larger geographic market area; and in the third is external demand for products of the exporting sector of the local economy. Models of the first type include linear and non-linear curves fit to historical trends. Models of the second type include stepdown allocation and shift and share models. Models of the third type include economic base technique, input-output and econometric models.

In a similar attempt to classify techniques, Hirsch (1973) labels our first two types "statistical-based" and our third type "theoretical-based." While our first two types are indeed statistical based, the trend extrapolations are based on a statistical relationship or ratio between employment levels and time. The market models are based on a statistical relationship or ratio between employment levels in, say, a county and a state. Models of the third type, such as input-output analysis and economic-base technique do tend to have more elaborate theoretical justification and reasoning behind them, but are not statistic free. They tend to be more complex in data and computational requirements, although not in every case. The more complex models are not necessarily the more accurate and reliable. In many instances, the simpler techniques will provide adequate projections at minimum cost.

It might be easier to understand these models in terms of the same kind of dichotomy used to distinguish among population projection models in Chapter 1, dividing them into non-component and component methods. Employment models might be similarly divided into non-sectoral and sectoral methods. The non-component and non-sectoral methods both forecast aggregates of population and employment respectively by means of simple time trend extrapolations and ratios or step--down methods that allocate from a larger area to smaller areas by proportional distribution. The component and sectoral methods look at the behavior of a functional part of the aggregate as a key determinant of how the whole will change. In population, the birth rates of women of childbearing age is a key component. In employment, the demand for export goods, investment activities, and the like are key sectors, generating future change in the total levels of employment.

Basic Data

The primary types of employment data used in economic models are historical employment trends in an area, historical employment trends in the larger region or state, and employment projections for the larger region. The data should be disaggregated to at least the Major Divisions of the Standard Industrial Classification (SIC) code. The SIC code is a data filing scheme that classifies all different kinds of economic activity in the United States and periodically publishes counts of employment and other measures of economic activity for each category in the system. In the *SIC Manual*, published by the U.S. Office of Management and Budget, all activity is first divided into eleven Major Divisions. Each Major Division is divided into sub-areas called Major Groups. Each Major Group is assigned a two-digit code number. Each Major Group is then subdivided into Groups, each assigned a three-digit code, and each Group is then subdivided into Industries. Each Industry is assigned a four-digit numerical code. All economic establishments fall under one of these Industry designations. These four levels of detail in the SIC code can be summarized as follows.

Levels of Classification	Range of Letter or Numerical Code	Examples: Code	Short Title
Major Divisions	A through K	B	Mining
Major Groups	01 – 99	10	Metal Mining
Groups	011 – 999	104	Gold & Silver Ores
Industries	0111 – 9999	1041	Gold Ores

Exhibit 9.1 presents a complete listing of the Major Divisions and Major Groups.

EXHIBIT 9.1
THE 1972 STANDARD INDUSTRIAL CLASSIFICATION (SIC): MAJOR DIVISIONS AND MAJOR GROUPS

SIC Code	Major Division / Major Group (2-digit code)
A	Agriculture, Forestry, and Fishing
01	Agricultural Production—Crops
02	Agricultural Production—Livestock
07	Agricultural Services
08	Forestry
09	Fishing, Hunting, and Trapping
B	Mining
10	Metal Mining
11	Anthracite Mining
12	Bituminous Coal and Lignite Mining
13	Oil and Gas Extraction
14	Nonmetallic Minerals, Except Fuels
C	Construction
15	General Building Contractors
16	Heavy Construction Contractors
17	Special Trade Contractors

EXHIBIT 9.1 (Continued)
THE 1972 STANDARD INDUSTRIAL CLASSIFICATION (SIC):
MAJOR DIVISIONS AND MAJOR GROUPS

SIC Code	Major Division Major Group (2-digit code)
D	Manufacturing
20	Food and Kindred Products
21	Tobacco Manufactures
22	Textile Mill Products
23	Apparel and Other Textile Products
24	Lumber and Wood Products
25	Furniture and Fixtures
26	Paper and Allied Products
27	Printing and Publishing
28	Chemicals and Allied Products
29	Petroleum and Coal Products
30	Rubber and Misc. Plastics Products
31	Leather and Leather Products
32	Stone, Clay and Glass Products
33	Primary Metal Industries
34	Fabricated Metal Products
35	Machinery, Except Electrical
36	Electric and Electronic Equipment
37	Transportation Equipment
38	Instruments and Related Products
39	Miscellaneous Manufacturing Industries
E	Transportation and Public Utilities
40	Railroad Transportation
41	Local and Interurban Passenger Transit
42	Trucking and Warehousing
43	U.S. Postal Service
44	Water Transportation
45	Transportation by Air
46	Pipe Lines, Except Natural Gas
47	Transportation Services
48	Communication
49	Electric, Gas, and Sanitary Services
F	Wholesale Trade
50	Wholesale Trade—Durable Goods
51	Wholesale Trade—Nondurable Goods

EXHIBIT 9.1 (Continued)
THE 1972 STANDARD INDUSTRIAL CLASSIFICATION (SIC):
MAJOR DIVISIONS AND MAJOR GROUPS

SIC Code	Major Division Major Group (2-digit code)
G	Retail Trade
52	Building Materials and Garden Supplies
53	General Merchandise Stores
54	Food Stores
55	Automotive Dealers and Service Stations
56	Apparel and Accessory Stores
57	Furniture and Home Furnishings Stores
58	Eating and Drinking Places
59	Miscellaneous Retail
H	Finance, Insurance, and Real Estate
60	Banking
61	Credit Agencies Other Than Banks
62	Security, Commodity Brokers and Services
63	Insurance Carriers
64	Insurance Agents, Brokers and Service
65	Real Estate
66	Combined Real Estate, Insurance, Etc.
67	Holding and Other Investment Offices
I	Services
70	Hotels and Other Lodging Places
72	Personal Services
73	Business Services
75	Auto Repair, Services, and Garages
76	Miscellaneous Repair Services
78	Motion Pictures
79	Amusement and Recreation Services
80	Health Services
81	Legal Services
82	Educational Services
83	Social Services
84	Museums, Botanical, Zoological Gardens
86	Membership Organizations
88	Private Households
89	Miscellaneous Services

EXHIBIT 9.1 (Continued)
THE 1972 STANDARD INDUSTRIAL CLASSIFICATION (SIC):
MAJOR DIVISIONS AND MAJOR GROUPS

SIC Code	Major Division Major Group (2-digit code)
J	Public Administration
91	Executive, Legislative, and General
92	Justice, Public Order, and Safety
93	Finance, Taxation and Monetary Policy
94	Administration of Human Resources
95	Environmental Quality and Housing
96	Administration of Economic Programs
97	National Security and Intl. Affairs
K	Nonclassifiable Establishments
99	Nonclassifiable Establishments

SOURCE: U.S. Executive Office of the President, Office of Management and Budget, *Standard Industrial Classification Manual – 1972.* Washington, D.C., U.S. Government Printing Office, 1972.

Models of Sectoral Interdependence

The most common and easy to understand model of sectoral interdependence is based on economic base theory and is called the economic base model. It supposes that we divide all economic activity (measured as either product, or employment or income or value added) into two sectors: that which produces for export consumption and that which produces for local consumption. A constant ratio between the amount of activity in each of these sectors is assumed to endure into the future. The model then depends on the availability of an exogenous forecast of demand for the export products. Local production in those export sector activities is then projected to change in response to the projected exogenous demand forecast for exports. Income brought into the community as a result of these export sales is then assumed to generate local consumption activities as it circulates through local buyers and sellers in cycles that multiply the initial export dollars. This "Keynesian" multiplier or ratio of export to local activities is the heart of the economic base model. The multiplier is estimated for current and historical periods and then held constant for projection purposes and applied to alternative forecasts of export activity.

A difficult technical problem in using this model is estimating for past and current periods—which activities are export and which activities are local? There are basically two approaches to this problem. One is to survey every economic establishment to determine the sources of all of their purchases and the destinations of all of their sales. This information is extremely costly to gather, but yields such a full picture of the workings of the economy that, indeed, much more than employment forecasts can be determined from these rich data. In fact, the analysis of such a table of data is subject to a whole branch of economic analysis called Input-Output analysis. If all one wanted was employment projections, the use of input-output analysis might be doing it the hard way.

The other approach to sectoring activities into export and local sectors is to use one of several short-cut techniques, such as location quotients and minimum requirements techniques. These techniques try, for each industry or group of industries, to determine an ideal or minimum proportion of a community's activity that is needed to meet local consumption needs. Any excess over that minimum proportion is presumed to be excess for export. The location quotient bases its standard on national averages. The minimum requirements technique bases its standard on a national minimum or near minimum proportion.

Input-output analysis is in fact also a kind of multiplier model but one so much more elaborate and detailed than economic base analysis as to be of a different kind. There are yet other models of sectoral interdependence employed to study metropolitan, regional, and state economies for planning and projection purposes that fall under the general rubric of econometric models. Mathematically, these models take the form of a set of linear equations, seldom less than 10 equations, sometimes more than 100. Complex linear regression models are used to calibrate the parameters of these equations, so that the many dependent variables might be simultaneously projected with a minimum of error. While they do sometimes have as one of their results a forecast of future employment, they tend to focus more on short-run policy variables such as rates of return, levels of taxes, business investment, aggregate unemployment rates, bank deposits, etc. For a survey of these see Gass and Sisson (1975).

Market Share Models

There are many relatively simple models that have been developed to project employment at the county levels. These models avoid the many data requirements and the expense of input-output and the chain of methods required in using economic base, location and population quotients, and minimum base requirements. Hewings (1976) reviewed twelve, which he labeled step-down models, because county projections were derived from multicounty, state, and national forecasts, with the latter serving as the exogenous input. With the exception of two of the techniques, the only data required are the standard historical employment series tabulations for all four geographic scales (county, multicounty, state, and nation) and the existing projections at the national level. Most of the models assume that the growth of the county is based on the growth of its multicounty region, which is based upon the growth of its state, which in turn is based upon the national growth. The different models operationalize this assumption via alternative procedures. Additionally, some approaches involve regression of the historical trends of an area's employment growth or regression of an area's changing shares of total employment activity in a region over time. Many of these methods are shift-share techniques, explicit or implicit.

Shift-share models (Ashby, 1965; Lasuen, 1971; Perloff, et al., 1960; Zimmerman, 1975), for the most part, consist of two components: (1) the share or ratio of county employment to state (or any larger region) employment; and (2) the shift or competitive component. This second component can be derived explicitly or implicitly. An explicitly determined shift component is one that is directly formulated from historical data of two time periods and presumably reflects the differentials between a county's economic growth and regional (or state) growth, for that time frame. The explicit variable can be population, the tax burden, labor force skills, income, or any other factor that causes the competitive component to change over time. It is, however, often unstable over time and, therefore, should be used with caution.

Alternatively, a shift increment that is operationalized implicitly is ascertained usually via a regression of a series of historical employment data against time, where the derived slope represents the shifting differences between county economic activity and regional (or state) growth. If the shift component is greater than zero, then the implication is that the economy (or industry) is growing faster in a particular county than in the region (or state), and vice versa.

Three of the market share models were chosen for this study: constant share, population/employment, and OBERS. The constant share model projects county employment at the same rate that the state's employment is expected to grow. The population/employment model, a modification of the constant share model, is based on a ratio of a county's population change to a state's population change. OBERS is technically the only shift-share model of the four. The competitive component is derived through a regression of the logarithm of the county share of state employment against the logarithm of time. These models will be discussed more fully in Chapter 10.

Trend Extrapolations

Models that simply plot the progress of a variable over time and extrapolate the trend into the future are, of course, not peculiar to employment studies. We saw them applied to population in Part I and they are widely used techniques throughout the social and physical sciences. They fall under a general category of curve-fitting techniques. The particular curve selected to represent a set of data can vary from a straight line, to various exponential curves, cyclical patterns, and to an almost infinite variety of geometric shapes.

For the purposes of this volume, a linear regression model was selected to represent this group. Because of its simplicity, the linear model is probably the most commonly used for simple trend extrapolation. It assumes that a constant absolute increment of employment change, evident in the past, will persist for each unit of time in the future. Linear regression analysis is used to determine what the size of an increment in the past has been and what the assumption implies for future points in time.

Elements Affecting Choice and Accuracy

Although no single employment projection model has been shown to be more consistently accurate than others, there are several factors that affect the results. The accuracy and choice of the models for a particular use depend on such variables as data availability, in terms of both type and quality, the length of the projection period, the validity of the model's assumptions, and time and budgetary constraints. Some models seem to be more appropriate than others for certain spatial configurations, and some perform better for certain classes of industries.

The data need to be consistent at all geographical scales and time periods. The *SIC Manual* is periodically revised. Thus, when using historical data spanning the revisions, adjustments must be made to ensure that the coding is consistent for all years.

The quality of employment data varies greatly. Disclosure policies (e.g., federal law mandates that data that disclose the operations of an individual employer be withheld) cause problems in most sources and are usually treated differently in each source. For example, in *County Business Patterns* data are not shown for any industry that does not have at least 100 employees or ten reporting units in the area covered by tabulations. However, data for an unpublished industry are included in the total shown for the broader industry group of which it is a part. In other sources, undisclosed establishments in a subcategory are not included in the larger group. The smaller the geographical area, the more cumbersome the problems with disclosure become.

County Business Patterns and *Employment and Earnings* are probably the easiest to use, but sometimes additional material is required to augment the information they provide. These and other data sources and definitions are detailed more fully in Chapter 11. Population data are needed for some models and the first part of this monograph may be referred to for a discussion of this material.

The quality of the control projections, i.e., the exogenous forecasts, affects the accuracy of small area projections for which the control projections serve as bases. Thus, the control projections should be examined to insure that the most recent available data have been utilized in formulating them. It may be necessary to adjust these control projections. Procedures suggested to accomplish this are presented in Chapter 11.

The length of the projection period should also be considered when choosing a model. As we will point out with respect to the regression techniques in the following chapters, more reliable short-term results may be produced by simple regression techniques than by step-down techniques because of the additive accumulation of measurement error in a series of ratio extrapolations. On the other hand, uncontrolled extrapolation of historical data is of dubious value for long-term projections.

Another consideration in model selection is the geographic scale of the study area. At the national level, employment projections are usually developed by large governmental agencies, such as the Bureau of Labor Statistics (BLS) and Bureau of Economic Analysis (BEA) (formerly Office of Business Economics), who can afford to become involved in major research programs. The BLS uses input-output analysis and the BEA has developed alternative techniques. Both agencies track their projections to examine their performance in relation to actual activity, and adjust them accordingly. Chapter 11 provides more details on these projections.

State agencies also become involved in employment projections. Some have their own input-output tables (e.g., Washington, West Virginia). Others use various other methods.

County projections, on the other hand, usually rely on national and/or state projections as controls. For example, as of early 1977, only six of the twenty-one New Jersey counties had prepared any employment projections. Additionally, as has been pointed out earlier, input-output analysis is more appropriate and economically feasible at the national level than at smaller geographic scales. At the state level, large-scale models may be applied; but there is evidence that, at the county level, the costlier and more time-consuming approaches do not provide results that are compensatingly better than those of less sophisticated models.

Activities are not driven by the same forces in all industrial sectors. Certain sectors interact with the local market; others are responsive only

EXHIBIT 9.2

COMPARISON OF EMPLOYMENT PROJECTION METHODS

Type of Model	Relative Complexity			Type of Data			Appropriate Projection Period		Appropriate Scale	Regional	
	Simple	Moderate	Complex	Historical Employment Data	Employment Projections	Population and Other Variables	Short	Long	Nation	State	and County
Extrapolation Type											
Linear Trend	✓	✓		✓			✓			✓	✓
Market Share Type											
Constant Share		✓			✓		✓			✓	✓
Population/Empl.		✓			✓	✓	✓	✓		✓	✓
OBERS		✓		✓	°		✓	✓		✓	✓
Sectoral Interdependence Type											
Economic Base		✓		✓	✓	✓	✓		✓	✓	
Input-Output & Econometric			✓	✓	✓	✓	✓		✓	✓	

to international demand. While it is appropriate for service employment to be projected using local population multipliers, projections for most durable products do not necessarily relate to the local market. Statistical testing by various researchers has shown the appropriateness of some models for specific industrial sectors (see Chapter 10).

Finally, other considerations in the choice of models include time and budgetary constraints. Input-output analysis is much more expensive in terms of time and money than are step-down models. Moreover, the step-down models can be hand calculated, although with the use of large-scale computers and, when many counties are involved, projections can be obtained relatively quickly.

Summary

This chapter has highlighted several alternative employment projection models and some of the elements that affect the accuracy and choice of models. Both the less and more complex models have been briefly reviewed. References have been made to other parts of this monograph where the subject matter has been presented in more detail. Exhibit 9.2 serves as a summary of some of the material covered in this and following chapters.

Exhibit 9.2 represents our collective judgments about the best and most feasible uses of the methods. Some of the judgments are based on actual comparative tests of different methods (Greenberg, 1972; Hewings, 1976) and others are based on theory and the feasibility of using certain methods in specific situations. An empty space signifies that we think that an application is not appropriate or not feasible, not that it cannot be made. For example, input-output and economic base studies can be done for a county. Such studies are, however, relatively rare because of cost. Regression projections can be made for infinite periods into the future. However, unless constrained by projections made at the federal and/or state scales, they may produce absurdly high projections or negative numbers. The chapter that follows outlines in detail the four models that have been included in the computer programs of this part.

Chapter 10
The Models

The four models described in this chapter are: Constant Share, Simple Linear Regression, Population/Employment, and OBERS. With the exception of Simple Regression, they are all step-down models and use national projections as constraints. They have been selected for inclusion in the study for three reasons: their underlying assumptions are different and simple; they are quite manageable in terms of data calibration and requirements; and their performance in statistical tests undertaken by various researchers has suggested that they produce relatively useful results. In this chapter each model will be analyzed with respect to the factors just listed. And the models will be fully illustrated at the state and county levels, using data from the State of New Jersey and Middlesex County, New Jersey.

The following notation will be used throughout the chapter:

$E =$ Employment
$P =$ Population
$i =$ Industrial Sector $(i = 1 \ldots 23)$
$n =$ Nation
$s =$ State $(s = 1 \ldots 6)$
$c =$ County $(c = 1 \ldots 600)$

$\text{t} =$ Base Time Period
$\text{m} =$ Number of Years in the Future
$\text{b} =$ Slope of least squares equation
$\text{a} =$ Intercept of least squares equation

Constant Share—Model 1

Of the four models included in the program package, constant share is perhaps the most simple in terms of assumptions, calibration, and data requirements. While the assumptions of the constant share model are simple, the results obtained are useful. Specifically, as will be demonstrated later, statistical testing of this model indicates that in some cases it has produced results superior to those of more elegantly designed alternatives.

The assumption of the constant share model is that an area's current share of regional employment will persist over time. This assumption implies that an area will grow at the same rate as its larger region. The method is a step-down technique in that exogenous national projections are used to calculate state projections, which in turn provide the bases for county projections. Using a two-step procedure the model is as follows:

State Projections

$$(10.1) \qquad E_{t+m}^{is} = \frac{E_t^{is}}{E_t^{in}} \cdot E_{t+m}^{in}$$

County Projections

$$(10.2) \qquad E_{t+m}^{ic} = \frac{E_t^{ic}}{E_t^{is}} \cdot E_{t+m}^{is}$$

An alternative approach to this model is to incorporate averages. This involves simply averaging an area's share of regional employment over three time periods. The effect of this procedure is to take into account trends and deviations that may have occurred during a particular time frame.

State Projections

$$(10.3) \qquad E_{t+m}^{is} = \left[\left(\frac{E_{t-2}^{is}}{E_{t-2}^{in}} + \frac{E_{t-1}^{is}}{E_{t-1}^{in}} + \frac{E_t^{is}}{E_t^{in}} \right) \div 3 \right] E_{t+m}^{in}$$

County Projections

$$(10.4) \qquad E_{t+m}^{ic} = \left[\left(\frac{E_{t-2}^{ic}}{E_{t-2}^{is}} + \frac{E_{t-1}^{ic}}{E_{t-1}^{is}} + \frac{E_{t}^{ic}}{E_{t}^{is}} \right) \div 3 \right] E_{t+m}^{is}$$

Exhibit 10.1 illustrates the calculation of the constant share model for wholesale and retail trade employment with and without averages, in New Jersey and Middlesex County. From the exhibit it can be seen that the procedure may be reduced to a one-step process if state projections are available. Or, county projections can be made directly from national projections. This latter approach, however, is rarely used.

EXHIBIT 10.1A
CALCULATION OF WHOLESALE AND RETAIL TRADE EMPLOYMENT
PROJECTIONS
NEW JERSEY AND MIDDLESEX COUNTY
1980–2000
MODEL 1—CONSTANT SHARE: WITHOUT AVERAGING
(employment in thousands)

New Jersey

(1) $E_{1980}^{is} = \dfrac{E_{1975}^{is}}{E_{1975}^{in}} \times E_{1980}^{in}$

$= \dfrac{621.2}{16,917.6} \times 18,765.0 = (.0367)(18,765.0)$

$= \underline{689.1}$

(2) $E_{1985}^{is} = \dfrac{E_{1975}^{is}}{E_{1975}^{in}} \times E_{1985}^{in}$

$= \dfrac{621.2}{16,917.6} \times 19,569.0 = (.0367)(19,569.0)$

$= \underline{718.6}$

EXHIBIT 10.1A (continued)
Calculation of Wholesale and Retail Trade Employment
Projections
New Jersey and Middlesex County
1980–2000
Model 1—Constant Share: Without Averaging
(employment in thousands)

$$(3) \quad E_{1990}^{is} = \frac{E_{1975}^{is}}{E_{1975}^{in}} \times E_{1990}^{in}$$

$$= \frac{621.2}{16,917.6} \times 20,340.0 = (.0367)(20,340.0)$$

$$= \underline{746.9}$$

$$(4) \quad E_{1995}^{is} = \frac{E_{1975}^{is}}{E_{1975}^{in}} \times E_{1995}^{in}$$

$$= \frac{621.2}{16,917.6} \times 21,069.6 = (.0367)(21,069.6)$$

$$= \underline{773.7}$$

$$(5) \quad E_{2000}^{is} = \frac{E_{1975}^{is}}{E_{1975}^{in}} \times E_{2000}^{in}$$

$$= \frac{621.2}{16,917.6} \times 21,789.3 = (.0367)(21,789.3)$$

$$= \underline{800.1}$$

EXHIBIT 10.1A
CALCULATION OF WHOLESALE AND RETAIL TRADE EMPLOYMENT
PROJECTIONS
NEW JERSEY AND MIDDLESEX COUNTY
1980–2000
MODEL 1—CONSTANT SHARE: WITHOUT AVERAGING
(employment in thousands)

Middlesex County

(1) $E_{1980}^{ic} = \dfrac{E_{1975}^{ic}}{E_{1975}^{is}} \times E_{1980}^{is}$

$= \dfrac{54.0}{621.2} \times 689.1 = (.0870)(689.1)$

$= \underline{59.9}$

(2) $E_{1985}^{ic} = \dfrac{E_{1975}^{ic}}{E_{1975}^{is}} \times E_{1985}^{is}$

$= \dfrac{54.0}{621.2} \times 718.6 = (.0870)(718.6)$

$= \underline{62.5}$

(3) $E_{1990}^{ic} = \dfrac{E_{1975}^{ic}}{E_{1975}^{is}} \times E_{1990}^{is}$

$= \dfrac{54.0}{621.2} \times 747.2 = (.0870)(747.2)$

$= \underline{65.0}$

EXHIBIT 10.1A (continued)
Calculation of Wholesale and Retail Trade Employment
Projections
New Jersey and Middlesex County
1980–2000
Model 1—Constant Share: Without Averaging
(employment in thousands)

$$(4)\ \ E^{ic}_{1995} = \frac{E^{ic}_{1975}}{E^{is}_{1975}} \times E^{is}_{1995}$$

$$= \frac{54.0}{621.2} \times 773.7 = (.0870)(773.7)$$

$$= \underline{67.3}$$

$$(5)\ \ E^{ic}_{2000} = \frac{E^{ic}_{1975}}{E^{is}_{1975}} \times E^{is}_{2000}$$

$$= \frac{54.0}{621.2} \times 800.1 = (.0870)(800.1)$$

$$= \underline{69.6}$$

EXHIBIT 10.1B
CALCULATION OF WHOLESALE AND RETAIL TRADE EMPLOYMENT
PROJECTIONS
NEW JERSEY AND MIDDLESEX COUNTY
1980–2000
MODEL 1—CONSTANT SHARE: WITH AVERAGING
(employment in thousands)

New Jersey

$$(1) \quad E^{is}_{1980} = \left[\left(\frac{E^{is}_{1965}}{E^{in}_{1965}} + \frac{E^{is}_{1970}}{E^{in}_{1970}} + \frac{E^{is}_{1975}}{E^{in}_{1975}} \right) \div 3 \right] \times E^{in}_{1980}$$

$$= \left[\left(\frac{455.9}{12,918.7} + \frac{557.1}{15,543.8} + \frac{621.2}{16,917.6} \right) \div 3 \right] \times 18,765.0$$

$$= \left[(.03529 + .03584 + .03672) \div 3 \right] \times 18,765.0$$

$$= \frac{.10785}{3} \times 18,765.0$$

$$= .03595 \times 18,765.0$$

$$= \underline{674.6}$$

$$(2) \quad E^{is}_{1985} = .03595 \times 19,569.0$$

$$= \underline{703.5}$$

$$(3) \quad E^{is}_{1990} = .03595 \times 20,340.0$$

$$= \underline{731.2}$$

$$(4) \quad E^{is}_{1995} = .03595 \times 21,069.6$$

$$= \underline{757.5}$$

EXHIBIT 10.1B (continued)
CALCULATION OF WHOLESALE AND RETAIL TRADE EMPLOYMENT
PROJECTIONS
NEW JERSEY AND MIDDLESEX COUNTY
1980–2000
MODEL 1—CONSTANT SHARE: WITH AVERAGING
(employment in thousands)

(5) E^{is}_{2000} = .03595 × 21,789.3

= 783.3

Middlesex County

(1) $E^{is}_{1980} = \left[\left(\dfrac{E^{ic}_{1965}}{E^{is}_{1965}} + \dfrac{E^{ic}_{1970}}{E^{is}_{1970}} + \dfrac{E^{ic}_{1975}}{E^{is}_{1975}} \right) \div 3 \right] \times E^{is}_{t+m}$

$= \left[\left(\dfrac{29.2}{455.9} + \dfrac{39.9}{557.1} + \dfrac{54.0}{621.2} \right) \div 3 \right] \times 674.6$

$= \left[\left(.06405 + .07161 + .08693 \right) \div 3 \right] \times 674.6$

= .22260/3 × 674.6

= .07420 × 674.6

= 50.1

(2) E^{ic}_{1985} = .07420 × 703.5

= 52.2

(3) E^{ic}_{1990} = .07420 × 731.2

= 54.3

EXHIBIT 10.1B (continued)
CALCULATION OF WHOLESALE AND RETAIL TRADE EMPLOYMENT
PROJECTIONS
NEW JERSEY AND MIDDLESEX COUNTY
1980–2000
MODEL 1—CONSTANT SHARE: WITH AVERAGING
(employment in thousands)

Middlesex County

(4) E^{ic}_{1995} = .07420 × 757.5

= $\underline{56.2}$

(5) E^{ic}_{2000} = .07420 × 783.3

= $\underline{58.1}$

SOURCES: The data base for this exhibit was U.S. Bureau of the Census, U.S., Department of Commerce, *County Business Patterns* (Washington, D.C.: U.S. Government Printing Office) and was adjusted to reflect self-employed and unpaid family workers. National projections were from U.S. Department of Commerce, *1972 OBERS Projections* (Washington, D.C.: U.S. Government Printing Office, 1974), and were adjusted to reflect actual 1975 employment activity.

The data requirements for the constant share model are minimal. If averages are not used, then only the most recent available endpoint data for each industrial sector in each geographic area, as well as base (national or state) projections, are needed. If averages are employed, then data for three years are necessary.

A major advantage of this method is the ease with which it can be calibrated and the minimal data research necessary. Additionally, statistical testing of this model against various other techniques has shown that it performs well in some instances, and in others performs better than some alternative tools. When Brown (1969) compared a three component shift-share model with constant share, it was found that "in every case the Super Ingrow Model (constant share) gives more precise projections than . . . the S and S (shift-share) model." James and Hughes (1973) tested an implicit shift-share model, which regressed the natural logarithm of county share against time, and the constant share model. When all industry employment series were combined over all states, the shift-share model produced predictions less accurate than those the constant share model produced. James and Hughes also found that when the models were estimated for individual two-digit industry groups, constant share outperformed the shift-share model in six sectors: wood products (SIC 24), electric and electronic equipment (36), transportation equipment (37), chemicals (28), petroleum (29), and miscellaneous manufacturing (39). Hewings (1976) tested twelve step-down employment models using Illinois data. Constant share again provided the best estimates of total state employment and performed best over a five-year period at the state level for the following industries: oil and gas extraction (13), mining and quarrying nonmetallic minerals, except fuels (14), food and kindred products (20), apparel and other textile products (23), lumber and wood products (24), stone, clay and glass products (32), primary metal industries (33), electric and electronic equipment (36), transportation (37), wholesale and retail trade (50-59), and finance, insurance, and real estate (60-67). At the multicounty level, constant share provided the best aggregate estimates for most urban areas in Illinois, a mixture of prosperous and less prosperous agriculturally-oriented counties, and an agricultural county with large urban centers.

However, the accuracy of the results of the constant share model are largely dependent upon exogeneous projections. Thus, any errors in these forecasts will increase the error of the models. Additionally, the model does not reflect any inter-regional relationships. This may cause a problem particularly with the projections at the county level. In examining the predictions of constant share at the two digit level, James and Hughes (1973, p. 230) observed that, in a simple majority of cases, the shift-share model they tested was "a superior forecasting technique to the constant share model." Greenberg (1972) tested the constant share method for six industries at the county scale, and of the four models in his analysis it ranked most accurate in three cases and second in three cases.

Simple Regression—Model 2

The simple regression model is unlike the three alternative models in that local employment projections are made independent of regional activity. Therefore, it does not involve a step-down process. It is a single variable extrapolation model that regresses historical employment data against time. The technique establishes employment trends using longitudinal series through simple, least squares linear regression. It produces annual employment changes that are represented by "b" in the equations. Also, the model forecasts by using the slope of the least squares line from the last point of observation rather than extrapolating the whole regression line "m" years into the future.

State Projections

Using (Ordinary Least Squares) OLS, regress

$$(10.5) \qquad E_t^{is} = a + b^{is}(t)$$

then

$$(10.6) \qquad E_{t+m}^{is} = E_t^{is} + b^{is}(m)$$

County Projections

Using OLS, regress

$$(10.7) \qquad E_t^{ic} = a + b^{ic}(t)$$

then

$$(10.8) \qquad E_{t+m}^{ic} = E^{ic} + b^{ic}(m)$$

A moving average approach may be employed in this model and involves the use of three-year averages instead of annual employment figures in the regression analysis. The effect is to diminish exaggerated activity and produce a better fit of the data to the trend line.

State Projections

Using OLS, regress

$$(10.9) \qquad \left[\left(E_{t-2}^{is} + E_{t-1}^{is} + E_t^{is} \right) \div 3 \right] =$$
$$a + b^{is} \left[\left((t - 2) + (t - 1) + (t) \right) \div 3 \right]$$

then

$$(10.10) \qquad E_{t+m}^{is} = E_t^{is} + b^{is}(m)$$

County Projections

Using OLS, regress

(10.11)

$$\left[\left(E_{t-2}^{ic} + E_{t-1}^{ic} + E_t^{ic} \right) \div 3 \right] = $$
$$a + b^{ic} \left[\left((t - 2) + (t - 1) + (t) \right) \div 3 \right]$$

then

(10.12)

$$E_{t+m}^{ic} = E_t^{ic} + b^{ic}(m)$$

The calibration of the model without moving averages is shown in Exhibit 10.2 for one industrial sector in New Jersey and Middlesex County. When activity in a sector has been extreme, including major decreases and/or increases in employment growth, this technique will produce absurd results.

EXHIBIT 10.2

CALCULATION OF WHOLESALE AND RETAIL TRADE EMPLOYMENT
PROJECTIONS
NEW JERSEY AND MIDDLESEX COUNTY
1980–2000
MODEL 2—SIMPLE LINEAR REGRESSION
(employment in thousands)

New Jersey

Year	T	T^2	E_t^{is}	(T) (E_t^{is})
1964	1	1	435.9	435.9
1965	2	4	455.9	911.9
1966	3	9	477.2	1,431.7
1967	4	16	486.8	1,947.2
1968	5	25	510.3	2,551.6
1969	6	36	530.4	3,182.6
1970	7	49	557.1	3,900.0
1971	8	64	566.7	4,533.5
1972	9	81	582.5	5,242.2
1973	10	100	607.6	6,076.3
1974	11	121	594.6	6,540.7
1975	12	144	621.1	7,454.5
	78	650	6,426.2	44,208.1

EXHIBIT 10.2 (continued)
CALCULATION OF WHOLESALE AND RETAIL TRADE
EMPLOYMENT PROJECTIONS
NEW JERSEY AND MIDDLESEX COUNTY
1980–2000
MODEL 2—SIMPLE LINEAR REGRESSION
(employment in thousands)

$$b^{is} = \frac{N\Sigma(T)(E_t^{is}) - \Sigma T \Sigma E_t^{is}}{N\Sigma T^2 - (\Sigma T)^2}$$

$$= \frac{(12)(44,208.1) - (78)(6,426.2)}{(12)(650) - (78)^2}$$

$$= \frac{530,497.2 - 501,243.6}{1716}$$

$$= \underline{17.05}$$

(1) $E_{1980}^{is} = E_{1975}^{is} + (b^{is})(5)$

$= 621.2 + (17.05)(5) = 621.2 + 85.3$

$= \underline{706.5}$

(2) $E_{1985}^{is} = E_{1975}^{is} + (b^{is})(10)$

$= 621.2 + (17.05)(10) = 621.2 + 170.5$

$= \underline{791.7}$

(3) $E_{1990}^{is} = E_{1975}^{is} + (b^{is})(15)$

$= 621.2 + (17.05)(15) = 621.2 + 255.8$

$= \underline{877.0}$

EXHIBIT 10.2 (continued)
CALCULATION OF WHOLESALE AND RETAIL TRADE EMPLOYMENT
PROJECTIONS
NEW JERSEY AND MIDDLESEX COUNTY
1980-2000
MODEL 2—SIMPLE LINEAR REGRESSION
(employment in thousands)

(4) $E^{is}_{1995} = E^{is}_{1975} + (b^{is})(20)$

$= 621.2 + (17.05)(20) = 621.2 + 341.0$

$= \underline{962.2}$

(5) $E^{is}_{2000} = E^{is}_{1975} + (b^{is})(25)$

$= 621.2 + (17.05)(25) = 621.2 + 426.3$

$= \underline{1,047.5}$

Middlesex County

Year	T	T^2	E^{ic}_t	$(T)(E^{ic}_t)$
1964	1	1	27.8	27.8
1965	2	4	29.2	58.4
1966	3	9	31.7	95.1
1967	4	16	32.7	130.6
1968	5	25	34.1	170.3
1969	6	36	36.3	218.1
1970	7	49	39.9	279.2
1971	8	64	44.1	353.2
1972	9	81	44.0	396.3
1973	10	100	46.7	466.8
1974	11	121	52.5	577.4
1975	12	144	54.0	648.5
	78	650	473.0	3,421.8

EXHIBIT 10.2 (continued)
CALCULATION OF WHOLESALE AND RETAIL TRADE EMPLOYMENT
PROJECTIONS
NEW JERSEY AND MIDDLESEX COUNTY
1980–2000
MODEL 2—SIMPLE LINEAR REGRESSION
(employment in thousands)

$$b = \frac{N\Sigma(T)(E_t^{ic}) - \Sigma T\Sigma E_t^{ic}}{N\Sigma T^2 - (\Sigma T)^2}$$

$$= \frac{(12)(3,411.8) - (78)(473.0)}{(12)(650) - (78)^2}$$

$$= \underline{2.36}$$

(1) $E_{1980}^{ic} = E_{1975}^{ic} + (b^{ic})(5)$

$$= 54.0 + (2.36)(5) = 54.0 + 11.8$$

$$= \underline{65.8}$$

(2) $E_{1985}^{ic} = E_{1975}^{ic} + (b^{ic})(10)$

$$= 54.0 + (2.36)(10) = 54.0 + 23.6$$

$$= \underline{77.6}$$

(3) $E_{1990}^{ic} = E_{1975}^{ic} + (b^{ic})(15)$

$$= 54.0 + (2.36)(15) = 54.0 + 35.4$$

$$= \underline{89.4}$$

EXHIBIT 10.2 (continued)
Calculation of Wholesale and Retail Trade Employment
Projections
New Jersey and Middlesex County
1980-2000
Model 2—Simple Linear Regression
(employment in thousands)

$$(4) \quad E^{ic}_{1995} = E^{ic}_{1975} + (b^{ic})(20)$$

$$= 54.0 + (2.36)(20) = 54.0 + 47.2$$

$$= \underline{101.2}$$

$$(5) \quad E^{ic}_{2000} = E^{ic}_{1975} + (b^{ic})(25)$$

$$= 54.0 + (2.36)(25) = 54.0 + 59.0$$

$$= \underline{113.0}$$

Source: The data base for this exhibit was U.S. Bureau of the Census, U.S., Department of Commerce, *County Business Patterns* (Washington, D.C.: U.S. Government Printing Office 1964-1975) and was adjusted to reflect self-employed and unpaid family workers.

The only data need of the simple regression method is annual historical data for the study area by industry group. It is suggested that there be at lease five years of employment data entered into the program to produce a five-year projection.

Although somewhat more difficult to calculate than the constant share model, simple regression is not cumbersome. Its results for the short-term appear adequate. Greenberg (1972) examined this model along with three other models at the county level in the New York Region and it ranked second or third in accuracy. In his statistical testing, Hewings (1976) used mean percentage error for analysis; for a five-year projection period simple regression forecasted well in certain instances. The technique produced reasonable estimates of total employment for the state, and the best results for paper and allied products (26) and chemicals and allied products (28).

Unlike the constant share model, simple regression does not take into account inter-regional economic activity. And sectors in which the employment growth has been very unstable are not suited for this approach.

Population/Employment—Model 3

The third employment projection model is a constant share model modified by an area's relative population change. It is a step-down technique and again is easily calculated. (Exhibit 10.3). The difference between this model and the three alternatives is that population plays a role in its operation by weighting the constant share results. Specifically, if the smaller political entity is projected to increase its share of the larger political unit's population, then the constant share employment is adjusted upwards to reflect its increased market share.

The basic assumption of population/employment goes beyond that of constant share. It is assumed that the changing market size affects an area's employment growth. The market is assumed to an important factor in the growth of local market oriented industries. Its insertion represents an improvement over the constant share method for local market oriented industries.

In the following equations the third term represents the area's changing population share. If this term is greater than 1.0, then the area's population growth rates are exceeding that of its region; if it is less than 1.0, the reverse is true.

State Projections

$$(10.13) \qquad E_{t+m}^{is} = \frac{E_t^{is}}{E_t^{in}} \cdot E_{t+m}^{in} \cdot \left[\frac{P_{t+m}^s}{P_t^s} \Big/ \frac{P_{t+m}^n}{P_t^n} \right]$$

County Projections

$$(10.14) \qquad E_{t+m}^{ic} = \frac{E_t^{ic}}{E_t^{is}} \cdot E_{t+m}^{is} \cdot \left[\frac{P_{t+m}^c}{P_t^c} \Big/ \frac{P_{t+m}^s}{P_t^s} \right]$$

Employment averages may be incorporated into this model in a manner similar to that in constant share.

State Projections

(10.15)

$$E_{t+m}^{is} = \left\{ \left[\frac{E_{t-2}^{is}}{E_{t-2}^{in}} + \frac{E_{t-1}^{is}}{E_{t-1}^{in}} + \frac{E_t^{is}}{E_t^{in}} \right] \middle/ 3 \right\} \cdot E_{t+m}^{in} \cdot \left[\frac{P_{t+m}^{s}}{P_t^{s}} \middle/ \frac{P_{t+m}^{n}}{P_t^{n}} \right]$$

County Projections

(10.16)

$$E_{t+m}^{ic} = \left\{ \left[\frac{E_{t-2}^{ic}}{E_{t-2}^{is}} + \frac{E_{t-1}^{ic}}{E_{t-1}^{is}} + \frac{E_t^{ic}}{E_t^{is}} \right] \middle/ 3 \right\} \cdot E_{t+m}^{is} \cdot \left[\frac{P_{t+m}^{c}}{P_t^{c}} \middle/ \frac{P_{t+m}^{s}}{P_t^{s}} \right]$$

Exhibit 10-3 depicts the operationalization of the population/ employment model again for New Jersey and Middlesex County.

Current employment data is again required for both the study area and for the larger region as well as regional employment projections. Additionally, both current and projected populations are necessary for all geographical entities. And, when using averages, two or more years of employment data are needed.

EXHIBIT 10.3
CALCULATION OF WHOLESALE AND RETAIL TRADE EMPLOYMENT
PROJECTIONS
NEW JERSEY AND MIDDLESEX COUNTY
1980–2000
MODEL 3—POPULATION/EMPLOYMENT

New Jersey

$$(1) \quad E_{1980}^{is} = \frac{E_{1970}^{is}}{E_{1970}^{in}} \times E_{1980}^{in} \times \left[\frac{P_{1980}^{s}}{P_{1970}^{s}} \middle/ \frac{P_{1980}^{n}}{P_{1970}^{n}} \right]$$

$$= \frac{557.1}{15,543.8} \times 18,765.0 \times \left[\frac{8,080.3}{7,195.0} \middle/ \frac{223,532.0}{203,857.9} \right]$$

$$= (.0358)(18,765.0)(1.0242)$$

$$= \underline{688.0}$$

EXHIBIT 10.3 (continued)
CALCULATION OF WHOLESALE AND RETAIL TRADE EMPLOYMENT
PROJECTIONS
NEW JERSEY AND MIDDLESEX COUNTY
1980–2000
MODEL 3—POPULATION/EMPLOYMENT

$$(2)\ E^{is}_{1990} = \frac{E^{is}_{1970}}{E^{in}_{1970}} \times E^{in}_{1990} \times \left[\frac{P^{s}_{1990}}{P^{s}_{1970}} \bigg/ \frac{P^{n}_{1990}}{P^{n}_{1970}} \right]$$

$$= \frac{557.1}{15{,}543.8} \times 20{,}349.8 \times \left[\frac{8{,}923.3}{7{,}195.0} \bigg/ \frac{246{,}039.0}{203{,}857.9} \right]$$

$$= (.0358)\ (20{,}349.7)\ (1.0276)$$

$$= \underline{748.6}$$

$$(3)\ E^{is}_{2000} = \frac{E^{is}_{1970}}{E^{in}_{1970}} \times E^{in}_{1970} \times \left[\frac{P^{s}_{2000}}{P^{s}_{1970}} \bigg/ \frac{P^{n}_{2000}}{P^{n}_{1970}} \right]$$

$$= \frac{557.1}{15{,}543.8} \times 21{,}789.3 \times \left[\frac{9{,}693.9}{7{,}195.0} \bigg/ \frac{263{,}830.0}{203{,}857.9} \right]$$

$$= (.0358)\ (21{,}789.3)\ (1.0410)$$

$$= \underline{812.0}$$

Middlesex County

$$(1)\ E^{ic}_{1980} = \frac{E^{ic}_{1970}}{E^{is}_{1970}} \times E^{is}_{1980} \times \left[\frac{P^{c}_{1980}}{P^{c}_{1970}} \bigg/ \frac{P^{s}_{1980}}{P^{s}_{1970}} \right]$$

$$= \frac{39.9}{557.1} \times 688.0 \times \left[\frac{676.5}{583.8} \bigg/ \frac{8{,}080.3}{7{,}195.0} \right]$$

$$= (.0716)\ (688.0)\ (1.0319)$$

$$= \underline{50.8}$$

EXHIBIT 10.3 (continued)
CALCULATION OF WHOLESALE AND RETAIL TRADE EMPLOYMENT
PROJECTIONS
NEW JERSEY AND MIDDLESEX COUNTY
1980-2000
MODEL 3—POPULATION/EMPLOYMENT

$$(2) \quad E^{ic}_{1990} = \frac{E^{ic}_{1970}}{E^{is}_{1970}} \times E^{is}_{1990} \times \left[\frac{P^c_{1990}}{P^c_{1970}} \bigg/ \frac{P^s_{1990}}{P^s_{1970}} \right]$$

$$= \frac{39.9}{557.1} \times 748.6 \times \left[\frac{767.5}{583.8} \bigg/ \frac{8,923.3}{7,195.0} \right]$$

$$= (.0716)(748.6)(1.0601)$$

$$= \underline{56.8}$$

$$(3) \quad E^{ic}_{2000} = \frac{E^{ic}_{1970}}{E^{is}_{1970}} \times E^{is}_{2000} \times \left[\frac{P^c_{2000}}{P^c_{1970}} \bigg/ \frac{P^s_{2000}}{P^s_{1970}} \right]$$

$$= \frac{39.9}{577.1} \times 812.0 \times \left[\frac{852.7}{583.8} \bigg/ \frac{9,693.9}{7,195.0} \right]$$

$$= (.0716)(812.0)(1.0841)$$

$$= \underline{63.0}$$

SOURCES: The data base for this exhibit is U.S. Bureau of the Census, U.S.,
Department of Commerce, *County Business Patterns* (Washington,
D.C.: U.S. Government Printing Office) and was adjusted to reflect
self-employed and unpaid family workers. National projections are from
U.S., Department of Commerce, *1972 OBERS Projections*
(Washington, D.C.: U.S. Government Printing Office, 1974) and were
adjusted to reflect actual 1975 employment activity.

The population/employment method is similar to the two techniques
outlined above in that it is easily calculated and its data requirements are
not overly demanding. The use of this model is suggested primarily for
industrial sectors that are most influenced by regional population growth.

However, Greenberg's results suggest that this model is the most accurate, not for the local-market oriented group, but the export industries (1972). And Hewings' (1976) analysis showed that of twelve step-down models, population/employment performed best in two industrial sectors: furniture and fixtures (25) and construction (15-17). Also, its accuracy was greatest in a comparatively wealthy, predominantly agricultural, county in Illinois (Hewings, 1976).

Because this technique relies on exogeneous employment and population projections, its errors may be greater than those of the two previous methods. Population data contain additional obstacles that are described in the first part of this monograph. Of the four models outlined, this one appears to be the least reliable for many industrial sectors, but theoretically useful for local market-oriented industries.

OBERS—Model 4 (U.S. Department of Commerce, 1974)

The OBERS shift-share model was developed by a research group drawn from the Office of Business Economics (now the Bureau of Economic Analysis) and the Economic Research Service of the U.S. Department of Commerce. Its purpose was to project employment activity at the regional level of the United States. It is a modified double exponential model whose "competitive" or shift component is implicit. The model combines the step-down character of model 1 (constant share) and the trend extrapolation device of model 2 (simple regression).

The OBERS model modifies the assumption of the constant share model via the shift component. This component measures the difference between the proportional growth accounted for by the constant share term and the attained level of economic activity. In other words, an area is assumed to grow faster or slower than the rest of its region with respect to the industry in question because of differences in the area's relative attractiveness to economic activity.

The technique yields a trend extrapolation of an area's historic percentage share of the regional employment total for a given industry. This is accomplished by fitting a least squares regression line to the logarithm of regional percentage shares versus the logarithm of time. The use of the logarithm of percentage shares converts the data to a ratio scale (where the slope of the line expresses the growth rate) so that the projected rate can be compared to the historic rate by observing the comparative slopes. The logarithm of time is used to smooth the slopes of rapidly rising or falling curves. The model assumes the following format:

State Projections

Using OLS, regress

(10.17)
$$\log \frac{E_t^{is}}{E_t^{in}} = a + b^{is} \log t$$

then

(10.18)
$$E_{t+m}^{is} = \left[\text{antilog} \left(\log \frac{E_t^{is}}{E_t^{in}} + b^{is} \log m \right) \right] E_{t+m}^{in}$$

County Projections

Using OLS, regress

(10.19)
$$\log \frac{E_t^{ic}}{E_t^{is}} = a + b^{ic} \log t$$

then

(10.20)
$$E_{t+m}^{ic} = \left[\text{antilog} \left(\log \frac{E_t^{ic}}{E_t^{is}} + b^{ic} \log m \right) \right] E_{t+m}^{is}$$

where: OLS = Ordinary Least Squares

Averages can be used in this model in a manner similar to that employed in model 2.

State Projections

Using OLS, regress

(10.21)

$$\log \left[\frac{E_{t-2}^{is}}{E_{t-2}^{in}} + \frac{E_{t-1}^{is}}{E_{t-1}^{in}} + \frac{E_t^{is}}{E_t^{in}} \right] \Bigg/ 3 = a + b^{is} \log \left[(t-2) + (t-1) + (t) \right] \Bigg/ 3$$

then

$$(10.22) \quad E_{t+m}^{is} = \left[\text{antilog} \left(\log \frac{E_t^{is}}{E_t^{in}} + b^{is} \log m \right) \right] E_{t+m}^{in}$$

County Projections

Using OLS, regress
(10.23)

$$\log \left[\frac{E_{t-2}^{ic}}{E_{t-2}^{is}} + \frac{E_{t-1}^{ic}}{E_{t-1}^{is}} + \frac{E_t^{ic}}{E_t^{is}} \right] \bigg/ 3 = a + b^{ic} \log \left[(t-2)+(t-1)+(t) \right] \bigg/ 3$$

then

$$(10.24) \quad E_{t+m}^{ic} = \left[\text{antilog} \left(\log \frac{E_t^{is}}{E_t^{in}} + b^{ic} \log m \right) \right] E_{t+m}^{is}$$

The calculation of this model is somewhat more cumbersome than that of the other three, and is illustrated in Exhibit 10.4. It is important to realize that when using OBERS the antilogarithm is taken of the entire series of terms (after the equal sign) before multiplying it by the base projection.

This technique requires employment data only. However, it is necessary to have a historical series of data for all geographical areas and industrial sectors. And control projections are needed as well.

There are several advantages to the OBERS model. One, of course, is that data inputs are manageable. With the use of large-scale computers, its calculation is not overly time-consuming and its cost is minimal. Only Hewings (1976) tested this model statistically. The results indicated that it performed particularly well in many instances and in some others fell only slightly behind alternative models. It was the best of twelve models for seven industrial sectors: bituminous coal and lignite mining (12), textile mill products (22), printing and publishing (27), rubber and misc. plastics products (30), leather and leather products (31), fabricated metal products (34), and instruments and related products (38). Additionally, along with

EXHIBIT 10.4
CALCULATION OF WHOLESALE AND RETAIL TRADE EMPLOYMENT
PROJECTIONS
NEW JERSEY AND MIDDLESEX COUNTY
1980–2000
MODEL 4—OBERS
(employment in thousands)

New Jersey

(1) Year	(2) T	(3) log T	(4) $(\log T)^2$	(5) $\dfrac{E_t^{is}}{E_t^{in}}$		(6) $\log \dfrac{E_t^{is}}{E_t^{in}}$	(3) × (6)
1964	1	0.0000	0.0000	$\dfrac{435.9}{12,429.0}$	= .03507	−1.4551*	.0000
1965	2	0.3010	0.0906	$\dfrac{455.9}{12,918.7}$	= .03529	−1.4523	−.4371
1966	3	0.4771	0.2276	$\dfrac{477.2}{13,551.4}$	= .03521	−1.4533	−.6934
1967	4	0.6021	0.3625	$\dfrac{486.8}{13,961.7}$	= .03487	−1.4575	−.8776
1968	5	0.6990	0.4886	$\dfrac{510.3}{14,488.5}$	= .03522	−1.4532	−1.0158
1969	6	0.7782	0.6056	$\dfrac{530.4}{15,067.3}$	= .03520	−1.4535	−1.1311
1970	7	0.8451	0.7142	$\dfrac{557.1}{15,543.8}$	= .03584	−1.4456	−1.2217
1971	8	0.9031	0.8156	$\dfrac{566.7}{15,527.6}$	= .03650	−1.4377	−1.2984
1972	9	0.9542	0.9105	$\dfrac{582.5}{16,171.6}$	= .03602	−1.4435	−1.3774

EXHIBIT 10.4 (continued)
CALCULATION OF WHOLESALE AND RETAIL TRADE EMPLOYMENT
PROJECTIONS
NEW JERSEY AND MIDDLESEX COUNTY
1980–2000
MODEL 4—OBERS
(employment in thousands)

1973	10	1.0000	1.0000	$\frac{607.6}{15,896.4} = .03822$	−1.4177	−1.4177
1974	11	1.0414	1.0845	$\frac{594.6}{16,589.3} = .03584$	−1.4456	−1.5054
1975	12	1.0792	1.1647	$\frac{621.2}{16,917.6} = .03672$	−1.4351	−1.4588
Σ		8.6804	7.4644		−17.3501	−12.5244

---

* Log .03507 = 8.5549 − 10 = −1.4551

$$b^{is} = \frac{N\Sigma(\log T)(\log \frac{E_t^{is}}{E_t^{in}}) - \Sigma(\log T)\Sigma(\log \frac{E_t^{is}}{E_t^{in}})}{N\Sigma(\log T)^2 - (\Sigma(\log T))^2}$$

$$= \frac{12(-12.5244) - (8.6804)(-17.3501)}{12(7.4644) - (8.6804)^2}$$

$$= \frac{-150.2928 + 150.6058}{89.5728 - 75.3493}$$

$$= \frac{+.3130}{14.2235} = .0220$$

EXHIBIT 10.4 (continued)
CALCULATION OF WHOLESALE AND RETAIL TRADE EMPLOYMENT
PROJECTIONS
NEW JERSEY AND MIDDLESEX COUNTY
1980–2000
MODEL 4—OBERS
(employment in thousands)

$$(1) \quad E^{is}_{1980} = \left[\text{antilog} \left(\log \frac{E^{is}_{1975}}{E^{in}_{1975}} + b^{is} \times \log 5 \right) \right] \times E^{in}_{1980}$$

$$= \left[\text{antilog} \left((-1.4351) + (.0220)(.6990) \right) \right] \times 18,765.0$$

$$= (.03804)(18,765.0)$$

$$= \underline{713.8}$$

$$(2) \quad E^{is}_{1985} = \left[\text{antilog} \left(\log \frac{E^{is}_{1975}}{E^{in}_{1975}} + b^{is} \times \log 10 \right) \right] \times E^{in}_{1985}$$

$$= \left[\text{antilog} \left((-1.4351) + (.0220)(1.0) \right) \right] \times 19,569.0$$

$$= (.03863)(19,569.0)$$

$$= \underline{756.0}$$

$$(3) \quad E^{is}_{1990} = \left[\text{antilog} \left(\log \frac{E^{is}_{1975}}{E^{in}_{1975}} + b^{is} \times \log 15 \right) \right] \times E^{in}_{1990}$$

$$= \left[\text{antilog} \left((-1.4351) + (.0220)(1.1761) \right) \right] \times 20,349.8$$

$$= (.03897)(20,349.8)$$

$$= \underline{793.0}$$

EXHIBIT 10.4 (continued)
CALCULATION OF WHOLESALE AND RETAIL TRADE EMPLOYMENT
PROJECTIONS
NEW JERSEY AND MIDDLESEX COUNTY
1980–2000
MODEL 4—OBERS
(employment in thousands)

$$(4) \quad E^{is}_{1995} = \left[\text{antilog} \left(\log \frac{E^{is}_{1975}}{E^{in}_{1975}} + b^{is} \times \log 20 \right) \right] \times E^{in}_{1995}$$

$$= \left[\text{antilog} \left((-1.4351) + (.0220)(1.3010) \right) \right] \times 21,069.6$$

$$= (.03922)(21,069.6)$$

$$= \underline{826.3}$$

$$(5) \quad E^{is}_{2000} = \left[\text{antilog} \left(\log \frac{E^{is}_{1975}}{E^{in}_{1975}} + b^{is} \times \log 25 \right) \right] \times E^{in}_{2000}$$

$$= \left[\text{antilog} \left((-1.4351) + (.0220)(1.3979) \right) \right] \times 21,789.3$$

$$= (.03941)(21,789.3)$$

$$= \underline{858.7}$$

Middlesex County

(1) Year	(2) T	(3) log T	(4) (log T)^2	(5) $\dfrac{E^{ic}_t}{E^{is}_t}$	(6) $\log \dfrac{E^{ic}_t}{E^{is}_t}$	(3) × (6)
1964	1	0.0000	0.0000	$\dfrac{27.8}{435.9} = .06378$	−1.1953	.0000
1965	2	0.3010	0.0906	$\dfrac{29.2}{455.9} = .06405$	−1.1935	−.3592

EXHIBIT 10.4 (continued)
CALCULATION OF WHOLESALE AND RETAIL EMPLOYMENT PROJECTIONS
NEW JERSEY AND MIDDLESEX COUNTY
1980–2000
MODEL 4—OBERS
(employment in thousands)

1966	3	0.4771	0.2276	$\frac{31.7}{477.2} = .06643$	−1.1776	−.5618
1967	4	0.6021	0.3625	$\frac{32.6}{486.8} = .06697$	−1.1741	−.7069
1968	5	0.6990	0.4886	$\frac{34.1}{510.3} = .06692$	−1.1751	−.8214
1969	6	0.7782	0.6056	$\frac{36.3}{530.4} = .06844$	−1.1647	−.9064
1970	7	0.8451	0.7142	$\frac{39.9}{557.1} = .07162$	−1.1450	−.9676
1971	8	0.9031	0.8156	$\frac{44.1}{566.7} = .07782$	−1.1089	−1.0014
1972	9	0.9542	0.9105	$\frac{44.0}{582.5} = .07554$	−1.1218	−1.0704
1973	10	1.0000	1.0000	$\frac{46.7}{607.6} = .07686$	−1.1143	−1.1143
1974	11	1.0414	1.0895	$\frac{52.5}{594.6} = .08829$	−1.0541	−1.0977
1975	12	1.0792	1.1647	$\frac{54.0}{621.2} = .08693$	−1.0608	−1.1448
	Σ	8.6804	7.4644		−13.6852	−9.7519

EXHIBIT 10.4 (continued)
CALCULATION OF WHOLESALE AND RETAIL TRADE EMPLOYMENT
PROJECTIONS
NEW JERSEY AND MIDDLESEX COUNTY
MODEL —OBERS
(employment in thousands)

$$b^{ic} = \frac{N\Sigma(\log T)(\log \frac{E_t^{ic}}{E_t^{is}}) - \Sigma(\log T)\Sigma(\log \frac{E_t^{ic}}{E_t^{is}})}{N\Sigma(\log T)^2 - (\Sigma(\log T))^2}$$

$$= \frac{12(-9.7519) - (8.6804)(-13.6842)}{12(7.4644) - (8.6804)^2}$$

$$= \frac{-117.0228 + 118.7930}{14.2235} = \frac{1.7702}{14.2235}$$

$$= \underline{.1245}$$

(1) $$E_{1980}^{ic} = \left[\text{antilog} \left(\log \frac{E_{1975}^{ic}}{E_{1975}^{is}} + b^{ic} \times \log 5 \right) \right] \times E_{1980}^{is}$$

$$= \left[\text{antilog} \left((-1.0608) + (.1245)(0.6990) \right) \right] \times 713.8$$

$$= (.1062)(713.8)$$

$$= \underline{75.8}$$

(2) $$E_{1985}^{ic} = \left[\text{antilog} \left(\log \frac{E_{1975}^{ic}}{E_{1975}^{is}} + b^{ic} \times \log 10 \right) \right] \times E_{1985}^{is}$$

$$= \left[\text{antilog} \left((-1.0608) + (.1245)(1.000) \right) \right] \times 756.0$$

$$= (.1158)(756.0)$$

$$= \underline{87.5}$$

EXHIBIT 10.4 (continued)
CALCULATION OF WHOLESALE AND RETAIL TRADE EMPLOYMENT
PROJECTIONS
NEW JERSEY AND MIDDLESEX COUNTY
MODEL—OBERS
(employment in thousands)

$$(3) \quad E^{ic}_{1990} = \left[\text{antilog} \left(\log \frac{E^{ic}_{1975}}{E^{is}_{1975}} + b^{ic} \times \log 15 \right) \right] \times E^{is}_{1990}$$

$$= \left[\text{antilog} \left((-1.0608) + (.1245)(1.1761) \right) \right] \times 793.0$$

$$= (.1218)(793.0)$$

$$= \underline{96.6}$$

$$(4) \quad E^{ic}_{1995} = \left[\text{antilog} \left(\log \frac{E^{ic}_{1975}}{E^{is}_{1975}} + b^{ic} \times \log 20 \right) \right] \times E^{is}_{1995}$$

$$= \left[\text{antilog} \left((-1.0608) + (.1245)(1.3010) \right) \right] \times 826.3$$

$$= (.1262)(826.3)$$

$$= \underline{104.3}$$

$$(5) \quad E^{ic}_{2000} = \left[\text{antilog} \left(\log \frac{E^{ic}_{1975}}{E^{is}_{1975}} + b^{ic} \times \log 25 \right) \right] \times E^{is}_{2000}$$

$$= \left[\text{antilog} \left((-1.0608) + (.1245)(1.3979) \right) \right] \times 858.7$$

$$= (.1298)(858.7)$$

$$= \underline{111.5}$$

SOURCES: The data base for this exhibit was U.S. Bureau of the Census, U.S. Department of Commerce, *County Business Pattersn* (Washington, D.C.: U.S. Government Printing Office) and was adjusted to reflect self-employed and unpaid family workers. National projections were from U.S. Department of Commerce, *1972 OBERS Projections* (Washington, D.C.: U.S. Government Printing Office, 1974) and were adjusted to reflect actual 1975 employment activity.

constant share, it dominated the selection of models that perform best at the multicounty level. And very importantly, both long-range and short-range projections derived from this method appear to be the most reasonable (Hewings, 1976).

Summary

Four economic forecasting techniques were outlined in this chapter—constant share, simple regression, population/employment, and OBERS. Each has been described in terms of its underlying assumptions, operation, data requirements, and applicability to various settings. The next chapter discusses some basic sources for the necessary data inputs of these models as well as alternative data adjustments that may be necessary.

Chapter 11
Data Sources and Adjustments

Introduction

The choice of basic input data plays a significant role in model selection, utility, and accuracy of the results. With several different published sources available, it is important to become acquainted with the contents of each, so that the most useful data are chosen. Sometimes it is necessary to augment the data from one source with that of another. Thus, the comparability between sources should also be noted.

In conjunction with the diversity of sources, data may have to be modified for several reasons. It may be necessary to adjust historical series so that the coverage is compatible with that of the base projections. For example, historical data may include only wage and salary employment, while the national projections include self-employed workers. In this case, the discrepancy would have to be eliminated. Or, the control projections may need to be adjusted upward or downward to account for economic activity that has occurred since the formulation of these projections.

The purpose, then, of this chapter is twofold: (1) to outline several sources of employment data, historical as well as projected; and (2) to examine various ways in which the data may be adjusted. To this end five employment data sources will be detailed in terms of coverage and comparability: *County Business Patterns* (annual), *Employment and Earnings* (monthly), *Employment and Wages* (quarterly), *Economic Censuses* (variable), and *Monthly Labor Review* (monthly). There are other published sets of employment data produced by various local agencies (Holleb, 1969), but the material presented in the above sources are perhaps the most useful and general. Two sets of national projections will also be outlined and compared: those prepared by the Office of Business Economics and those of the Bureau of Labor Statistics. Finally, various data adjustment procedures will be suggested for preparing the data for use in the projection models.

Four Information Concepts

Before proceeding with a description of employment data sources, it is important to note the distinctions among four concepts: jobs, workers, establishment data, and household data.

The number of jobs in an area is not equivalent to the number of workers. A count of jobs represents the number of employment positions; and, more than one position may be held by one person. On the other hand, a count of workers is the number of people working. A worker may have more than one job.

Establishment data are usually obtained via required reporting forms, such as U.S. Treasury Form 941, or direct surveys of establishments. Establishment data usually represent, therefore, a count of jobs. In contrast, household data are usually compiled through sample surveys comprising questionnaires sent to residents in an area (who indicate type and location of their employment), and consist of the number of workers. Some sources provide separate tables covering all of these; while others provide information covering one type. For example, *County Business Patterns* details the number of jobs at establishments located in a county; however, *Employment and Earnings* provides both the number of jobs at establishments located in various geographical delineations (counties and labor market areas) and the number of workers in such areas.

Data Sources

Since there are several published sources of employment data available, a brief overview of their major characteristics is warranted. Included will be the publishing agency, the technique for gathering the data, the coverage, and the comparability of each source with the other sources. In addition, existing sources of national employment projections will be presented.

SOURCES OF TIME SERIES EMPLOYMENT DATA

Exhibit 11.1 presents a summary of the description of the following sources.

County Business Patterns (CBP)

County Business Patterns is published by the U.S. Department of Commerce, Bureau of the Census. The series was first published in 1946 and has been issued annually since 1964.

Sources of Data: The reports are derived from employment and payroll information reported on U.S. Treasury Form 941, Schedule A, supplemented by a special survey of multiunit companies. The survey was designed to provide industry and county detail that is not provided on Form 941.

Coverage: Employment and payroll statistics (as of the mid-March pay period) are included for major Standard Industrial Classification code industry groups. There is a 2, 3, and 4 digit classification for the counties, states, and the nation, and a 2 digit breakdown for SMSAs. The following types of employment covered by the Federal Insurance Contributions Act are presented: all covered wage and salary employment of private nonfarm employees and of nonprofit membership organizations under compulsory coverage; and all employment of religious organizations covered under the elective provisions of the act. Not included are: government workers; self-employed persons; farm workers; domestic service workers; and railroad workers.

Comparability:

Employment and Earnings: Differences exist because *Employment and Earnings* estimates are adjusted to levels indicated by social insurance statistics, primarily state unemployment insurance data supplemented by small firm data from *County Business Patterns.* Other differences are those of overall scope, definition of reporting unit, and industry classification.

Economic Censuses: CBP differs from this publication with respect to pay period, classification of some employees, and reporting unit for multiunit firms in nonmanufacturing industries.

Employment and Earnings

Employment and Earnings is a monthly publication issued by the Bureau of Labor Statistics, U.S. Department of Labor.

Sources of Data: The statistics in this publication are compiled from three major sources: (1) household interviews; (2) reports from employers; and (3) administrative statistics of unemployment insurance systems. Data based on household interviews are obtained from a sample survey of the population sixteen years of age and over. Data based on establishment records are compiled each month from mail questionnaires. And data based on administrative records of unemployment insurance systems are obtained from weekly reports by the states.

Coverage: This publication reports household and establishment data for the United States, the states, selected SMSAs, and major labor market areas. There is a 1 digit SIC detail for all geographical areas, and 2 digit detail for the United States. The data collected are based on activity or status reported for the calendar week including the 12th of the month. Establishment data cover only wage and salary employees on the payrolls of nonagricultural establishments. Salaried officers of corporations are included; government employment is also included, but only of civilian employees. The data do not include proprietors, the self-employed, unpaid volunteer or family workers, farm workers, or domestic workers in households.

Comparability:

Economic Censuses: Two major reasons for noncomparability between the *Economic Censuses* and *Employment and Earnings* are the different treatments of business units considered parts of an establishment and the different scope of the industries covered.

County Business Patterns: Data in CBP differ from the establishment statistics of this publication in the treatment of central administrative offices and auxillary units. Also, industrial classification and reporting practices are dissimilar. And, CBP excludes interstate railroads and government, and coverage is incomplete for some of the nonprofit activities.

Employment and Wages: Certain activities such as interstate railroads, parochial schools, churches and most local government activities are not covered in *Employment and Wages.*

Employment and Wages

The Bureau of Labor Statistics, Department of Labor has issued this publication on a quarterly basis since the first quarter of 1950.

Sources of Data: The data in *Employment and Wages* are compiled from the quarterly contribution (tax) reports submitted to state employment security agencies by employers subject to state unemployment insurance laws and by federal installations subject to the Unemployment Compensation for Federal Employees program. State employment security agencies compile the data for their states which are then summarized for the nation by the Bureau of Labor Statistics.

Coverage: This publication contains national totals of all covered employment and wage data by ten broad industry divisions, seventy-eight

EXHIBIT 11.1

Comparison of Employment Data Sources

Source	Publishing Agency	Technique	Coverage		
			SIC-Level	Geographic Scale	Type of Employment
County Business Patterns (CBP)	U.S. Dept. of Commerce, Bureau of the Census (annual)	U.S. Treasury Form 941 and Special Multi-unit Survey	1,2,3,4-digit for all	Nation, State, County, SMSA, Large Cities	Nonfarm Wage & Salary, Federal Civilian Government
Employment and Earnings	U.S. Dept. of Labor, Bureau of Labor Statistics (monthly)	Employment Reports, Household Interviews, Administrative Statistics	1 & 2-digit for U.S.; 1-digit for all others	Nation, State, SMSA, Labor Market Areas	Nonfarm Wage & Salary, Civilian Government
Employment and Wages	U.S. Dept. of Labor, Bureau of Labor Statistics (quarterly)	Employers Tax Reports	1,2, & 3-digit for U.S.; 1-digit for States	Nation, State, Region	Nonfarm Wage & Salary, Civilian Government
Economic Censuses	U.S. Dept. of Commerce, Bureau of the Census (quinquennially)	Employer Survey and Sample of Tax Returns	1,2,3 & 4-digit for Business & Manufacturing; 1,2,3-digit for Mineral Industries	Nation, State, SMSA, Counties, Large Cities	Nonfarm Wage & Salary
Monthly Labor Review	U.S. Dept. of Labor, Bureau of Labor Statistics (monthly)	(See Employment and Earnings)	1 & 2-digit	Nation	Nonfarm Wage & Salary, Civilian Government

major industry groups, and 384 three-digit industry groups. The data also are distributed by state and region, but in less detail. The employment data represent the number of workers earning wages during the pay period including the 12th of the month. The count of workers in private industry includes all corporation officials, executives, supervisory personnel, clerical workers, and wage earners. It excludes proprietors, the self-employed, unpaid family workers, most farmworkers, and most domestics in private households.

Comparability:

County Business Patterns: The differences between *Employment and Wages* and *CBP* are primarily: (1) those that arise in industrial classification because of differences in what constitutes the reporting unit; and (2) differences in the coverage of nonprofit organizations.

Employment and Earnings: Coverage between these sources may not be comparable because certain activities are not included in *Employment and Wages.*

Economic Censuses: Employment totals will differ because of exclusions from coverage in the unemployment insurance program, differences in industrial classifications, and differences in pay periods.

Economic Censuses

The Economic Censuses are published every five years by the U.S. Department of Commerce, Bureau of the Census, and are partitioned into three subsets: *Census of Business, Manufactures, and Mineral Industries.* The *Census of Business* is a seven volume analysis of the volume and characteristics of retail, wholesale, and service trade activity in the United States, regions, divisions, states, SMSAs, counties, and selected municipalities. The three volume *Census of Manufactures* provides the coverage of industrial activity in these areas. The *Census of Mineral Industries* details by county a listing of the number of mining establishments.

Sources of Data: Information for establishments with payrolls is gathered by a mail canvass of all firms included in the active records of the Internal Revenue Service as subject to payment of Federal Insurance Contribution Act taxes and classified in the records of the Social Security Administration as wholly or partly engaged in economic activity. Data for the remainder (i.e., the nonemployer universe) are compiled from an analysis of a 50 percent sample of tax returns from those businesses not in Federal Insurance Contribution Act files whose sales exceeded $2,500 in the surveyed year.

Coverage: The various volumes of the *Census of Business* provide detailed information on 2, 3 and 4-digit SIC code establishments, such as the number of establishments (total with and total without payrolls), dollar volume of sales for establishments with and without payroll, dollar volume of payrolls for the year and for the week ending nearest November 15, total paid employment as of November 5, and the number of active proprietors of unincorporated businesses. Not all volumes disaggregate this information by SIC code for all geographical areas. Basic data reproduced for states, SMSAs, counties, and cities of 10,000 inhabitants or more in the *Census of Manufactures* include the number of industrial establishments, total industrial employment and dollar payroll, total number of production workers, production man-hours and total wages, value added by manufacturing, and new capital expenditures. The basic data are also reproduced for 2, 3, and selected 4-digit SIC code industrial categories for selected SMSAs, standard consolidated areas, and counties in each state. The *Census of Mineral Industries* provides details on the number of mining establishments, including: total employment and payroll (in dollars), number of production, development, and exploration workers, production man-hours and total wages, value added in mining, value of shipments and receipts, cost of supplies purchased and machinery installed, and new capital expenditures for 2 and 3-digit SIC code mining groups.

Comparability:

County Business Patterns: In addition to the differences discussed previously, the Economic Censuses are published only every five years, whereas *CBP* is an annual publication. Also, the Economic Censuses, in terms of employment data, do not cover all the industrial sectors presented in *CBP*.

Employment and Earnings: Employment and Earnings is published more frequently than the Economic Censuses. See the description of this publication for other differences in coverage.

Employment and Wages: This publication is also published more often; and details at various SIC levels and geographical scales differ.

Monthly Labor Review:

The Monthly Labor Review is issued monthly by the U.S. Department of Labor, Bureau of Labor Statistics. In addition to feature articles on conditions and trends in the labor market, it presents statistical information derived from the BLS household, establishment, price, and work stoppage surveys. All data are presented in summary form for the U.S. as a whole.

Sources of Data: Employment data in this publication are compiled from payroll records reported monthly on a voluntary basis to the Bureau of Labor Statistics and its cooperating state agencies by over 100,000 establishments, representing all industries except agriculture.

Coverage: Employed persons are all persons who received pay for any part of the payroll period including the 12th of the month. Persons holding more than one job are counted in each establishment that reports them. Self-employed persons and others not on a regular civilian payroll are outside the scope of this survey because they are excluded from establishment records.

Comparability: The data in the *Monthly Labor Review* are comparable to that in *Employment and Earnings* with the exception that only U.S. figures are given in the former.

SOURCES OF NATIONAL EMPLOYMENT PROJECTIONS

The two major sources of national employment projections are those prepared by the Bureau of Economic Analysis (OBERS) and those of the Bureau of Labor Statistics (BLS). Both sets of projections will be described in some detail with respect to content, method, and, where possible, the track record to date. Additionally, a comparison will be made between these two sets of forecasts to pinpoint specific differences.

1972 OBERS PROJECTIONS

The OBERS projection set consists of seven volumes on historical and projected regional economic activity in the United States prepared by the Bureau of Economic Analysis (BEA), U.S. Department of Commerce and the Economic Research Service, and the U.S. Department of Agriculture for the Water Resources Council. Volume 1 contains a description of the concepts and method and a set of summary tables. Volume 2 presents historical and projected data for the 173 BEA economic areas. Volume 3 presents data for the water resources regions and subareas. Volume 4 presents data for the individual states. Volume 5 presents data for the Standard Metropolitan Statistical Areas. Volume 6 presents data for the non-SMSA portions of the BEA economic areas, and volume 7 presents data for the non-SMSA portions of the water resources subareas.

Included in these volumes are data on population, personal income, total employment, earnings by thirty-seven industry groups, per capita incomes, earnings per worker, and employment/population ratios for all geographical areas. And employment by thirty-three industry groups is provided for the United States.

The U.S. Water Resources Council's (1972, Vol. 4, p.iii) position on the use of these projections is as follows:

> The OBERS projections are intended as a planning tool, as a contribution to planning decisions. . . .
>
> The OBERS projections are not a goal. It is not intended that they be used as assigned shares or quotas. They are not intended as a constraint on any region's economic activity. They do not express what is desirable or undesirable.

The first set of projections published in 1972 used the Census Bureau's 1967 "Series C" national population projections. The more recent edition incorporates the Census Bureau's 1972 "Series E" national population projections. Seven other changes in the more recent report contributed to the differences between that and the earlier one:

1. The hours worked per year are projected to decline at the rate of 0.35 percent per year. The "Series C" report used a 0.25 percent rate.

2. The projected rate of increase in product per man per hour in the private economy is lowered in the second report from 3.0 percent to 2.9 percent.

3. Earnings per worker in the individual industries at the national level are projected to converge toward the all-industry rate more slowly in the "Series E" report than in the "Series C" report.

4. Income data for 1970 and 1971 and total employment data for 1970 have been included in the recent report. Use of this additional information, which was not available for the first report, has caused significant changes in some area projections.

5. On the basis of the President's 1974 budget message to Congress, a smaller military establishment has been assumed.

6. The method of projecting population as a function of projected employment has been revised to treat each of three age groups separately.

7. Employment projections by industry, included in the previous report, are excluded from the more recent one because the information contained in the 1970 Census is not directly comparable with that of previous censuses.

However, the overall method for producing the national employment projections in the "Series E" and "Series C" reports is the same.

OBERS Method

In order to obtain industrially disaggregated projections of earnings in dollars of constant purchasing power that were comparable with the industrial distributions of constant dollar GNP, current dollar projections were established for both GNP and total earnings. Projected GNP in real terms was put on a current dollar basis through use of a deflator. An extension of the relationship between total earnings and GNP in current dollars when applied to projected GNP in current dollars gave projected total earnings in current dollars.

Historical trends in the industrial distribution of GPO (Gross Product Originating—each industry expressed as a percent of the all-industry total), earnings of persons by industry, and employment by industry were calculated and extended to 2020. The projected industrial percent shares in GPO, earnings, and employment were examined for consistency and plausibility in the light of historical trends in the shares. Application of the projected shares to the projected all-industry totals of GNP, earnings of persons, and employment yielded absolute values of each by industry. The industry projections of GPO and earnings of persons so derived were expressed in current dollars. These three series for each industry were then reconciled.

Employment on a Decennial Census Basis

The OBERS national employment projections were converted to the Census employment concepts. There are several differences in the "persons engaged" concept and the Census concept. First, the Census classifies government workers in the industry that describes their activity. Thus most, if not all, industries contain some government workers. In the "persons engaged" series, however, all government workers are in the single category of government. And the "persons engaged" series is on an annual average basis, whereas the Census series relates to early April and varies in seasonal character both industrially and by area.

The national conversion from a "persons engaged" to a Census concept was accomplished by first eliminating the number of government workers in each industry from the Census-based national totals. The private industry national totals were then moved forward to the projected years by the change in the national total of the corresponding industry in the "persons engaged" series. The projected number of government workers were then redistributed between those classified in government and those in private industries in terms of the Census classifications. Merging of the two projected series yielded national totals for each industry on a Census classification. (OBERS, 1972, Vol. 1, p.19)

Performance of the OBERS Projection Series

Exhibit 11.2 shows 1960 actual and 1980 to 2000 national projections for major industries of the OBERS "Series E" and "Series C" reports. Series E projections are lower for total employment in 1990 and 2000, but Series C shows slower growth for 1980. However, this pattern is not retained in all of the industrial groupings. In fact, only the mining sector reflects a similar pattern. The Series E projections for Transportation, Communications, and Public Utilities, and Wholesale and Retail Trade in 1980 and 1990 are higher than those in the Series C set, while in 2000 they are lower. On the other hand, all of the outcomes of Series E are higher for F.I.R.E. and Services. Conversely, Construction, Manufacturing and Civilian Government (Public Administration) employment are projected to grow less rapidly in all years in the Series E set.

The Bureau of Economic Analysis of the U.S. Department of Commerce has been monitoring the Series C projections with respect to actual economic activity. The analysts are primarily studying total earnings by industrial sector, not employment. Their findings, however, are important because, with respect to employment, estimates are derived from total earnings. Their findings show that for 1975 total earnings were overestimated in the Series C set. In fact, the only two major industrial sectors in which earnings were underestimated were in agriculture and mining. At present neither the OBERS Series C nor Series E employment projections have been adjusted to reflect these findings.

BLS PROJECTIONS

The Structure of the U.S. Economy in 1980 and 1985, published by the U.S. Department of Labor, Bureau of Labor Statistics (1975) provides detailed projections for 1980 and 1985 of the following: gross national product (GNP); the income and demand composition of GNP; the industrial composition of demand; input-output coefficients; and output, man-hours, productivity, and employment by industry. The projections were developed for the 1968–1980 and 1980–1985 periods. BLS chose the year 1968 as a base because 1968 was characterized by full employment of resources and by productivity advances at or near assumed long-run potential. The projection periods 1968–1980 and 1955–1968 are treated as periods of comparable length when the economy was operating near capacity. In contrast, to focus more on the current period when growth has been slower in most cases, the implied 1972–1980 growth is also shown (BLS, 1975, p.1).

This 1975 BLS study is similar in content to its earlier research in which projections were developed for 1970, 1975, and 1980. The 1980 projections in this study replace or update the earlier projections for 1980.

> The bulletin is part of a comprehensive coordinated program of the Bureau of Labor Statistics to provide information on what the U.S. economy might be like in coming years under certain assumptions. The primary use of the employment projections by industry is to provide a framework for the occupational outlook program of the Bureau. The detailed projections of demand, output, and employment have important uses in providing insight into the effects of alternative government policies on the composition of demand, on employment by industry, and, through the use of an industry-occupational matrix, on employment by occupation (p. iii).

These projections are not forecasts, but rather are projections of what the U.S. economy might be like in 1980 and 1985 under given assumptions. Some of the assumptions are explicit. Others, even more numerous, are implicit. The most important assumptions are as follows (pp. 1–2):

1. The projections assume a 4 percent unemployment rate (of the civilian labor force) and a 3 percent annual rate of increase in the implicit GNP price deflator. It is assumed that this unemployment rate and this rate of price increase will be reached in 1975 and that these rates will remain the same through 1985.

2. The institutional framework of the American economy will not change radically.

3. Economic, social, technological, and scientific trends will continue, including values placed on work, education, income, and leisure.

4. Efforts to solve major domestic problems such as air and water pollution, solid waste disposal, congestion in large urban areas, and inadequate safety conditions in industry may preempt a larger share of the Nation's productive resources but not enough to have a more than marginal effect on the long-term economic growth rate.

5. Bureau of the Census "Series E" projections are assumed.

6. Future labor force participation rates for each age-sex group are derived by extrapolating the trend for the period 1955–1972 and tapering this trend so that in fifty years all changes are reduced to approximately zero.

7. Average annual hours (paid) are assumed to decline by 0.5 percent a year in the agricultural sector; in the private nonagricultural sector they are assumed to decline by 0.3 percent a year.

8. Productivity in the private nonfarm economy is assumed to grow at its long-term rate—2.7 percent a year. The annual trend rate of 5.5 percent for the farm sector is assumed to continue throughout the projection period.

EXHIBIT 11.2

COMPARISON OF "SERIES C" AND "SERIES E" OBERS EMPLOYMENT PROJECTIONS
UNITED STATES: MAJOR INDUSTRIAL SECTORS
(employment in thousands)

Industrial Sector	1960[1]	1980 "Series C"	1980 "Series E"	1990 "Series C"	1990 "Series E"	2000 "Series C"	2000 "Series E"
Total	66,372.6	93,820.0	96,114.0	106,917.0	106,388.0	124,641.0	117,891.0
Agriculture	4,469.6	2,915.9	2,527.0	2,516.0	2,104.0	1,885.0	1,849.0
Mining	674.7	571.0	609.0	550.0	547.0	534.0	501.0
Contract Construction	3,968.3	5,767.0	5,589.0	6,659.0	6,015.0	7,847.0	6,586.0
Manufacturing	18,244.9	24,769.0	22,112.0	27,422.0	23,106.0	30,951.0	24,169.0
Transportation, Communities, and Public Utilities	4,650.6	5,878.0	6,105.0	6,572.0	6,723.0	7,518.0	7,409.0
Wholesale and Retail Trade	12,287.9	17,229.0	19,396.0	19,536.0	21,034.0	22,667.0	22,522.0
Finance, Insurance, and Real Estate	2,820.5	4,226.0	5,240.0	4,840.0	6,178.0	5,663.0	7,198.0
Services	14,123.7	24,749.0	27,705.0	30,143.0	32,765.0	37,110.0	38,881.0
Government (Civilian)	3,341.9	6,034.0	5,275.0	7,021.0	6,330.0	8,396.0	7,209.0

NOTE: 1. In this table 1960 is used as the base year in this comparison because the 1970 data were not available for both series.
SOURCE: U.S. Department of Commerce, *1972 OBERS Projections* (Washington, D.C.: U.S. Government Printing Office, 1972 and 1974).

9. All levels of government will expand efforts to meet a wide variety of domestic requirements but state and local government activity will continue to grow relative to federal government activity. It has been further assumed that federal, state, and local budgets will be close to being in balance by 1980 and 1985.

10. Estimates assume that the Nation will meet its housing goals by 1978. Thereafter, residential construction is projected to remain a constant proportion of real GNP.

11. In international trade, it is assumed that by 1980 and 1985 the United States will have achieved a slight surplus in its net export balance, in spite of increased imports of oil (p.3).

The BLS projections were developed using the following sequence:

1. Labor force projections were developed through separate projections of the population and labor force participation rates for various groups in the population sixteen years and over, by age and sex.

2. Potential output (GNP) was projected as the product of three major variables: (a) employment, based on the projected labor force and an assumption of a 4 percent unemployment rate; (b) annual hours per job; and (c) output per man hour.

3. Distribution of potential GNP into major categories of demand was projected through the use of a macroeconometric model that starts with potential GNP and develops estimates of government revenue, personal income, and business income. The income estimates were then used to develop projections of government purchases of goods and services, personal consumption, and investment expenditures.

4. Conversion of projected major components of demand into detailed industry employment estimates was done in three substages: (a) major final demand components were distributed into detailed "bills of goods" on an item-by-item basis; (b) the potential demand for all final goods and services was converted into industry output requirements through the use of inter-industry (input-output) relationships projected to 1980 and 1985; and (c) projected industry output was derived and subsequently converted into employment requirements based on projections of annual hours per job and output per man hour.

The projection system involves a number of checkpoints to see that projections made at different stages in the sequence are mutually consistent. Important among these checks is the balancing of the employment projections with the total employment used in the initial stage.

Performance of the BLS Projection Series

Exhibit 11.3 depicts national employment estimates for 1965 and a comparison of three sets of BLS projections for major industrial sectors. The first set is from *Patterns of the U.S. Economy*, Bulletin 1672. The second represent those published in Bulletin 1831 and discussed above. And, Set III are more recent revisions which were summarized in the March 1976 and November 1976 issues of the *Monthly Labor Review*. At present, however, a more detailed version of this latter set is not available. Moreover, the new set of projections "should be thought of as an interim revision, because the underlying data base and the basic projection model have not changed." (Kutscher 1976, p.3). The basic methodology for these series is the same, however, some of the underlying assumptions have changed.

From the exhibit it can be seen that total employment both in 1980 and 1985 has been forecasted to increase. From the overall employment perspective, Set III is the highest and Set I the lowest. This pattern is caused primarily by two sectors (Trade and F.I.R.E.) which are projected to increase in each revision.

In all cases, agriculture employment is estimated to decrease in growth. For the year 1980, Set I is the most optimistic for agriculture followed by Set III and II. For the year 1985, agricultural employment is projected to decline less under Set III's assumptions.

The pattern of projected employment in the government sector is similar to that for agriculture, but in reverse, i.e., it is expected to increase. Sets I and II project mining activity to decline, while Set III shows it increasing. All sets indicate increased growth in the contract construction group; Set II, however, indicates faster growth in 1985. Manufacturing employment shows growth under all assumption alternatives, but at a slower rate under the most recently revised set of projections. The patterns of forecasts for transportation, communications, and public utilities and services are similar in that Set II is the most optimistic in 1980, followed by Set III and Set I; and in 1985 (III) indicates a faster growth.

In the words of Ronald E. Kutscher, Assistant Commissioner for Economic Growth, Bureau of Labor Statistics:

> Projections of the state of a nation's economy are subject to changes in a large number of factors. A set of projections, at least one covering a period of ten or twelve years, cannot be developed and then never reviewed or updated. . . . The present program calls for new economic and employment projections every two years (previously, every four).

> The Bureau's program for the next four-year cycle anticipates preparation of a full-scale new set of projections for 1980, 1985, and 1990, based on incorporating into the system the input-output table developed from 1967 data

and on reestimated macro and final demand models based on rebenchmarked GNP data. About two years later, according to present plans, revised projections to 1985 and 1990 will be prepared, using the model, input-output tables, and substantially the same data base, but altering assumptions in light of intervening events (p.8).

Comparison of OBERS and BLS Projections

Although the differences between these two series of national employment projections can be ascertained from the above discussions, it is perhaps useful to mention some of the specific differences that are pertinent to their use as inputs to the programmed models. Additionally, the graph in Exhibit 11.4 compares total employment as projected by OBERS and BLS. In all cases, the OBERS series are lower than BLS. Comparisons of the major industry sectors cannot be made in a like manner because the delineation of employment into these sectors is not consistent between the two series.

Both sets include the self-employed and unpaid family workers in their projections. However, as previously detailed, OBERS includes government employees in its associated activity sector, while BLS keeps all government workers separate. This is a major and important difference between these two series.

BLS has projected only to the year 1985, while OBERS provides series to 2020. BLS plans to update its series to extend further in the future, but long-range projection modeling will have to rely on the OBERS series at present.

Additionally, OBERS details only thirty-three industrial groups. BLS, on the other hand, provides projections to 2, 3 and sometimes 4 digit SIC level.

While neither set has detailed employment projections below the national scale, OBERS has forecasted total employment (and total earnings by industry) for various geographical levels.

Finally, other differences exist because of the underlying assumptions and methods used by BLS and OBERS. For a study of these differences, the reader is referred to the source documents.

Data Adjustments

This section describes various ways in which employment data may need to be adjusted. As is discussed later, the control (or base) projections can be adjusted directly within the program. However, it may be necessary to make adjustments to the time series data as well. Both types of manipulation will be reviewed.

EXHIBIT 11.3
COMPARISON OF BLS EMPLOYMENT PROJECTIONS
UNITED STATES: MAJOR INDUSTRIAL SECTORS
(employment in thousands)

Industrial Sector	1965*	1980			1985**	
		I[1]	II[2]	III[3]	II[2]	III[3]
Total	74,568	98,600	101,186	101,866	107,609	109,565
Agriculture	4,671	3,156	2,720	2,750	1,900	2,300
Mining	667	584	655	788	632	823
Contract Construction	3,994	5,427	4,908	5,178	5,184	5,798
Manufacturing	18,454	22,133	22,529	21,937	23,499	22,597
Transportation, Communications, and Public Utilities	4,250	4,925	5,317	5,186	5,368	5,381
Wholesale and Retail Trade	15,352	20,282	21,695	22,457	22,381	23,187
Finance, Insurance and Real Estate	3,367	4,598	5,349	5,392	5,932	5,964
Services	13,722	20,867	21,428	21,378	23,913	24,165
Government (Civilian)	10,091	16,632	16,585	18,490	18,800	21,145

NOTES: *1965 was the only comparable base year for all three series.
       **Series I did not project to 1985.

SOURCES: 1. Bureau of Labor Statistics, U.S. Department of Labor, *Patterns of the U.S. Economy*, Bulletin 1672 (Washington, D.C.: U.S. Government Printing Office, 1970).
         2. Bureau of Labor Statistics, U.S. Department of Labor, *The Structure of the U.S. Economy in 1980, 1985* Bulletin 1831 (Washington, D.C.: U.S. Government Printing Office, 1975).
         3. Bureau of Labor Statistics, U.S. Department of Labor, *Monthly Labor Review* March and November 1976 issues (Washington, D.C.: U.S. Government Printing Office).

EXHIBIT 11.4
COMPARISON OF U.S.
EMPLOYMENT (TOTAL)
PROJECTIONS

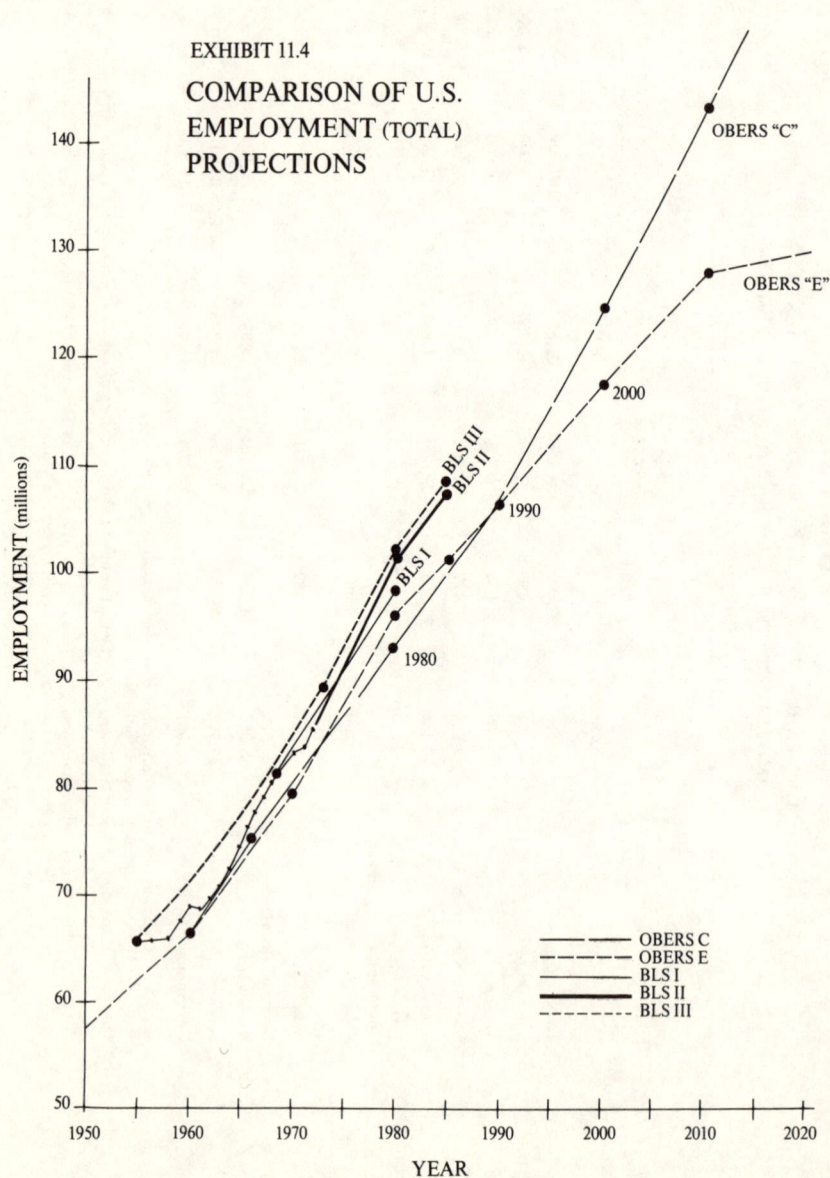

EXHIBIT 11.4

**COMPARISON OF U.S.
EMPLOYMENT (TOTAL)
PROJECTIONS**

ADJUSTMENTS TO TIME SERIES DATA

Most employment series data exclude the self-employed and unpaid family workers. But, it may be desirable to include these employees. There are two suggested methods for incorporating these workers into time series data. One method assumes that the proportion of self-employed and unpaid family workers in each industrial sector is the same each year and for each geographical area. The decennial Census of Population (1970) provides the necessary information to develop these multipliers. Then, each year of data is multiplied by the same ratio vector to increase an area's employment to include the self-employed and unpaid family workers. Exhibit 11.5 provides sample calculations.

The second method is similar to the first. The total number of self-employed and unpaid family workers for each year for each geographical area is obtained. For example, in New Jersey, the state Department of Labor and Industry can supply this data. Then, using the census information, ratios of the number of these employees for each industrial sector to the total number of self-employed and unpaid family workers are developed. The vector formulated is multiplied by the total for each year and added into each industrial sector (see Exhibit 11.6).

Another difficulty may arise with regard to government employment. For example, *County Business Patterns* does not include government employment. One solution is to augment the CBP data with tabulations from another source (such as *Employment and Earnings*). This procedure is sufficient when the base projections being used are consistent with the time series. However, OBERS follows the census delineations of industrial sectors. And the census delineations include some government employment within several industrial breakdowns, particularly the service sector. Thus, either a method similar to that outlined above for self-employed and unpaid family workers will have to be utilized, or the government and service sectors will have to be aggregated.

ADJUSTMENTS TO BASE (NATIONAL OR STATE) PROJECTIONS

The program routines of this volume provide a means for adjusting the national or state projections within the program. There are two ways in which these projections can be manipulated. One is by a vertical matrix which can be filled with ratios to be multiplied by the industrial sectors. This may be useful if recent economic activity indicates that the national projections are overly optimistic or pessimistic. For example, in a New Jersey study, the OBERS 1970 and 1980 national estimates were extrapolated to determine estimates for 1975. These, in turn, were compared to

EXHIBIT 11.5

ADJUSTMENTS TO EMPLOYMENT TIME SERIES DATA
USING SELF-EMPLOYMENT AND UNPAID FAMILY WORKERS MULTIPLIERS
METHOD 1
(employment in thousands)

Industrial Sector	(1) U.S. 1970 Total Employment[1]	(2) U.S. 1970 Wage and Salary Employment[2]	(3) N.J. Multiplier $\frac{(1)}{(2)}$	(4) N.J. 1975 Wage and Salary Employment[3]	(5) 1975 Total Adjusted Employment (3) x (4)
Agriculture	2,758	1,179	2.34	7.5	17.6
Mining	626	606	1.03	3.8	3.9
Contract Construction	4,065	3,429	1.19	91.4	108.8
Manufacturing	19,489	19,201	1.01	749.7	757.2
Transportation, Communications, and Public Utilities	3,965	3,801	1.04	165.7	172.3
Wholesale and Retail Trade	15,222	13,678	1.11	605.4	672.0
Finance, Insurance, and Real Estate	3,700	3,457	1.07	132.8	142.1
Services	13,790	11,947	1.15	400.5	460.6
Total	63,615	57,298		2,156.8	2,334.5

SOURCES: 1., 2. U.S. Bureau of the Census, Census of Population: 1970, Vol. 1, Characteristics of the Population, Part 1, U.S. Summary—Section 2, Table 238.

3. Bureau of the Census, U.S. Department of Commerce, *County Business Patterns,* New Jersey.

EXHIBIT 11.6

ADJUSTMENTS TO EMPLOYMENT TIME SERIES DATA
USING SELF-EMPLOYMENT AND UNPAID FAMILY WORKERS MULTIPLIERS
METHOD 2
(employment in thousands)

Industrial Sector	(1) U.S. 1970 Number of Self-Employed and Unpaid Family Workers[1]	(2) Percent of Total Self-Employed and Unpaid Family Workers	(3) N.J. 1975 Total Self-Employed and Unpaid Family Workers	(4) N.J. 1975 Self-Employed and Unpaid Family Workers (2) x $\sum$ (3)	(5) N.J. 1975 Wage and Salary Employment[2]	(6) N.J. 1975 Total Adjusted Employment (4)+ (5)
Agriculture	1,579	22.7	n.a.	42.7	7.5	50.2
Mining	20	0.3	n.a.	0.6	3.8	4.4
Contract Construction	636	9.1	n.a.	17.1	91.4	108.5
Manufacturing	924	13.3	n.a.	25.0	749.7	774.7
Transportation Communications, and Public Utilities	164	2.4	n.a.	4.6	165.7	170.2
Wholesale and Retail Trade	1,544	22.2	n.a.	41.8	605.4	647.2
Finance, Insurance and Real Estate	243	3.5	n.a.	6.6	132.8	139.4
Services	1,843	26.5	n.a.	49.9	400.5	450.4
Total	6,953	100.0	188.3	188.3	2,156.8	2,345.0

NOTE: N.A. = not applicable

SOURCES: 1. U.S. Bureau of the Census, Census of Population: 1970, Vol. 1, Characteristics of the Population, Part 1, U.S. Summary—Section 2, Table 238.
2. Bureau of the Census, U.S. Department of Commerce, *County Business Patterns*, New Jersey.

EXHIBIT 11.7
Adjustments to Base (National) Employment Projections
Using Actual to Estimated Employment Ratios
(employment in thousands)

Industrial Sector	(1) U.S. 1975 Actual Employment[1]	(2) U.S. 1975 OBERS Estimated Employment[2]	(3) Multiplier $\frac{(1)}{(2)}$	(4) U.S. 1980 OBERS Projections[3]	(5) U.S. 1980 Revised OBERS Projections (3) × (4)	(6) U.S. 1990 OBERS Projections[2]	(7) U.S. 1990 Revised OBERS Projections (3) × (6)
Agriculture	2,912	2,715	1.07	2,516	2,692	2,123	2,272
Mining	724	620	1.17	609	713	547	640
Contract Construction	4,611	5,100	0.90	5,589	5,030	6,015	5,414
Manufacturing	18,191	20,975	0.87	22,112	19,237	23,106	20,102
Transportation Communications, and Public Utilities	5,219	5,088	1.03	6,105	6,288	6,723	6,925
Wholesale and Retail Trade	16,918	17,486	0.97	19,396	18,814	21,034	20,403
Fire, Insurance, and Real Estate	4,286	4,539	0.94	5,240	4,926	6,178	5,807
Services and Government	28,469	28,846	0.99	32,980	32,650	39,095	38,704
Total	81,330	85,369	—	94,547	90,350	104,821	100,267

SOURCES: 1. The data base is Bureau of Census, U.S. Department of Commerce, *County Business Patterns* (Washington, D.C.: U.S. Government Printing Office), augmented by Bureau of Labor Statistics, U.S. Department of Labor, *Employment and Earnings* (Washington, D.C.: U.S. Government Printing Office) for government employment; and adjusted to reflect self-employed and unpaid family workers.
2. Extrapolation between 1966 and 1980 OBERS estimates.
3. U.S. Department of Commerce, *1972 OBERS Projections* (Washington, D.C.: U.S. Government Printing Office, 1974).

EXHIBIT 11.8
ADJUSTMENTS TO BASE (STATE) EMPLOYMENT PROJECTIONS
USING SERIES II TO SERIES E POPULATION RATIOS
(employment in thousands)

Industrial Sector	(1) N.J. 1980 Employment Projections[1]	(2) N.J. 1980 Multiplier[2]	(3) N.J. 1980 Revised Employment Projections (1) × (2)	(4) N.J. 1990 Employment Projections[1]	(5) N.J. 1990 Multipliers[3]	(6) N.J. 1990 Revised Employment Projections (4) × (5)
Agriculture	16.4	.96	15.7	12.1	.93	11.3
Mining	4.2	.96	4.0	3.6	.93	3.3
Contract Construction	144.9	.96	139.1	150.7	.93	140.2
Manufacturing	734.1	.96	704.7	727.7	.93	676.8
Transportation, Communications, and Public Utilities	196.2	.96	188.4	212.0	.93	197.2
Wholesale and Retail Trade	713.9	.96	685.3	793.2	.93	737.7
Finance, Insurance, and Real Estate	158.3	.96	152.0	185.6	.93	172.6
Services and Government	1,004.2	.96	964.0	1,198.9	.93	1,115.0
Total	2,972.3		2,853.2	3,283.7		3,054.1

SOURCES: 1. Derived from the New Jersey study using Model 4—OBERS and national projections that were adjusted to reflect actual 1975 employment activity.

2. $\dfrac{1980 \text{ N.J. Series II Population}}{1980 \text{ N.J. Series E Population}} = \dfrac{7,780,250}{8,080,300} = .96$

3. $\dfrac{1990 \text{ N.J. Series II Population}}{1990 \text{ N.J. Series E Population}} = \dfrac{8,283,890}{8,923,300} = .93$

1975 actual data. Ratios were then derived that reflected the difference between the projected and actual employment levels. These ratios were then applied to the respective industrial sectors for the years 1980–2000 (see Exhibit 11.7).

The other approach is an horizontal matrix which can be filled with scalars to be multiplied by the projection years, e.g., all of 1980's base (in this case, state) projections would be adjusted by one multiplier and all of 1985's by another. This method was also used in the New Jersey analysis. The state projections were modified via the ratios of the Census Series II New Jersey population projections to those of Series II, for 1980, 1990, and 2000. (see Exhibit 11.8).

Summary

The focus of this chapter has been on sources for data inputs necessary for the programmed models and on suggested techniques for data modifications. Five alternative sources of historical data have been reviewed and two different national projection sets outlined. Adjustments to time series and projected data have been illustrated with examples from the New Jersey study.

Chapter 12
The Employment Program:
The Options

There are five options available in the program presented in Chapter 14. This chapter will briefly describe each option and explain how to use it.

1. Models

As indicated in Chapter 10, four models have been programmed. In many instances the user will not desire or need four sets of projections. Thus, the program is written to permit any one model or combination of models to be run. The user simply indicates on the first option card (see Chapter 13 for format) which models are to be run.

2. Averages

Each model is programmed to run with or without averages. If the user wishes to have projections estimated both with and without averages, the program must be run twice. In other words, the program is designed so that projections are made *either* with *or* without averages. There is space on the second option card to indicate which method is preferred.

3. Projection Levels

There are two alternative projection levels available. Employment projections may be made in a two-step process (national to state to county) or in one step (state to county). If only national projections are available, then the former method should be chosen. In this case, data will be needed for all three geographical areas. However, if acceptable state projections are available, then the one-step procedure can be followed. Then, data are required for only two geographical areas (state and county). The selection of this option is indicated on the second option card.

4. Vertical Vector

This vector has been incorporated into the program so that the base (national or state, depending on the number of steps chosen) employment projections for each industrial sector may be adjusted by a multiplier. It can be used to adjust the projections upward or downward. We incorporated this capability in order to be able to adjust one or more of the geographical areas to employment counts that are not available for all of them. For example, a more recent count may suggest that some blue collar sector should receive a higher percentage of the projected employment, while others should get a lower share. Whether this option is to be employed or not is indicated on the second option card.

5. Horizontal Vector

This vector is used to multiply the projections for different years by a single scalar and it enters the program only at the state level. The purpose of this option is to adjust projections that may be out-of-date but must be used because they are the only available projections. For example, projections made from a 1969 base for the year 1990 seem high from the 1975–1977 perspective. The 1969 based projections would overproject employment for 1975. The difference between the 1975 actual employment and 1975 projected employment would be converted into a percentage scale that would be used to lower the 1980, 1985, 1990 projections. This option is selected on the first option card.

Chapter 13
The Employment Program:
Job Deck Set-Up

The program, reproduced in Chapter 14 and demonstrated in Chapter 15, is written in Fortran IV and all constructions and testing were run at the Center for Computer Information and Services at Rutgers University, New Brunswick, New Jersey on an IBM 370/168.

The job deck set-up has fourteen components that are listed below in their mandatory order. The system cards, set 1, 3 and 14, may vary from system to system, but it is imperative that the input data, sets 4 through 14, be in order given. Sets 11 through 13 are needed only if Model 3 (Population/Employment) is being run.

Set 1, System Cards. These cards are written in Job Control Language (JCL).

Set 2, Main Program. These are written in Fortran IV and exhibited in Chapter 14.

Set 3, System Cards. These JCL cards set up three scratch files: one for county employment data and two for county employment projections.

Set 4, Option Cards. There are two cards in this set, whose format is specified later.

Set 5, Vertical Vector. These three cards contain one multiplier for each industrial sector. This format is specified later.

Set 6, Horizontal Vector. This card contains one multiplier for each projection year. This format is specified later.

Set 7, National Employment Data. There are three cards for each industrial sector. They must be in the order shown in Exhibit 13.2. This format is specified later.

Set 8, State Employment Data. There are three cards for each industrial sector and one complete set for each state. There can be six state sets. This format is specified later.

Set 9, County Employment Data. There are two cards for each industrial sector and one complete set for each county. All counties within a state must be grouped together and in the identical order as the states. There can be 600 county sets. This format is specified later.

Set 10, County Total Employment Data. There are two cards for each county. All counties within a state must be grouped together and in the identical order as the states. This format is specified later.

Set 11, National Population Data. This is one card, whose format is specified later.

Set 12, State Population Data. This is one card for each state. The states must be in the same order as used for the employment data. This format is specified later.

Set 13, County Population Data. This is one card for each county. The counties must be in the same order as used for the employment data. This format is specified later.

Set 14, System Card. This card signals the end of the job.

EXHIBIT 13.1
JOB DECK SET-UP;
EMPLOYMENT PROJECTIONS

SET 14. SYSTEM CARD

SET 13. COUNTY
POPULATION DATA

SET 12. STATE
POPULATION DATA

SET 11. NATIONAL
POPULATION DATA

SET 10. COUNTY
TOTAL EMPLOYMENT.

SET 9. COUNTY
EMPLOYMENT DATA

SET 8. STATE
EMPLOYMENT DATA

SET 7. NATIONAL
EMPLOYMENT DATA

SET 6. HORIZONTAL VECTOR

SET 5. VERTICAL VECTOR

SET 4. OPTION CARDS

SET 3. SYSTEM CARDS

SET 2. MAIN PROGRAM

SET 1. SYSTEM CARDS

EXHIBIT 13.2
INDUSTRIAL DIVISIONS AND GROUPS
SPECIFIED FOR INPUT AND OUTPUT
OF COMPUTER PROGRAM

1972 SIC Codes	Labels on Computer Printout	Major Division SIC Titles Major Group SIC Titles	Sector Index Number (i) in Computer Program
01-09	AGRI	Agriculture, Forestry, and Fishing	1
10-14	MINI	Mining	2
15-17	CONS	Construction	3
20-39	MANU	Manufacturing	4
20	FD&K	Food and Kindred Products	5
22	TEXT	Textile Mill Products	6
23	APPL	Apparel and Other Textile Products	7
24,25	LUM&	Lumber & Wood Products; Furniture & Fixtures	8
26	PAPR	Paper and Allied Products	9
27	PRNT	Printing and Publishing	10
28	CHEM	Chemicals and Allied Products	11
29	PETR	Petroleum and Coal Products	12
33	PRIM	Primary Metals	13
34	FABM	Fabricated Metal Products	14
35	MACH	Machinery, Except Electrical	15
36	ELMA	Electric and Electronic Equipment	16
37	TRAN	Transportation Equipment	17
21,30 31,32 38,39	OTHR	(All other Major Groups of Manufacturing)	18
40-49	TCPU	Transportation and Public Utilities	19
50-59	WHRT	Wholesale Trade; Retail Trade	20
60,67	FIRE	Finance, Insurance, and Real Estate	21
70-89	SERV	Services	22
91-97	GOVT	Public Administration	23

Note: The user may of course use the 23 sectors or categories of the program to analyze any 23 items, disregarding the labels we have programmed into the printout. The only restriction in the program is that
items 5 through 18, when summed, must not exceed item 4,
MANU. This is a built-in safety check over the manufacturing industries.

Input Formats

PROGRAM OPTIONS CONTROL CARDS FORMAT

Card 1

Columns

1	Blank
2	"1" if Model 1 (Constant Share) is to be run; blank if it is not
3	Blank
4	"1" if Model 2 (Simple Regression) is to be run; blank if it is not
5	Blank
6	"1" if Model 3 (Population/Employment) is to be run; blank if it is not
7	Blank
8	"1" if Model 4 (OBERS) is to be run; blank if it is not
9	Blank
10	"1" if the horizontal vector is to be applied; blank if it is not
11–80	Blank

Card 2

Columns

Note: The number in Columns 6–8 should be the total number of counties *plus* 1 for each state. This is to take into account dummy counties that are created. The numbers in columns 10–32 must be 1 *plus* the actual number of counties.

1–3	Blank
4	s=number of states; $1 \leq s \leq 6$
5	Blank
6–8	c = number of counties; $1 \leq c \leq 600$ (right justified)
9	Blank

10–12   Total number of counties in state 1; must be greater than 1 (right justified)

13   Blank

14–16   Total number of counties in states 1 *and* 2; may be blank if only one state (right justified)

17   Blank

18–20   Total number of counties in states 1 through 3; may be blank if less than three states (right justified)

21   Blank

22–24   Total number of counties in states 1 through 4; may be blank if less than four states (right justified)

25   Blank

26–28   Total number of counties in states 1 through 5; may be blank if less than five states (right justified)

29   Blank

30–32   Total number of counties in states 1 through 6; may be blank if less than six states (right justified)

33–35   Blank

36   Blank if using two projection steps (nation to state to county) and there are no state projections; "1" if using one step (state to county) and there are state projections.

37–39   Blank

40   Blank if the chosen models are to be run *without* averages; "1" if they are to be run *with* averages.

41–42   Blank

43–44   Number of years of historical data; must not be greater than fifteen (right justified)

45–47   Blank

48   "1" if the vertical vector is to be applied; blank if it is not

49–80   Blank

VERTICAL VECTOR CARDS FORMAT

Note: (1) If this option is *not* utilized three blank cards must be substituted here.
(2) The field width for these multipliers is nine. The first two columns are for the whole numbers; the third column must be a decimal point; and the remaining six columns are for the decimal digits.

Card 1

Columns

1–9	Agriculture, Forestry, & Fishing Employment Multiplier
10–18	Mining Employment Multiplier
19–27	Construction Employment Multiplier
28–36	Manufacturing Employment Multiplier
37–45	Food and Kindred Products Employment Multiplier
46–54	Textile Mill Products Employment Multiplier
55–63	Apparel and Other Textile Products Employment Multiplier
64–72	Lumber Products and Furniture Employment Multiplier
73–80	Blank

Card 2

Columns

1–9	Paper and Allied Products Employment Multiplier
10–18	Printing and Publishing Employment Multiplier
19–27	Chemicals and Allied Products Employment Multiplier
28–36	Petroleum Employment Multiplier
37–45	Primary Metals Employment Multiplier
46–54	Fabricated Metal Products Employment Multiplier
55–63	Machinery, Except Electrical, Employment Multiplier
64–72	Electric and Electronic Equipment Employment Multiplier
73–80	Blank

Card 3

Columns

1–9	Transportation Equipment Employment Multiplier
10–18	Other Manufacturing Employment Multiplier
19–27	Transportation, and Public Utilities Employment Multiplier
28–36	Wholesale and Retail Trade Employment Multiplier
37–45	Finance, Insurance, and Real Estate Employment Multiplier
46–54	Services Employment Multiplier
56–63	Public Administration Employment Multiplier
64–80	Blank

HORIZONTAL VECTOR CARD FORMAT

Note: (1) If this option is not utilized, one blank card must be substituted here.

(2) The field width for these multipliers is nine. The first two columns are for the whole numbers; the third column must be a decimal point; and the remaining six columns are for the decimal digits.

Columns

1–9	1980 Multiplier
10–18	1985 Multiplier
19–27	1990 Multiplier
28–36	1995 Multiplier
37–45	2000 Multiplier
46–80	Blank

(IN ALL OF THE FOLLOWING CARD SETS, DATA ARE RIGHT JUSTIFIED)

NATIONAL EMPLOYMENT DATA CARDS FORMAT

Note: 3 cards per industrial sector × 23 industrial sectors = 69 cards.

These are not necessary if only a one-step (state to county) projection series is being used.

Example:

This example illustrates the data format for agriculture employment. There are twelve years of historical data and five five-year projections. Up to fifteen years of historical data may be used, as well as less than twelve years. Also, less than five years of projections are acceptable. Projections may be in ten-year increments, but they must be punched so that there are nine blank spaces between the last historical year data and nine blank spaces between each projection. It should be noted that, regardless of the number of historical years of data, the projections are punched immediately following the last historical datum in fields of nine.

Set 1: National Agriculture Employment Data

Card 1

Columns

1–9	Agriculture Employment for first year
10–18	Agriculture Employment for second year
19–27	Agriculture Employment for third year
28–36	Agriculture Employment for fourth year
37–45	Agriculture Employment for fifth year
46–54	Agriculture Employment for sixth year
55–63	Agriculture Employment for seventh year
64–72	Agriculture Employment for eighth year
73–80	Blank

Card 2

Columns

1–9	Agriculture Employment for ninth year
10–18	Agriculture Employment for tenth year
19–27	Agriculture Employment for eleventh year

28–36   Agriculture Employment for twelfth year

37–45   Projected Agriculture Employment for five years beyond last historical data year

46–54   Projected Agriculture Employment for ten years beyond last historical data year

55–63   Projected Agriculture Employment for fifteen years beyond last historical data year

64–72   Projected Agriculture Employment for twenty years beyond last historical data year

73–80   Blank

Card 3

Columns

1–9   Projected Agriculture Employment for twenty-five years beyond last historical data year

10–80   Blank

STATE EMPLOYMENT DATA CARDS FORMAT

3 cards/industrial sector × 23 industrial sectors/state × number of states = 69 cards/state × number of states

The format for these cards for each state is exactly the same as for the National Employment Data Cards *if* state projections are used as the base projections. If this is not the case, the format is then the same with the exception that there will be blank columns replacing the projections.

COUNTY EMPLOYMENT DATA CARDS FORMAT

2 cards/industrial sector × 23 industrial sectors/county × number of counties = 46 cards/county × number of counties

The format for these cards is similar to that for the State Employment Data Cards. However, only two cards are needed per industrial sector because county projections will not be used.

COUNTY TOTAL EMPLOYMENT DATA CARDS FORMAT

Card 1

Columns

1–9	County Total Employment for the first year
10–18	County Total Employment for the second year
19–27	County Total Employment for the third year
28–36	County Total Employment for the fourth year
37–45	County Total Employment for the fifth year
46–54	County Total Employment for the sixth year
55–63	County Total Employment for the seventh year
64–72	County Total Employment for the eighth year
73–80	Blank

Card 2

Columns

1–9	County Total Employment for the ninth year
10–18	County Total Employment for the tenth year
19–27	County Total Employment for the eleventh year
28–36	County Total Employment for the twelfth year
37–80	Blank

Note: If there are more than twelve years, the additional data must be punched in nine-space fields. There must be 2 data cards for total employment for the dummy counties. Two blank cards may be used and are to be placed at the end of each group of counties, even if all counties are covered.

NATIONAL POPULATION DATA CARD FORMAT

Columns

1–10	Population for five years prior to last employment data year

11–20   Population for last employment data year

21–30   Projected population for five years after last employment data year

31–40   Projected population for ten years after last employment data year

41–50   Projected population for fifteen years after last employment data year

51–60   Projected population for twenty years after last employment data year

61–70   Projected population for twenty-five years after last employment data year

71–80   Blank

STATE POPULATION DATA CARD FORMAT

One for each state with the same format as the National Population Data Card, plus one representing the difference between the total of the states' populations and that of the nation.

COUNTY POPULATION DATA CARD FORMAT

One for each county with the same format as the National Population Data Card, plus one for each dummy county to be created. If all counties within a state are used, a card with the appropriate state's total population should be inserted.

Chapter 14
The Employment Program: Input, a Listing of the Program and a Sample Problem Data Set

This chapter consists of a listing of the input deck for a sample problem. The job set up is as described in Chapter 13, including the complete set of models presented in Chapter 10.

The data set consists of one state and one county. Twelve historical years of employment data were used for the nation, state, and county, as well as five-year national projections. The government and services sectors were aggregated. Zeros in the employment input may indicate undisclosed data. The total of the 2 digit manufacturing major groups $(i = 5-18)$ may not sum to total manufacturing employment because of disclosure problems.

The state and county are projected on all four models. The averaging technique was not used. And the national projections were adjusted via the vertical matrix.

EMPLOYMENT PROJECTIONS FOR COUNTIES
BY CONNIE O MICHAELSON
RUTGERS UNIVERSITY, CENTER FOR URBAN POLICY RESEARCH
NEW BRUNSWICK, NEW JERSEY

```
      DIMENSION XNE(24,20),SE(6,24,20),CE(24,15),SP(6,7),SEP3(6,24,5)
      DIMENSION XNP(7),CP(600,7),SEP1(6,24,5),CEP1(24,5),CEP3(24,5)
      DIMENSION SEP2(6,24,5),CEP2(24,5),CEP2T(600,5),CEP1T(600,5)
      DIMENSION CET(600,15),IND(24),T(15),X(15),TT(15),CEP3T(600,5)
      DIMENSION SEP4(6,24,5),CEP4(24,5),CB(600,24),CEP4T(600,5)
      DIMENSION SB(6,24),P(23),TX(20),CT(24,15)
      DATA IND/4HAGRI,4HMINI,4HCONS,4HMANU,4HFD#K,4HTEXT,4HAPPL,4HLUM#,4
     2HPAPR,4HPRNT,4HCHEM,4HPETR,4HPRIM,4HFABM,4HMACH,4HELMA,4HTRAN,4HOT
     3HR,4HTCPU,4HWHRT,4HFIRE,4HSERV,4HGOVT,4HTOTL/
      XMAVG(X1,Y1,X2,Y2,X3,Y3,Z)=(X1/Y1+X2/Y2+X3/Y3)/Z
      READ(5,10) IM1,IM2,IM3,IM4,IX
   10 FORMAT(5I2)
      READ(5,11) INS,INC,NCS1,NCS2,NCS3,NCS4,NCS5,NCS6,ISEP,IMAVG,IY,IP
   11 FORMAT (12I4)
      READ(5,16)(P(I),I=1,23)
   16 FORMAT(8F9.6/8F9.6/7F9.6)
      READ(5,12)(TT(K),K=1,5)
   12 FORMAT(5F9.6)
      IF(ISEP .EQ. 1) GO TO 1111
      READ(5,13)((XNE(I,J),J=1,20),I=1,23)
   13 FORMAT(8F9.0/8F9.0/4F9.0)
      IF(IP .EQ. 0) GO TO 1112
      DO 1023 I=1,23
      DO 1023 J=1,5
      XNE(I,J+IY)=XNE(I,J+IY)*P(I)
 1023 CONTINUE
 1112 CONTINUE
      DO 8500 J=1,20
      TX(J)=0.
      IN=0
      DO 8500 I=5,18
      IF(XNE(I,J) .EQ. 0.) GO TO 8550
      IN=IN+1
      TX(J)=TX(J)+XNE(I,J)
 8550 CONTINUE
      IF(IN .LT. 14 .AND. I .EQ. 18) TX(J)=0.
 8500 CONTINUE
      DO 8501 I=5,18
      DO 8501 J=1,20
      IF(TX(J) .EQ. 0.) GO TO 8502
      XNE(I,J)=(XNE(I,J)/TX(J))*XNE(4,J)
 8502 CONTINUE
 8501 CONTINUE
      DO 6090 I=1,20
      XNE(24,I)=XNE(1,I)+XNE(2,I)+XNE(3,I)+XNE(4,I)+XNE(19,I)+XNE(20,I)+
     2XNE(21,I)+XNE(22,I)+XNE(23,I)
 6090 CONTINUE
 1111 DO 14 I=1,INS
      READ(5,13)((SE(I,J,K),K=1,20),J=1,23)
   14 CONTINUE
      DO 1021 I=1,INS
```

```
      DO 1021 J=1,23
      DO 1021 K=1,5
      IF(IP .EQ. 0) GO TO 1025
      SE(I,J,K+IY)=SE(I,J,K+IY)*P(J)
1025  CONTINUE
      IF(IX .EQ. 0) GO TO 1024
      SE(I,J,K+IY)=SE(I,J,K+IY)*TT(K)
1024  CONTINUE
1021  CONTINUE
      DO 6505 I=1,INS
      DO 6505 K=1,20
      SB(I,K)=0.
      IN=0
      DO 6505 J=5,18
      IF(SE(I,J,K) .EQ. 0.) GO TO 1026
      IN=IN+1
      SB(I,K)=SB(I,K)+SE(I,J,K)
1026  CONTINUE
      IF(IN .LT. 14 .AND. J .EQ. 18) SB(I,K)=0.
6505  CONTINUE
      DO 6506 I=1,INS
      DO 6506 J=5,18
      DO 6506 K=1,20
      IF(SB(I,K) .EQ. 0.) GO TO 6507
      SE(I,J,K)=(SE(I,J,K)/SB(I,K))*SE(I,4,K)
6507  CONTINUE
6506  CONTINUE
      DO 8510 J=1,23
      DO 8510 K=1,20
      CB(J,K)=0.
      DO 8510 I=1,INS
      CB(J,K)=CB(J,K)+SE(I,J,K)
8510  CONTINUE
      IF(ISEP .EQ. 1) GO TO 8515
      DO 8511 I=1,23
      DO 8511 J=1,20
      SE(INS+1,I,J)=XNE(I,J)-CB(I,J)
8511  CONTINUE
      INS=INS+1
8515  CONTINUE
      DO 6091 I=1,INS
      DO 6091 J=1,20
      SE(I,24,J)=SE(I,1,J)+SE(I,2,J)+SE(I,3,J)+SE(I,4,J)+SE(I,19,J)+SE(I
     2,20,J)+SE(I,21,J)+SE(I,22,J)+SE(I,23,J)
6091  CONTINUE
      DO 8542 J=1,23
      DO 8542 K=1,15
      CT(J,K)=0.
8542  CONTINUE
      DO 100 I=1,INC
      DO 100 J=1,23
      IF(I .EQ. NCS1) GO TO 8540
      IF(NCS2 .GT. 0 .AND. I .EQ. NCS2) GO TO 8540
      IF(NCS3 .GT. 0 .AND. I .EQ. NCS3) GO TO 8540
      IF(NCS4 .GT. 0 .AND. I .EQ. NCS4) GO TO 8540
      IF(NCS5 .GT. 0 .AND. I .EQ. NCS5) GO TO 8540
      IF(NCS6 .GT. 0 .AND. I .EQ. NCS6) GO TO 8540
      READ(5,24)(CE(J,K),K=1,15)
  24  FORMAT(8F9.0/7F9.0)
      DO 8543 K=1,15
      CT(J,K)=CT(J,K)+CE(J,K)
```

```
8543 CONTINUE
     GO TO 8544
8540 CONTINUE
     DO 8541 K=1,15
     IST=IT(I,NCS1,NCS2,NCS3,NCS4,NCS5,NCS6)
     CE(J,K)=SE(IST,J,K)-CT(J,K)
8541 CONTINUE
     DO 8250 K=1,15
     CT(J,K)=0.
9250 CONTINUE
8544 CONTINUE
     WRITE(4)(CE(J,K),K=1,15)
 100 CONTINUE
     READ(5,24)((CET(I,J),J=1,15),I=1,INC)
     IF(IM3 .EQ. 0) GO TO 1000
     READ(5,15)(XNP(L),L=1,7)
  15 FORMAT(7F10.0)
  20 READ(5,15)((SP(I,J),J=1,7),I=1,INS)
     READ(5,15)((CP(I,J),J=1,7),I=1,INC)
1000 CONTINUE
     IF(ISEP .EQ. 1) GO TO 8002
     WRITE(6,5000)
5000 FORMAT(1H1,2X,;NATIONAL EMPLOYMENT;/)
     WRITE(6,50)
  50 FORMAT(10X,4H1964,6X,4H1965,6X,4H1966,6X,4H1967,6X,4H1968,6X,4H196
    29,6X,4H1970,6X,4H1971,6X,4H1972,6X,4H1973,6X,4H1974,6X,4H1975/)
     DO 6001 I=1,24
     WRITE(6,6000) IND(I),(XNE(I,J),J=1,IY)
6000 FORMAT(2X,1A4,12F10.0)
6001 CONTINUE
     WRITE(6,7000)
7000 FORMAT(1H1,2X,;NATIONAL EMPLOYMENT PROJECTIONS;/)
     WRITE(6,30)
  30 FORMAT(10X,4H1980,6X,4H1985,6X,4H1990,6X,4H1995,6X,4H2000/)
     DO 7100 I=1,24
     MM=IY+1
     LM=IY+5
     WRITE(6,8000)IND(I),(XNE(I,J),J=MM,LM)
8000 FORMAT(2X,1A4,5F10.0)
7100 CONTINUE
8002 DO 4090 I=1,INS
     WRITE(6,5001) I
5001 FORMAT(1H1,2X,;STATE;,I3,;EMPLOYMENT;)
     WRITE(6,50)
     DO 4090 J=1,24
     WRITE(6,6000)IND(J),(SE(I,J,K),K=1,IY)
4090 CONTINUE
     ENDFILE 4
     REWIND 4
     DO 9000 K=1,INC
     WRITE(6,5002) K
5002 FORMAT(1H1,2X,;COUNTY;,2X,I4,;EMPLOYMENT;)
     WRITE(6,50)
     DO 9208 I=1,23
     READ(4)(CE(I,J),J=1,IY)
     WRITE(6,6000) IND(I),(CE(I,J),J=1,IY)
9208 CONTINUE
     WRITE(6,6000)IND(24),(CET(K,J),J=1,IY)
9000 CONTINUE
     DO 5 I=1,INC
     DO 5 J=1,5
```

```
      CEP1T(I,J)=0.
      CEP2T(I,J)=0.
      CEP3T(I,J)=0.
      CEP4T(I,J)=0.
    5 CONTINUE
      IA=IY
      CC=3.
      IF(ISEP .EQ. 0) GO TO 251
      DO 250 I=1,INS
      DO 250 J=1,23
      DO 250 K=1,5
      SEP1(I,J,K)=SE(I,J,K+IY)
      SEP2(I,J,K)=SE(I,J,K+IY)
      SEP3(I,J,K)=SE(I,J,K+IY)
      SEP4(I,J,K)=SE(I,J,K+IY)
  250 CONTINUE
  251 CONTINUE
  200 IF(IM1 .EQ. 0) GO TO 2000
      REWIND 4
      IF(ISEP .EQ. 1) GO TO 4100
      DO 4001 I=1,INS
      DO 4001 L=1,23
      DO 4001 J=1,5
      K=J+IY
      IF(IMAVG .EQ. 1) GO TO 4200
      IF(XNE(L,IA) .EQ. 0.) SEP1(I,L,J)=0.
      IF(XNE(L,IA) .EQ. 0.) GO TO 666
      SEP1(I,L,J)=(SE(I,L,IA)/XNE(L,IA))*XNE(L,K)
      GO TO 666
 4200 CONTINUE
      ID=IY
      IC=IY-1
      IB=IY-2
      IF(XNE(L,IB) .EQ. 0.) SEP1(I,L,J)=0.
      IF(XNE(L,IB) .EQ. 0.) GO TO 666
      IF(XNE(L,IC) .EQ. 0.) SEP1(I,L,J) =0.
      IF(XNE(L,IC) .EQ. 0.) GO TO 666
      IF(XNE(L,ID) .EQ. 0.) SEP1(I,L,J)=0.
      IF(XNE(L,ID) .EQ. 0.) GO TO 666
      SEP1(I,L,J)=XMAVG(SE(I,L,IB),XNE(L,IB),SE(I,L,IC),XNE(L,IC),SE(I,L
     2,ID),XNE(L,ID),CC)*XNE(L,K)
  666 CONTINUE
 4001 CONTINUE
      IF(IX .EQ. 0) GO TO 4100
      DO 4120 I=1,INS
      DO 4120 J=1,23
      DO 4120 K=1,5
      SEP1(I,J,K)=SEP1(I,J,K)*TT(K)
 4120 CONTINUE
 4100 CONTINUE
      CALL CON(INS,5,SEP1)
      DO 6093 I=1,INS
      DO 6093 J=1,5
      SEP1(I,24,J)=SEP1(I,1,J)+SEP1(I,2,J)+SEP1(I,3,J)+SEP1(I,4,J)+SEP1(
     2I,19,J)+SEP1(I,20,J)+SEP1(I,21,J)+SEP1(I,22,J)+SEP1(I,23,J)
 6093 CONTINUE
      DO 4101 I=1,INC
      DO 4101 J=1,23
      READ(4)(CE(J,K),K=1,15)
      DO 4102 K=1,5
      IK=K+IY
```

```
      IST=IT(I,NCS1,NCS2,NCS3,NCS4,NCS5,NCS6)
      IF(ISEP .EQ. 1) SEP1(IST,J,K)=SE(IST,J,IK)
      IF(IMAVG .EQ. 1) GO TO 4201
      IF(SE(IST,J,IA) .EQ. 0.) CEP1(J,K)=0.
      IF(SE(IST,J,IA) .EQ. 0.) GO TO 8001
      CEP1(J,K)=(CE(J,IA)/SE(IST,J,IA))*SEP1(IST,J,K)
      GO TO 8001
 4201 CONTINUE
      IF(SE(IST,J,IB) .EQ. 0.) CEP1(J,K)=0.
      IF(SE(IST,J,IB) .EQ. 0.) GO TO 8001
      IF(SE(IST,J,IC) .EQ. 0.) CEP1(J,K)=0.
      IF(SE(IST,J,IC) .EQ. 0.) GO TO 8001
      IF(SE(IST,J,ID) .EQ. 0.) CEP1(J,K)=0.
      IF(SE(IST,J,ID) .EQ. 0.) GO TO 8001
      CEP1(J,K)=XMAVG(CE(J,IB),SE(IST,J,IB),CE(J,IC),SE(IST,J,IC),CE(J,I
     2D),SE(IST,J,ID),CC)*SEP1(IST,J,K)
 8001 CONTINUE
      IF(J .LE. 4 .OR. J .GE. 19) GO TO 6590
      CEP2T(I,K)=CEP2T(I,K)+CEP1(J,K)
 6590 CONTINUE
      IF(J .GT. 4 .AND. J .LT. 19) GO TO 8012
      CEP1T(I,K)=CEP1T(I,K)+CEP1(J,K)
 8012 CONTINUE
 4102 CONTINUE
      WRITE(3)(CEP1(J,K),K=1,5)
 4101 CONTINUE
      ENDFILE 3
      REWIND 3
      DO 5500 I=1,INC
      DO 5510 J=1,23
      READ(3)(CEP1(J,K),K=1,5)
 5510 CONTINUE
      DO 5520 J=1,23
      DO 5501 K=1,5
      IF(J .LE. 4 .OR. J .GE. 19) CEP1(J,K)=CEP1(J,K)
      IF(J .LE. 4 .OR. J .GE. 19) GO TO 6592
      IF(CEP2T(I,K) .LE. CEP1(4,K)) CEP1(J,K)=CEP1(J,K)
      IF(CEP2T(I,K) .LE. CEP1(4,K)) GO TO 6592
      CEP1(J,K)=(CEP1(J,K)/CEP2T(I,K))*CEP1(4,K)
 6592 CONTINUE
 5501 CONTINUE
      WRITE(2)(CEP1(J,K),K=1,5)
 5520 CONTINUE
 5500 CONTINUE
      DO 4092 I=1,INS
      WRITE(6,4093)I
 4093 FORMAT(1H1,2X,;STATE;,2X,I4,;EMPLOYMENT PROJECTIONS;)
      WRITE(6,4094)
 4094 FORMAT(2X,;MODEL 1;)
      WRITE(6,30)
      DO 4092 J=1,24
      WRITE(6,4096) IND(J),(SEP1(I,J,K),K=1,5)
 4096 FORMAT(2X,1A4,5F10.0)
 4092 CONTINUE
      ENDFILE 2
      REWIND 2
      DO 9003 K=1,INC
      WRITE(6,9002) K
 9002 FORMAT(1H1,2X,;COUNTY;,2X,I4,;EMPLOYMENT PROJECTIONS;)
      WRITE(6,4094)
      WRITE(6,30)
```

```
      DO 9005 I=1,23
      READ(2)(CEP1(I,J),J=1,5)
      WRITE(6,4096) IND(I),(CEP1(I,J),J=1,5)
9005 CONTINUE
      WRITE(6,4096) IND(24),(CEP1T(K,J),J=1,5)
9003 CONTINUE
2000 IF(IM2 .EQ. 0) GO TO 3000
      IF(ISEP .EQ. 0) GO TO 55
      DO 201 I=1,INS
      DO 201 J=1,23
      DO 201 K=1,5
      SEP2(I,J,K)=SE(I,J,IY+K)
 201 CONTINUE
  55 CONTINUE
      DO 9940 I=1,INC
      DO 9940 J=1,5
      CEP2T(I,J)=0.
9940 CONTINUE
      IF(ISEP .EQ. 1) GO TO 2222
      DO 4222 I=1,INS
      DO 4222 J=1,23
      SUMT=0
      SUMT2=0.
      XN=0.
      WN=0.
      SUMSE=0.
      SUMTSE=0.
      DO 4222 K=1,IY
      IF(SE(I,J,K) .EQ. 0.) SB(I,J)=0.
      IF(SE(I,J,K) .EQ. 0.) GO TO 8200
      TK=K
      IF(IMAVG .EQ. 1) GO TO 590
      XN=XN+1.
      SUMT=SUMT+TK
      SUMT2=SUMT2+TK*TK
      SUMSE=SUMSE+SE(I,J,K)
      SUMTSE=SUMTSE+TK*SE(I,J,K)
      IF((XN*SUMT2-SUMT**2) .EQ. 0.) GO TO 8200
      SB(I,J)=(XN*SUMTSE-SUMT*SUMSE)/(XN*SUMT2-SUMT**2)
      GO TO 8200
 590 IF((K+1) .GT. IY) GO TO 992
      IF((K+2) .GT. IY) GO TO 992
      TK=K
      WN=WN+1.
      SUMT=SUMT+((TK+TK+1.+TK+2.)/3.)
      SUMT2=SUMT2+((TK*TK+(TK+1.)*(TK+1.)+(TK+2.)*(TK+2.))/3.)
      SUMSE=SUMSE+((SE(I,J,K)+SE(I,J,K+1)+SE(I,J,K+2))/3.)
      SUMTSE=SUMTSE+((TK+TK+1.+TK+2.)/3.)*((SE(I,J,K)+SE(I,J,K+1)+SE(I,J
     2,K+2))/3.)
      IF((WN*SUMT2-SUMT**2) .EQ. 0.) GO TO 992
      SB(I,J)=(WN*SUMTSE-SUMT*SUMSE)/(WN*SUMT2-SUMT**2)
 992 CONTINUE
8200 CONTINUE
4222 CONTINUF
      DO 555 I=1,INS
      DO 555 J=1,23
      DO 555 K=1,5
      XL=K*5
      SEP2(I,J,K)=SE(I,J,IA)+SB(I,J)*XL
 555 CONTINUE
2222 CONTINUE
```

```
      DO 3160 I=1,INS
      DO 3160 J=1,5
      SEP2(I,24,J)=SEP2(I,1,J)+SEP2(I,2,J)+SEP2(I,3,J)+SEP2(I,4,J)+SEP2(
     2I,19,J)+SEP2(I,20,J)+SEP2(I,21,J)+SEP2(I,22,J)+SEP2(I,23,J)
3160  CONTINUE
      REWIND 4
      DO 4204 I=1,INC
      DO 4204 J=1,23
      SUMT=0.
      SUMT2=0.
      ZN=0.
      XN=0.
      SUMCE=0.
      SUMTCE=0.
      READ(4)(CE(J,K),K=1,15)
      DO 4224 K=1,IY
      IF(CE(J,K) .EQ. 0.) CB(I,J)=0.
      IF(CE(J,K) .EQ. 0.) GO TO 8201
      TK=K
      ZN=ZN+1.
      IF(IMAVG .EQ. 1) GO TO 7201
      SUMT=SUMT+TK
      SUMT2=SUMT2+TK*TK
      SUMCE=SUMCE+CE(J,K)
      SUMTCE=SUMTCE+TK*CE(J,K)
      IF((ZN*SUMT2-SUMT**2) .EQ. 0.) GO TO 8201
      CB(I,J)=(ZN*SUMTCE-SUMT*SUMCE)/(ZN*SUMT2-SUMT**2)
      GO TO 8201
7201  IF((K+1) .GT. IY) GO TO 7233
      IF((K+2) .GT. IY) GO TO 7233
      TK=K
      XN=XN+1.
      SUMT=SUMT+((TK+TK+1.+TK+2.)/3.)
      SUMT2=SUMT2+((TK*TK+(TK+1.)*(TK+1.)+(TK+2.)*(TK+2.))/3.)
      SUMCE=SUMCE+((CE(J,K)+CE(J,K+1)+CE(J,K+2))/3.)
      SUMTCE=SUMTCE+((TK+TK+1.+TK+2.)/3.)*((CE(J,K)+CE(J,K+1)+CE(J,K+2))
     2/3.)
      IF((XN*SUMT2-SUMT**2) .EQ. 0.) GO TO 7233
      CB(I,J)=(XN*SUMTCE-SUMT*SUMCE)/(XN*SUMT2-SUMT**2)
7233  CONTINUE
8201  CONTINUE
4224  CONTINUE
4204  CONTINUE
      REWIND 3
      REWIND 4
      DO 7500 I=1,INC
      DO 7500 J=1,23
      READ(4)(CE(J,K),K=1,15)
      DO 3161 K=1,5
      XL=K*5
      CEP2(J,K)=CE(J,IA)+CB(I,J)*XL
      IF(J .GT. 4 .AND. J .LT. 19) GO TO 7561
      CEP2T(I,K)=CEP2T(I,K)+CEP2(J,K)
7561  CONTINUE
3161  CONTINUE
      WRITE(3)(CEP2(J,K),K=1,5)
7500  CONTINUE
      DO 4098 I=1,INS
      WRITE(6,4093) I
      WRITE(6,4099)
4099  FORMAT(2X,;MODEL 2;)
```

```
      WRITE(6,30)
      DO 4098 J=1,24
      WRITE(6,4096) IND(J),(SEP2(I,J,K),K=1,5)
 4098 CONTINUE
      ENDFILE 3
      REWIND 3
      DO 7652 K=1,INC
      WRITE(6,9002) K
      WRITE(6,4099)
      WRITE(6,30)
      DO 7765 I=1,23
      READ(3)(CEP2(I,J),J=1,5)
      WRITE(6,4096) IND(I),(CEP2(I,J),J=1,5)
 7765 CONTINUE
      WRITE(6,4096) IND(24),(CEP2T(K,J),J=1,5)
 7652 CONTINUE
 3000 IF(IM3 .EQ. 0) GO TO 4000
      REWIND 2
      REWIND 3
      REWIND 4
      IF(ISEP .EQ. 1) GO TO 140
      DO 8100 I=1,INS
      DO 8100 J=1,23
      DO 8100 M=1,5
      L=IY+M
      IA=IY-5
      IF(XNE(J,IA) .EQ. 0.) SEP3(I,J,M)=0.
      IF(XNE(J,IA) .EQ. 0.) GO TO 8110
      IF((XNP(M+2)/XNP(1)) .EQ. 0.) SEP3(I,J,M)=0.
      IF((XNP(M+2)/XNP(1)) .EQ. 0.) GO TO 8110
      IF(IMAVG .EQ. 1) GO TO 8119
      SEP3(I,J,M)=(XNE(J,L)/XNE(J,IA))*SE(I,J,IA)*((SP(I,M+2)/SP(I,1))/(
     2XNP(M+2)/XNP(1)))
      GO TO 8110
 8119 IC=IY-10
      IB=IY
      IF(XNE(J,IC) .EQ. 0.) SEP3(I,J,M)=0.
      IF(XNE(J,IC) .EQ. 0.) GO TO 8110
      IF(XNE(J,IB) .EQ. 0.) SEP3(I,J,M)=0.
      IF(XNE(J,IB) .EQ. 0.) GO TO 8110
      SEP3(I,J,M)=(XNE(J,L)/((XNE(J,IC)+XNE(J,IB)+XNE(J,IA))/3.))*((SE(I
     2,J,IC)+SE(I,J,IB)+SE(I,J,IA))/3.)*((SP(I,M+2)/SP(I,1))/(XNP(M+2)/X
     3NP(1)))
 8110 CONTINUE
 8100 CONTINUE
      CALL CCON(INS,SEP3,XNE,IY)
      IF(IX .EQ. 0) GO TO 140
      DO 8120 I=1,INS
      DO 8120 J=1,23
      DO 8120 K=1,5
      SEP3(I,J,K)=SEP3(I,J,K)*TT(K)
 8120 CONTINUE
  140 CONTINUE
      CALL CON(INS,5,SEP3)
      DO 8220 I=1,INS
      DO 8220 J=1,5
      SEP3(I,24,J)=SEP3(I,1,J)+SEP3(I,2,J)+SEP3(I,3,J)+SEP3(I,4,J)+SEP3(
     2I,19,J)+SEP3(I,20,J)+SEP3(I,21,J)+SEP3(I,22,J)+SEP3(I,23,J)
      DO 8251 K=1,23
      SEP2(I,K,J)=0.
 8251 CONTINUE
```

```
8220 CONTINUE
     DO 8130 I=1,INC
     DO 8130 J=1,23
     READ(4)(CE(J,K),K=1,15)
     DO 8131 M=1,5
     L=IY+M
     IA=IY-5
     IST=IT(I,NCS1,NCS2,NCS3,NCS4,NCS5,NCS6)
     IF(ISEP .EQ. 1) SEP3(IST,J,M)=SE(IST,J,L)
     IF(SE(IST,J,IA) .EQ. 0.) CEP3(J,M)=0.
     IF(SE(IST,J,IA) .EQ. 0.) GO TO 8140
     IF((SP(IST,M+2)/SP(IST,1)) .EQ. 0.) CEP3(J,M)=0.
     IF((SP(IST,M+2)/SP(IST,1)) .EQ. 0.) GO TO 8140
     IF(IMAVG .EQ. 1) GO TO 8118
     CEP3(J,M)=(SEP3(IST,J,M)/SE(IST,J,IA))*CE(J,IA)*((CP(I,M+2)/CP(I,1
    2))/(SP(IST,M+2)/SP(IST,1)))
     GO TO 8140
8118 IC=IY-10
     IB=IY
     IF(SE(IST,J,IC) .EQ. 0.) CEP3(J,M)=0.
     IF(SE(IST,J,IC) .EQ. 0.) GO TO 8140
     IF(SE(IST,J,IB) .EQ. 0.) CEP3(J,M)=0.
     IF(SE(IST,J,IB) .EQ. 0.) GO TO 8140
     CEP3(J,M)=(SEP3(IST,J,M)/((SE(IST,J,IC)+SE(IST,J,IB)+SE(IST,J,IA))
    2/3.))*((CE(J,IC)+CE(J,IB)+CE(J,IA))/3.)*((CP(I,M+2)/CP(I,1))/(SP(I
    3ST,M+2)/SP(IST,1)))
8140 CONTINUE
     IF(I .LE. NCS1)SEP2(1,J,M)=SEP2(1,J,M)+CEP3(J,M)
     IF(I .GT. NCS1 .AND. I .LE. NCS2)SEP2(2,J,M)=SEP2(2,J,M)+CEP3(J,M)
     IF(I .GT. NCS2 .AND. I .LE. NCS3)SEP2(3,J,M)=SEP2(3,J,M)+CEP3(J,M)
     IF(I .GT. NCS3 .AND. I .LE. NCS4)SEP2(4,J,M)=SEP2(4,J,M)+CEP3(J,M)
     IF(I .GT. NCS4 .AND. I .LE. NCS5)SEP2(5,J,M)=SEP2(5,J,M)+CEP3(J,M)
     IF(I .GT. NCS5 .AND. I .LE. NCS6)SEP2(6,J,M)=SEP2(6,J,M)+CEP3(J,M)
8131 CONTINUE
     WRITE(2)(CEP3(J,K),K=1,5)
8130 CONTINUE
     ENDFILE 2
     REWIND 2
     DO 3500 I=1,INC
     DO 3500 J=1,23
     READ(2)(CEP3(J,K),K=1,5)
     DO 3501 M=1,5
     IST=IT(I,NCS1,NCS2,NCS3,NCS4,NCS5,NCS6)
     IF(SEP2(IST,J,M) .EQ. 0.) CEP3(J,M)=CEP3(J,M)
     IF(SEP2(IST,J,M) .EQ. 0.) GO TO 4125
     CEP3(J,M)=(CEP3(J,M)/SEP2(IST,J,M))*SEP3(IST,J,M)
4125 CONTINUE
     IF(J .LE. 4 .OR. J .GE. 19) GO TO 6500
     CEP4T(I,M)=CEP4T(I,M)+CEP3(J,M)        •
6500 CONTINUE
     IF(J .GT. 4 .AND. J .LT. 19) GO TO 8129
     CEP3T(I,M)=CEP3T(I,M)+CEP3(J,M)
8129 CONTINUE
3501 CONTINUE
     WRITE(3)(CEP3(J,K),K=1,5)
3500 CONTINUE
     ENDFILE 3
     REWIND 3
     REWIND 2
     DO 5502 I=1,INC
     DO 5512 J=1,23
```

```
      READ(3) (CEP3(J,K),K=1,5)
5512 CONTINUE
      DO 5522 J=1,23
      DO 5503 M=1,5
      IF(J .LE. 4 .OR. J .GE. 19) CEP3(J,M)=CEP3(J,M)
      IF(J .LE. 4 .OR. J .GE. 19) GO TO 6501
      IF(CEP4T(I,M) .LE. CEP3(4,M))CEP3(J,M)=CEP3(J,M)
      IF(CEP4T(I,M) .LE. CEP3(4,M)) GO TO 6501
      CEP3(J,M)=(CEP3(J,M)/CEP4T(I,M))*CEP3(4,M)
6501 CONTINUE
5503 CONTINUE
      WRITE(2)(CEP3(J,K),K=1,5)
5522 CONTINUE
5502 CONTINUE
      DO 2891 I=1,INS
      WRITE(6,4093) I
      WRITE(6,2091)
2091 FORMAT(2X,;MODEL 3;)
      WRITE(6,30)
      DO 2891 J=1,24
      WRITE(6,4096) IND(J),(SEP3(I,J,K),K=1,5)
2891 CONTINUE
      ENDFILE 2
      REWIND 2
      DO 766 K=1,INC
      WRITE(5,9002) K
      WRITE(6,2091)
      WRITE(6,30)
      DO 765 I=1,23
      READ(2)(CEP3(I,M),M=1,5)
      WRITE(6,4096) IND(I),(CEP3(I,J),J=1,5)
 765 CONTINUE
      WRITE(6,4096) IND(24),(CEP3T(K,J),J=1,5)
 766 CONTINUE
4000 IF(IM4 .EQ. 0) GO TO 9999
      DO 9055 I=1,600
      DO 9055 K=1,5
      CEP3T(I,K)=0.
      CEP4T(I,K)=0.
9055 CONTINUE
      IF(ISEP .EQ. 1) GO TO 9995
      DO 161 I=1,INS
      DO 161 J=1,23
      SUMX=0.
      SUMX2=0.
      WN=0.
      SUMSE=0.
      SUMTSE=0.
      DO 161 K=1,IY
      IF(XNE(J,K) .EQ. 0.) SB(I,J)=0.
      IF(XNE(J,K) .EQ. 0.) GO TO 162
      IF(SE(I,J,K) .EQ. 0.) SB(I,J)=0.
      IF(SE(I,J,K) .EQ. 0.) GO TO 162
      IF(IMAVG .EQ. 1) GO TO 9990
      WN=WN+1.
      T(K)=K
      X(K)=ALOG10(T(K))
      SUMX=SUMX+X(K)
      SUMX2=SUMX2+X(K)*X(K)
      SY=ALOG10(SE(I,J,K)/XNE(J,K))
      SUMSE=SUMSE+SY
```

```
      SUMTSE=SUMTSE+X(K)*SY
      IF((WN*SUMX2-SUMX**2) .EQ. 0.) GO TO 162
      SB(I,J)=(WN*SUMTSE-SUMX*SUMSE)/(WN*SUMX2-SUMX**2)
      GO TO 162
 9990 KK=K+1
      KL=K+2
      IF(KK .GT. IY) GO TO 182
      IF(KL .GT. IY) GO TO 182
      IF(XNE(J,KK) .EQ. 0.) SB(I,J)=0.
      IF(XNE(J,KK) .EQ. 0.) GO TO 182
      IF(SE(I,J,KK) .EQ. 0.) SB(I,J)=0.
      IF(SE(I,J,KK) .EQ. 0.) GO TO 182
      IF(XNE(J,KL) .EQ. 0.) SB(I,J)=0.
      IF(XNE(J,KL) .EQ. 0.) GO TO 182
      IF(SE(I,J,KL) .EQ. 0.) SB(I,J)=0.
      IF(SE(I,J,KL) .EQ. 0.) GO TO 182
      WN=WN+1.
      T(K)=(K+KK+KL)/3.
      X(K)=ALOG10(T(K))
      SUMX=SUMX+X(K)
      SUMX2=SUMX2+X(K)*X(K)
      SYY=((SE(I,J,K)/XNE(J,K))+(SE(I,J,KK)/XNE(J,KK))+(SE(I,J,KL)/XNE(J
     2,KL)))/3.
      SY=ALOG10(SYY)
      SUMSE=SUMSE+SY
      SUMTSE=SUMTSE+X(K)*SY
      IF((WN*SUMX2-SUMX**2) .EQ. 0.) GO TO 182
      SB(I,J)=(WN*SUMTSE-SUMX*SUMSE)/(WN*SUMX2-SUMX**2)
  182 CONTINUE
  162 CONTINUE
  161 CONTINUE
      DO 164 I=1,INS
      DO 164 J=1,23
      DO 164 K=1,5
      IK=IY
      XL=K*5
      IF(XNE(J,IK) .EQ. 0.) SEP4(I,J,K)=0.
      IF(XNE(J,IK) .EQ. 0.) GO TO 165
      IF(SE(I,J,IK) .EQ. 0.) SEP4(I,J,K)=0.
      IF(SE(I,J,IK) .EQ. 0.) GO TO 165
      SEP4(I,J,K)=(10.**(ALOG10(SE(I,J,IK)/XNE(J,IK))+SB(I,J)*ALOG10(XL)
     2))*XNE(J,IY+K)
  165 CONTINUE
  164 CONTINUE
      CALL CCON(INS,SEP4,XNE,IY)
      IF(IX .EQ. 0) GO TO 9995
      DO 9920 I=1,INS
      DO 9920 J=1,23
      DO 9920 K=1,5
      SEP4(I,J,K)=SEP4(I,J,K)*TT(K)
 9920 CONTINUE
 9995 CONTINUE
      CALL CON(INS,5,SEP4)
      DO 1796 I=1,INS
      DO 1796 J=1,5
      SEP4(I,24,J)=SEP4(I,1,J)+SEP4(I,2,J)+SEP4(I,3,J)+SEP4(I,4,J)+SEP4(
     2I,19,J)+SEP4(I,20,J)+SEP4(I,21,J)+SEP4(I,22,J)+SEP4(I,23,J)
      DO 8252 K=1,23
      SEP2(I,K,J)=0.
 8252 CONTINUE
 1796 CONTINUE
```

```
      REWIND 4
      DO 167 I=1,INC
      DO 167 J=1,23
      READ(4)(CE(J,K),K=1,15)
      SUMX=0.
      SUMX2=0.
      WN=0.
      SUMCE=0.
      SUMTCE=0.
      DO 1671 K=1,IY
      IST=IT(I,NCS1,NCS2,NCS3,NCS4,NCS5,NCS6)
      IF(SE(IST,J,K) .EQ. 0.) CB(I,J)=0.
      IF(SE(IST,J,K) .EQ. 0.) GO TO 168
      IF(CE(J,K) .EQ. 0.) CB(I,J)=0.
      IF(CE(J,K) .EQ. 0.) GO TO 168
      IF(IMAVG .EQ. 1) GO TO 184
      WN=WN+1
      T(K)=K
      X(K)=ALOG10(T(K))
      SUMX=SUMX+X(K)
      SUMX2=SUMX2+X(K)*X(K)
      Y=ALOG10(CE(J,K)/SE(IST,J,K))
      SUMCE=SUMCE+Y
      SUMTCE=SUMTCE+X(K)*Y
      IF((WN*SUMX2-SUMX**2) .EQ. 0.) GO TO 168
      CB(I,J)=(WN*SUMTCE-SUMX*SUMCE)/(WN*SUMX2-SUMX**2)
      GO TO 168
  184 KK=K+1
      KL=K+2
      IF(KK .GT. IY) GO TO 188
      IF(KL .GT. IY) GO TO 188
      IF(SE(IST,J,KK) .EQ. 0.) CB(I,J)=0.
      IF(SE(IST,J,KK) .EQ. 0.) GO TO 188
      IF(CE(J,KK) .EQ. 0.) CB(I,J)=0.
      IF(CE(J,KK) .EQ. 0.) GO TO 188
      IF(SE(IST,J,KL) .EQ. 0.) CB(I,J)=0.
      IF(SE(IST,J,KL) .EQ. 0.) GO TO 188
      IF(CE(J,KL) .EQ. 0.) CB(I,J)=0.
      IF(CE(J,KL) .EQ. 0.) GO TO 188
      WN=WN+1.
      T(K)=(K+KK+KL)/3.
      X(K)=ALOG10(T(K))
      SUMX=SUMX+X(K)
      SUMX2=SUMX2+X(K)*X(K)
      YY=((CE(J,K)/SE(IST,J,K))+(CE(J,KK)/SE(IST,J,KK))+(CE(J,KL)/SE(IST
     2,J,KL)))/3.
      Y=ALOG10(YY)
      SUMCE=SUMCE+Y
      SUMTCE=SUMTCE+X(K)*Y
      IF((WN*SUMX2-SUMX**2) .EQ. 0.) GO TO 188
      CB(I,J)=(WN*SUMTCE-SUMX*SUMCE)/(WN*SUMX2-SUMX**2)
  188 CONTINUE
  187 CONTINUE
  168 CONTINUE
 1671 CONTINUE
  167 CONTINUE
      REWIND 2
      REWIND 3
      REWIND 4
      DO 170 I=1,INC
      DO 170 J=1,23
```

```
      READ(4)(CE(J,K),K=1,15)
      DO 1701 K=1,5
      IST=IT(I,NCS1,NCS2,NCS3,NCS4,NCS5,NCS6)
      IK=IY
      XL=K*5
      IF(SE(IST,J,IK) .EQ. 0.) CEP4(J,K)=0.
      IF(SE(IST,J,IK) .EQ. 0.) GO TO 171
      IF(CE(J,IK) .EQ. 0.) CEP4(J,K)=0.
      IF(CE(J,IK) .EQ. 0.) GO TO 171
      IF(ISEP .EQ. 1) SEP4(IST,J,K)=SE(IST,J,K+IY)
      CEP4(J,K)=(10.**(ALOG10(CE(J,IK)/SE(IST,J,IK))+CB(I,J)*ALOG10(XL))
     2)*SEP4(IST,J,K)
  171 CONTINUE
      IF(I .LE. NCS1)SEP2(1,J,K)=SEP2(1,J,K)+CEP4(J,K)
      IF(I .GT. NCS1 .AND. I .LE. NCS2)SEP2(2,J,K)=SEP2(2,J,K)+CEP4(J,K)
      IF(I .GT. NCS2 .AND. I .LE. NCS3)SEP2(3,J,K)=SEP2(3,J,K)+CEP4(J,K)
      IF(I .GT. NCS3 .AND. I .LE. NCS4)SEP2(4,J,K)=SEP2(4,J,K)+CEP4(J,K)
      IF(I .GT. NCS4 .AND. I .LE. NCS5)SEP2(5,J,K)=SEP2(5,J,K)+CEP4(J,K)
      IF(I .GT. NCS5 .AND. I .LE. NCS6)SEP2(6,J,K)=SEP2(6,J,K)+CEP4(J,K)
 1701 CONTINUE
      WRITE(2)(CEP4(J,K),K=1,5)
  170 CONTINUE
      ENDFILE 2
      REWIND 2
      DO 3550 I=1,INC
      DO 3550 J=1,23
      READ(2)(CEP4(J,K),K=1,5)
      DO 3551 M=1,5
      IST=IT(I,NCS1,NCS2,NCS3,NCS4,NCS5,NCS6)
      IF(SEP2(IST,J,M) .EQ. 0.) CEP4(J,M)=CEP4(J,M)
      IF(SEP2(IST,J,M) .EQ. 0.) GO TO 8225
      CEP4(J,M)=(CEP4(J,M)/SEP2(IST,J,M))*SEP4(IST,J,M)
 8225 CONTINUE
      IF(J .LE. 4 .OR. J .GE. 19) GO TO 6502
      CEP3T(I,M)=CEP3T(I,M)+CEP4(J,M)
 6502 CONTINUE
      IF(J .GT. 4 .AND. J .LT. 19) GO TO 1791
      CEP4T(I,M)=CEP4T(I,M)+CEP4(J,M)
 1791 CONTINUE
 3551 CONTINUE
      WRITE(3)(CEP4(J,K),K=1,5)
 3550 CONTINUE
      REWIND 2
      ENDFILE 3
      REWIND 3
      DO 5505 I=1,INC
      DO 5515 J=1,23
      READ(3)(CEP4(J,K),K=1,5)
 5515 CONTINUE
      DO 5525 J=1,23
      DO 5506 M=1,5
      IF(J .LE. 4. OR. J .GE. 19) CEP4(J,M)=CEP4(J,M)
      IF(J .LE. 4 .OR. J .GE. 19) GO TO 6503
      IF(CEP3T(I,M) .LE. CEP4(4,M)) CEP4(J,M)=CEP4(J,M)
      IF(CEP3T(I,M) .LE. CEP4(4,M)) GO TO 6503
      CEP4(J,M)=(CEP4(J,M)/CEP3T(I,M))*CEP4(4,M)
 6503 CONTINUE
 5506 CONTINUE
      WRITE(2)(CEP4(J,K),K=1,5)
 5525 CONTINUE
 5505 CONTINUE
```

```
      DO 2094 I=1,INS
      WRITE(6,4093) I
      WRITE(6,2095)
 2095 FORMAT(2X,;MODEL 4;)
      WRITE(6,30)
      DO 2094 J=1,24
      WRITE(6,4096) IND(J),(SEP4(I,J,K),K=1,5)
 2094 CONTINUE
      ENDFILE 2
      REWIND 2
      DO 767 K=1,INC
      WRITE(6,9002) K
      WRITE(6,2095)
      WRITE(6,30)
      DO 7767 I=1,23
      READ(2)(CEP4(I,J),J=1,5)
      WRITE(6,4096) IND(I),(CEP4(I,J),J=1,5)
 7767 CONTINUE
      WRITE(6,4096) IND(24),(CEP4T(K,J),J=1,5)
  767 CONTINUE
 9999 CONTINUE
      STOP
      END
      SUBROUTINE CON(JI,N,SJ)
      DIMENSION SJ(6,24,5),ST(6,5)
      DO 8505 I=1,JI
      DO 8505 K=1,N
      ST(I,K)=0.
      IN=0.
      DO 8505 J=5,18
      IF(SJ(I,J,K) .EQ. 0.) GO TO 8552
      IN=IN+1
      ST(I,K)=ST(I,K)+SJ(I,J,K)
 8552 CONTINUE
      IF(IN .LT. 14 .AND. J .EQ. 18) ST(I,K)=0.
 8505 CONTINUE
      DO 8506 I=1,JI
      DO 8506 J=5,18
      DO 8506 K=1,N
      IF(ST(I,K) .EQ. 0.) SJ(I,J,K)=SJ(I,J,K)
      IF(ST(I,K) .EQ. 0.) GO TO 8507
      SJ(I,J,K)=(SJ(I,J,K)/ST(I,K))*SJ(I,4,K)
 8507 CONTINUE
 8506 CONTINUE
      RETURN
      END
      FUNCTION IT(II,I1,I2,I3,I4,I5,I6)
      IF(II. LE. I1)   IT = 1
      IF(II .GT. I1 .AND. II .LE. I2) IT=2
      IF(II .GT. I2 .AND. II .LE. I3) IT=3
      IF(II .GT. I3 .AND. II .LE. I4) IT=4
      IF(II .GT. I4 .AND. II .LE. I5) IT=5
      IF(II .GT. I5 .AND. II .LE. I6) IT=6
      RETURN
      END
      SUBROUTINE CCON(JII,SJJ,XEJ,JIY)
      DIMENSION CJI(24,5),SJJ(6,24,5),XEJ(24,20)
      DO 9950 J=1,23
      DO 9950 K=1,5
      CJI(J,K)=0.
      DO 9950 I=1,JII
```

```
      CJI(J,K)=CJI(J,K)+SJJ(I,J,K)
 9950 CONTINUE
      DO 9951 I=1,JII
      DO 9951 J=1,23
      DO 9951 K=1,5
      IF(CJI(J,K) .EQ. 0.) SJJ(I,J,K)=SJJ(I,J,K)
      IF(CJI(J,K) .EQ. 0.) GO TO 9952
      SJJ(I,J,K)=(SJJ(I,J,K)/CJI(J,K))*XEJ(J,K+JIY)
 9952 CONTINUE
 9951 CONTINUE
      RETURN
      END
//GO.FT04F001 DD DSN=##A,DISP=(NEW,DELETE),UNIT=S2314,
// DCB=(RECFM=VBS,LRECL=24,BLKSIZE=1924),SPACE=(TRK,(50,10),RLSE)
//GO.FT03F001 DD DSN=##B,DISP=(NEW,DELETE),UNIT=S2314,
// DCB=(RECFM=VBS,LRECL=24,BLKSIZE=1924),SPACE=(TRK,(50,10),RLSE)
//GO.FT02F001 DD DSN=##C,DISP=(NEW,DELETE),UNIT=S2314,
// DCB=(RECFM=VBS,LRECL=24,BLKSIZE=1924),SPACE=(TRK,(50,10),RLSE)
//GO.SYSIN DD *
 1 1 1 1
   1     2     2                      0     0    12     1
 1.072106  1.167341   .904124   .867304   .849813   .938437   .883319   .970811
  .859698   .824036   .922405   .691626  1.066865   .811648  1.018414   .818019
  .727972   .817062  1.025616   .967470   .944162   .986930
  .962866  0.0        .928344  0.0        .906501
 3210766  3172621  3124604  2644033  2659891  2744166  2723986  2754041
 2811381  2854323  2842427  2911776  2516000  2313000  2123000  1986000
 1849000
  630283   632708   635190   622226   610132   626544   628732   619067
  626042   629170   671906   723628   609000   578000   547000   524000
  501000
 4226286  4390294  4587322  4243772  4395480  4515131  4512060  4462978
 4750298  4512802  4661409  4611301  5589000  5807000  6015000  6301000
 6586000
17020496 17678864 18854016 19505328 19787552 20264880 19831856 18485088
18768672 19464208 19767552 18191360 22112000 22609000 23106000 23638000
24169000
 1546287  1552510  1579040  1591773  1584254  1594460  1601149  1545594
 1542248  1676204  1690505  1594819  1871000  1815000  1758000  1710000
 1661000
  861635   887324   931543   928420   965886   968969   951106   907774
  939545  1022345  1025865   855999   919000   898000   875000   855000
  835000
 1286053  1340012  1382398  1395749  1393569  1412793  1381253  1330031
 1354217  1351583  1311112  1180926  1395000  1396000  1393000  1388000
 1383000
  950161   984525  1027253  1013498  1013661  1046003  1004151   968790
 1051399  1130251  1153935   977797  1036000  1024000  1010000   999000
  988000
  586610   598825   624231   643670   644436   664951   670464   637316
  634031   707360   725161   645036   814000   839000   863000   890000
  916000
  930034   959893   993181  1032719  1046135  1069244  1086204  1063899
 1060422  1086988  1112282  1090457  1455000  1516000  1592000  1662000
 1732000
  752052   779222   827119   870258   862802   883140   884410   856463
  853256  1015419  1037608  1023283  1231000  1320000  1412000  1506000
 1599000
  151337   147700   142223   139000   140980   137284   136654   137169
  139766   184995   188893   183449   274000   269000   264000   260000
  256000
```

```
1157637    1252374    1277737    1307660    1268974    1285461    1272854    1195634
1148753    1283928    1333092    1243885    1120000    1068000    1017000     977000
 937000
1329770    1351697    1466963    1578719    1740510    1807361    1702782    1527863
1538402    1630633    1650457    1497923    1954000    2012000    2066000    2122000
2177000
1535241    1643345    1821650    1949979    1921155    1969126    2003172    1750260
1776582    1991791    2136742    2135127    2202000    2254000    2302000    2344000
2386000
1473130    1547372    1760610    1911887    1899576    1937746    1887775    1666907
1705294    1941903    2033864    1774252    2433000    2631000    2836000    3050000
3263000
1635773    1716977    1911619    1950235    1986408    2027714    1823958    1664390
1707300    1841225    1682775    1568009    2169000    2274000    2174000    2177000
2179000
2072344    2155190    2281560    2305222    2319448    2411321    2360845    2208463
2290102    2599878    2685757    2420595    3239000    3393000    3544000    3701000
3857000
3857209    4006892    4135922    4170089    4249162    4370493    4499425    4472212
4575793    5210785    5286548    5218603    5627000    5991000    6364000    6752000
7140000
12429022   12918692   13551362   13961675   14488508   15067311   15543759   15527635
16171591   15896445   16589330   16917568   19396000   20227000   21034000   21778000
22522000
3098826    3195326    3286875    3349371    3501068    3662444    3826888    3867612
4080401    4134246    4242814    4285732    5240000    5698000    6178000    6688000
7198000
16884240   17800144   19191152   20336448   21363728   22676320   23014464   23639120
24404064   26226000   27206000   28468992   32980000   35916000   39095000   42592000
46090000


 31439.     26480.     22915.     19743.     20333.     18248.     17531.     18461.
 18691.     18385.     22953.     21521.         0.         0.         0.         0.
     0.         0.         0.         0.
  4973.      4807.      4732.      3903.      3827.      4034.      4299.      3783.
  3788.      3754.      6023.      4776.         0.         0.         0.         0.
     0.         0.         0.         0.
149261.    154051.    156085.    141748.    145391.    148846.    149341.    149999.
151911.    161806.    159908.    138980.         0.         0.         0.         0.
     0.         0.         0.         0.
804534.    817042.    853894.    884720.    878680.    901677.    886550.    821982.
804208.    829566.    830399.    752209.         0.         0.         0.         0.
     0.         0.         0.         0.
 59989.     60324.     63279.     61638.     62119.     62030.     61852.     58142.
 56794.     54855.     57108.     51126.

 27156.     28488.     29922.     29694.     32140.     31092.     29644.     29232.
 31626.     32367.     28321.     23173.

 79454.     84273.     84477.     83727.     85275.     84846.     81759.     77193.
 75283.     75816.     63744.     53747.

 14723.     14345.     15957.     16305.     14743.     15704.     16743.     16354.
 15907.     17480.     15030.     13028.

 32206.     31312.     33354.     34313.     35490.     36934.     35517.     33470.
 31745.     34396.     37701.     32466.

 37268.     38217.     39692.     42099.     41398.     43620.     44421.     43947.
```

43867.	44904.	46885.	46663.				
89446.	91186.	96520.	104955.	106749.	112539.	116076.	114026.
112761.	112954.	123320.	121222.				
11010.	8649.	7925.	7414.	7210.	7924.	6894.	7101.
6804.	7144.	11006.	11569.				
36240.	37480.	39036.	41096.	36658.	39199.	38585.	33899.
31796.	32927.	32124.	27371.				
61559.	60798.	64782.	68631.	69309.	71806.	71181.	63445.
62450.	65158.	67296.	60173.				
62317.	65600.	70168.	79273.	81146.	82207.	80319.	69711.
70444.	74141.	75358.	70488.				
131562.	126428.	136116.	143368.	139482.	132892.	128575.	112536.
103785.	106730.	109314.	90930.				
38689.	40062.	39435.	37666.	35425.	36767.	32358.	29729.
29106.	30607.	27453.	27588.				
122914.	129880.	133232.	134539.	131536.	144119.	142625.	133197.
131840.	140086.	135740.	122665.				
159631.	161302.	167828.	165785.	167477.	170936.	183244.	182404.
180842.	185377.	199188.	189698.	0.	0.	0.	0.
0.	0.	0.	0.				
435922.	455938.	477224.	486842.	510323.	530438.	557129.	566683.
582465.	607626.	594607.	621212.	0.	0.	0.	0.
0.	0.	0.	0.				
101577.	105868.	108986.	111141.	116030.	118454.	123218.	125778.
131866.	139413.	138938.	138348.	0.	0.	0.	0.
0.	0.	0.	0.				
519500.	547243.	583118.	623489.	659487.	686136.	718539.	739719.
776262.	813485.	844567.	869244.	0.	0.	0.	0.
0.	0.	0.	0.	0.	0.	0.	0.
0.	0.	0.	0.	0.	0.	0.	0.
0.	0.	0.	0.				
1509.	1186.	1018.	916.	966.	856.	899.	891.
918.	923.	1119.	1075.	0.	0.	0.	
273.	403.	382.	338.	165.	173.	187.	184.
235.	211.	345.	299.	0.	0.	0.	
9604.	10269.	10620.	10256.	10345.	10734.	10479.	10143.
10794.	11327.	11873.	11452.	0.	0.	0.	
73952.	73658.	78855.	85397.	84114.	86163.	87175.	83430.
80173.	82375.	92591.	84464.	0.	0.	0.	
1882.	2266.	3221.	3216.	3013.	2965.	3362.	2859.
2946.	3095.	4034.	3566.	0.	0.	0.	
1084.	1163.	1101.	1185.	945.	922.	936.	968.
1044.	1119.	891.	656.	0.	0.	0.	
5874.	6484.	6200.	5746.	5739.	5412.	5139.	4841.
4830.	5181.	5346.	4471.	0.	0.	0.	
590.	643.	729.	249.	898.	826.	792.	548.
564.	646.	556.	624.	0.	0.	0.	
4478.	4055.	4343.	4615.	4728.	4849.	4972.	4394.
4213.	4913.	8032.	7648.	0.	0.	0.	
2507.	2462.	2617.	2898.	2906.	1525.	1430.	1719.
1594.	1607.	2149.	2663.	0.	0.	0.	

14501.	14636.	17337.	18901.	18351.	18166.	19635.	19613.
18798.	17731.	20927.	20210.	0.	0.	0.	
1202.	891.	758.	841.	626.	994.	608.	623.
424.	472.	2123.	2602.	0.	0.	0.	
7809.	7964.	8052.	8515.	5976.	8025.	7726.	7182.
6288.	6729.	7495.	5728.	0.	0.	0.	
3274.	3259.	3482.	3245.	3215.	3818.	4321.	4177.
3637.	3943.	6735.	6136.	0.	0.	0.	
2405.	2533.	2461.	4277.	5211.	5948.	6390.	5815.
5712.	5270.	9124.	6436.	0.	0.	0.	
7855.	6689.	7855.	8687.	8699.	7019.	6592.	6065.
5919.	6407.	4276.	3573.	0.	0.	0.	
3251.	3505.	3761.	4319.	4239.	4149.	4043.	3837.
3733.	3720.	3720.	3720.	0.	0.	0.	
6959.	6745.	6565.	6837.	10027.	10699.	10719.	10220.
9837.	10592.	6383.	10642.	0.	0.	0.	
9006.	8763.	9127.	9394.	9552.	9951.	11658.	13582.
13916.	14674.	18896.	17357.	0.	0.	0.	
27815.	29203.	31713.	32657.	34061.	36343.	39891.	44147.
44034.	46681.	52490.	54041.	0.	0.	0.	
3901.	4132.	4435.	4480.	4703.	4827.	5359.	5648.
5685.	6130.	7059.	6800.	0.	0.	0.	
33595.	35343.	38894.	41949.	46603.	50247.	53230.	55936.
59281.	62630.	67618.	69956.	0.	0.	0.	
0.	0.	0.	0.	0.	0.	0.	
0.	0.	0.	0.	0.	0.	0.	0.
159655.	162957.	175044.	185387.	190509.	199294.	208878.	213961.
215036.	224951.	251991.	245444.	0.	0.	0.	

203235298		223532000		246039000		263830000
7195000.	0. 8080300.		0. 8923300.		0. 9693900.	
196040298	0 215451700		0 237116700		0 254136100	
583813.	0. 676517.		0. 767542.		0. 852690.	
// 6611187.	7403783.		8155758.		8841210.	

Chapter 15
The Employment Program: Output, the Sample Problem Printout

This chapter consists of the printout generated by the sample problem data listed in Chapter 14 run on the IBM System 370/168, at Rutgers University. State 2 and County 2 represent the dummy state and county generated by the program.

NATIONAL EMPLOYMENT

	1964	1965	1966	1967	1968	1969	1970	1971	1972	1973	1974	1975
AGRI	3210766.	3172621.	3124604.	2644033.	2659891.	2744166.	2723986.	2754041.	2811381.	2854323.	2842427.	2911776.
MINI	630283.	632708.	635190.	622226.	610132.	626544.	628732.	619067.	626042.	629170.	671906.	723628.
CONS	4226286.	4390294.	4587322.	4243772.	4395480.	4515131.	4512060.	4462978.	4750298.	4512802.	4661409.	4611301.
MANU	17020496.	17678864.	18854016.	19505328.	19787552.	20264880.	19831856.	18485088.	18768672.	19464208.	19767552.	18191360.
FD&K	1617805.	1622431.	1651468.	1667566.	1668557.	1681529.	1692019.	1636285.	1631555.	1676178.	1690463.	1594801.
TEXT	901487.	927287.	974272.	972627.	1017284.	1021883.	1005085.	961040.	993952.	1022330.	1025840.	855990.
APPL	1345535.	1400362.	1445806.	1462207.	1467725.	1489942.	1459643.	1408073.	1432636.	1351562.	1311079.	1180912.
LUM&	994108.	1028866.	1074372.	1061756.	1067601.	1103123.	1061140.	1025636.	1112283.	1130234.	1153906.	977787.
PAPR	613742.	625795.	652864.	674319.	678729.	701263.	708515.	674712.	670746.	707350.	725143.	645029.
PRNT	973050.	1003125.	1038738.	1081892.	1101803.	1127633.	1147850.	1126326.	1121828.	1086971.	1112254.	1090445.
CHEM	786836.	814316.	865059.	911696.	908714.	931367.	934604.	906718.	902666.	1015404.	1037583.	1023272.
PETR	158337.	154352.	148747.	145619.	148482.	144781.	144410.	145218.	147859.	184992.	188888.	183447.
PRIM,	1211179.	1308777.	1336345.	1369924.	1336499.	1355656.	1345092.	1265790.	1215274.	1283908.	1333059.	1243870.
FABM	1391273.	1412574.	1534251.	1653890.	1833127.	1906056.	1799421.	1617514.	1627487.	1630607.	1650416.	1497906.
MACH	1606248.	1717357.	1905207.	2042828.	2023385.	2076655.	2116859.	1852960.	1879459.	1991761.	2136689.	2135103.
ELMA	1541264.	1617061.	1841367.	2002921.	2000657.	2043561.	1994913.	1764716.	1804043.	1941873.	2033814.	1774232.
TRAN	1711430.	1794305.	1999303.	2043095.	2092110.	2138443.	1927473.	1762052.	1806165.	1841197.	1682733.	1567992.
OTHR	2168193.	2252254.	2386213.	2414985.	2442873.	2542998.	2494831.	2338049.	2422716.	2599839.	2685690.	2420569.
TCPU	3857209.	4006892.	4135922.	4170089.	4249162.	4370493.	4499425.	4472212.	4575793.	5210785.	5286548.	5218603.
WHRT	12429022.	12918692.	13551362.	13961675.	14488508.	15067311.	15543759.	15527635.	16171591.	15896445.	16589330.	16917568.
FIRE	3098826.	3195326.	3286875.	3349371.	3501068.	3662444.	3826888.	3867612.	4080401.	4134246.	4242814.	4285732.
SERV	16884240.	17800144.	19191152.	20336448.	21363728.	22676320.	23014464.	23639120.	24404064.	26226000.	27206000.	28468992.
GOVT	0.	0.	0.	0.	0.	0.	0.	0.	0.	0.	0.	0.
TOTL	61357088.	63795504.	67366416.	68832896.	71055472.	73927248.	74581136.	73827728.	76188224.	78927952.	81267952.	81328944.

NATIONAL EMPLOYMENT PROJECTIONS

	1980	1985	1990	1995	2000
AGRI	2697417.	2479779.	2276079.	2129201.	1982322.
MINI	710910.	674723.	638535.	611686.	584837.
CONS	5053148.	5250247.	5438305.	5696885.	5954560.
MANU	19177824.	19608864.	20039920.	20501328.	20961856.
FD&K	1592041.	1540407.	1499252.	1459642.	1419384.
TEXT	863532.	841623.	824036.	805932.	787950.
APPL	1233811.	1231512.	1234813.	1231498.	1228420.
LUM&	1007052.	992821.	993986.	974153.	964493.
PAPR	700693.	720351.	744543.	768534.	791860.
PRNT	1200511.	1247617.	1316503.	1375636.	1435162.
CHEM	1136938.	1215994.	1307039.	1395317.	1483122.
PETR	189749.	185806.	183235.	180622.	178040.
PRIM	1196423.	1137932.	1088337.	1046962.	1005209.
FABM	1587997.	1630915.	1682792.	1729974.	1776778.
MACH	2245427.	2292525.	2352675.	2397776.	2443439.
ELMA	1992796.	2149414.	2328102.	2506051.	2684031.
TRAN	1580999.	1653259.	1588206.	1591841.	1595067.
OTHR	2649862.	2768693.	2905905.	3037393.	3168922.
TCPU	5771139.	6144463.	6527018.	6924957.	7322896.
WHRT	18765040.	19568992.	20349760.	21069552.	21789344.
FIRE	4947408.	5379834.	5833032.	6314555.	6796077.
SERV	32548944.	35446576.	38584016.	42035312.	45487600.
GOVT	0.	0.	0.	0.	0.
TOTL	89671824.	94553440.	99686640.	105283440.	110879472.

STATE	1EMPLOYMENT											
	1964	1965	1966	1967	1968	1969	1970	1971	1972	1973	1974	1975
AGRI	31439.	26480.	22915.	19743.	20333.	18248.	17531.	18461.	18691.	18385.	22953.	21521.
MINI	4973.	4807.	4732.	3903.	3827.	4034.	4299.	3783.	3788.	3754.	6023.	4776.
CONS	149261.	154051.	156085.	141748.	145391.	148846.	149341.	149999.	151911.	161808.	159908.	138980.
MANU	804534.	817042.	853894.	884720.	878680.	901677.	886550.	821982.	804208.	829566.	830399.	752209.
FD&K	59989.	60324.	63279.	61638.	62119.	62030.	61852.	58142.	56794.	54855.	57108.	51126.
TEXT	27156.	28488.	29922.	29694.	32140.	31092.	29464.	29232.	31626.	32367.	28321.	23173.
APPL	79454.	84273.	84477.	83727.	85275.	84846.	81759.	77193.	75283.	75816.	63744.	53747.
LUM&	14723.	14345.	15957.	16305.	14743.	15704.	16743.	16354.	15907.	17480.	15030.	13028.
PAPR	32206.	31312.	33354.	34313.	35490.	36934.	35517.	33470.	31745.	34396.	37701.	32466.
PRNT	37268.	38217.	39692.	42099.	41398.	43620.	44421.	43947.	43867.	44904.	46885.	46663.
CHEM	89446.	91186.	96520.	104955.	106749.	112539.	116076.	114026.	112761.	112954.	123320.	121222.
PETR	11010.	8649.	7925.	7414.	7210.	7924.	6894.	7101.	6804.	7144.	11006.	11569.
PRIM	36240.	37480.	39036.	41096.	36658.	39199.	38585.	33899.	31796.	32927.	32124.	27371.
FABM	61559.	60798.	64782.	68631.	69309.	71806.	71181.	63445.	62450.	65158.	67296.	60173.
MACH	62317.	65600.	70168.	79273.	81146.	82207.	80319.	69711.	70444.	74141.	75358.	70488.
ELMA	131562.	126428.	136116.	143368.	139482.	132892.	128575.	112536.	103785.	106730.	109314.	90930.
TRAN	38689.	40062.	39435.	37666.	35425.	36767.	32358.	29729.	29106.	30607.	27453.	27588.
OTHR	122914.	129880.	133232.	134539.	131536.	144119.	142625.	133197.	131840.	140086.	135740.	122665.
TCPU	159631.	161302.	167828.	165785.	167477.	170936.	183244.	182404.	180842.	185377.	199188.	189698.
WHRT	435922.	455938.	477224.	486842.	510323.	530438.	557129.	566683.	582465.	607626.	594607.	621212.
FIRE	101577.	105868.	108986.	111141.	116030.	118454.	123218.	125778.	131866.	139413.	138938.	138348.
SERV	519500.	547243.	583118.	623489.	659487.	686136.	718539.	739719.	776262.	813485.	844567.	869244.
GOVT	0.	0.	0.	0.	0.	0.	0.	0.	0.	0.	0.	0.
TOTL	2206837.	2272731.	2374782.	2437371.	2501548.	2578769.	2639851.	2608809.	2650033.	2759414.	2796583.	2735988.

STATE 2EMPLOYMENT

	1964	1965	1966	1967	1968	1969	1970	1971	1972	1973	1974	1975
AGRI	3179327.	3146141.	3101689.	2624290.	2639558.	2725918.	2706455.	2735580.	2792690.	2835938.	2819474.	2890255.
MINI	625310.	627901.	630458.	618323.	606305.	622510.	624433.	615284.	622254.	625416.	665883.	718852.
CONS	4077025.	4236243.	4431237.	4102024.	4250089.	4366285.	4362719.	4312979.	4598387.	4350994.	4501501.	4472321.
MANU	16215962.	16861808.	18000112.	18620608.	18908864.	19363200.	18945296.	17663104.	17964464.	18634640.	18937152.	17439136.
FD&K	1557815.	1562107.	1588189.	1605927.	1606438.	1619499.	1630167.	1578143.	1574761.	1621323.	1633355.	1543675.
TEXT	874331.	898799.	944350.	942933.	985144.	990791.	975441.	931808.	962326.	989963.	997519.	832817.
APPL	1266081.	1316089.	1361329.	1378479.	1382450.	1405096.	1377883.	1330880.	1357353.	1275745.	1247335.	1127165.
LUM&	979385.	1014521.	1058415.	1045451.	1052858.	1087419.	1044397.	1009282.	1096376.	1112754.	1138876.	964759.
PAPR	581536.	594483.	619510.	640006.	643239.	664329.	672998.	641242.	639001.	672953.	687442.	612563.
PRNT	935782.	964908.	999046.	1039793.	1060405.	1084013.	1103429.	1082379.	1077961.	1042067.	1065369.	1043782.
CHEM	697390.	723131.	768539.	806741.	801966.	818828.	818528.	792692.	789905.	902450.	914263.	902050.
PETR	147327.	145703.	140822.	138204.	141272.	136857.	137516.	138117.	141055.	177848.	177882.	171878.
PRIM	1174939.	1271297.	1297309.	1328827.	1299841.	1316457.	1306507.	1231891.	1183478.	1250981.	1300935.	1216499.
FABM	1329714.	1351776.	1469469.	1585258.	1763818.	1834250.	1728239.	1554069.	1565037.	1565449.	1583120.	1437733.
MACH	1543931.	1651757.	1835039.	1963554.	1942239.	1994448.	2036539.	1783249.	1809015.	1917620.	2061331.	2064615.
ELMA	1409701.	1490633.	1705251.	1859552.	1861175.	1910669.	1866337.	1652180.	1700258.	1835142.	1924500.	1683302.
TRAN	1672741.	1754243.	1959868.	2005428.	2056685.	2101676.	1895115.	1732323.	1777059.	1810590.	1655280.	1540404.
OTHR	2045278.	2122374.	2252981.	2280445.	2311337.	2398879.	2352205.	2204852.	2290876.	2459752.	2549950.	2297904.
TCPU	3697578.	3845590.	3968094.	4004304.	4081685.	4199557.	4316181.	4289808.	4394951.	5025408.	5087360.	5028905.
WHRT	11993100.	12462754.	13074138.	13474833.	13978185.	14536873.	14986630.	14960952.	15589126.	15288819.	15994723.	16296356.
FIRE	2997249.	3089458.	3177889.	3238230.	3385038.	3543990.	3703670.	3741834.	3948535.	3994833.	4103876.	4147384.
SERV	16364740.	17252896.	18608032.	19712944.	20704240.	21990176.	22295920.	22899392.	23627792.	25412512.	26361424.	27599744.
GOVT	0.	0.	0.	0.	0.	0.	0.	0.	0.	0.	0.	0.
TOTL	59150256.	61522768.	64991616.	66395536.	68553936.	71348480.	71941280.	71218912.	73538176.	76168544.	78471376.	78592928.

COUNTY	EMPLOYMENT											
	1964	1965	1966	1967	1968	1969	1970	1971	1972	1973	1974	1975
AGRI	1509.	1186.	1018.	916.	966.	856.	899.	891.	918.	923.	1119.	1075.
MINI	273.	403.	382.	338.	165.	173.	187.	184.	235.	211.	345.	299.
CONS	9604.	10269.	10620.	10256.	10345.	10734.	10479.	10143.	10794.	11327.	11873.	11452.
MANU	73952.	73658.	78855.	85397.	84114.	86163.	87175.	83430.	80173.	82375.	92591.	84464.
FD&K	1882.	2266.	3221.	3216.	3013.	2965.	3362.	2859.	2946.	3095.	4034.	3566.
TEXT	1084.	1163.	1101.	1185.	945.	922.	936.	968.	1044.	1119.	891.	656.
APPL	5874.	6484.	6200.	5746.	5739.	5412.	5139.	4841.	4830.	5181.	5346.	4471.
LUMB	590.	643.	729.	249.	898.	826.	792.	548.	564.	646.	556.	624.
PAPR	4478.	4055.	4363.	4615.	4728.	4849.	4972.	4394.	4213.	4913.	8032.	7648.
PRNT	2507.	2462.	2617.	2898.	2906.	1525.	1430.	1719.	1594.	1607.	2149.	2663.
CHEM	14501.	14636.	17337.	18901.	18351.	18166.	19635.	19613.	18798.	17731.	20927.	20210.
PETR	1202.	891.	758.	841.	626.	994.	608.	623.	424.	472.	2123.	2602.
PRIM	7809.	7964.	8052.	8515.	5976.	8025.	7726.	7182.	6288.	6729.	7495.	5728.
FABM	3274.	3259.	3482.	3245.	3215.	3818.	4321.	4177.	3637.	3943.	6735.	6136.
MACH	2405.	2533.	2461.	4277.	5211.	5948.	6390.	5815.	5712.	5270.	9124.	6436.
ELMA	7855.	6689.	7855.	8687.	8699.	7019.	6592.	6065.	5919.	6407.	4276.	3573.
TRAN	3251.	3505.	3761.	4319.	4239.	4149.	4043.	3837.	3733.	3720.	3720.	3720.
OTHR	6959.	6745.	6565.	6837.	10027.	10699.	10719.	10220.	9837.	10592.	6383.	10642.
TCPU	9006.	8763.	9127.	9394.	9552.	9951.	11658.	13582.	13916.	14674.	18896.	17357.
WHRT	27815.	29203.	31713.	32657.	34061.	36343.	39991.	44148.	44034.	46681.	52490.	54041.
FIRE	3901.	4132.	4435.	4480.	4703.	4827.	5359.	5648.	5685.	6130.	7059.	6800.
SERV	33595.	35343.	38894.	41949.	46603.	50247.	53230.	55936.	59281.	62630.	67618.	69956.
GOVT	0.	0.	0.	0.	0.	0.	0.	0.	0.	0.	0.	0.
TOTL	159655.	162957.	175044.	185387.	190509.	199294.	208878.	213961.	215036.	224951.	251991.	245444.

	COUNTY 1964	2EMPLOYMENT 1965	1966	1967	1968	1969	1970	1971	1972	1973	1974	1975
AGRI	29930.	25294.	21897.	18827.	19367.	17392.	16632.	17570.	17773.	17462.	21834.	20446.
MINI	4700.	4404.	4350.	3565.	3662.	3861.	4112.	3599.	3553.	3543.	5678.	4477.
CONS	139657.	143782.	145465.	131492.	135046.	138112.	138862.	139856.	141117.	150481.	148035.	127528.
MANU	730582.	743384.	775039.	799323.	794566.	815514.	799375.	738552.	724035.	747191.	737808.	667745.
FD&K	58107.	58058.	60058.	58422.	59106.	59065.	58490.	55283.	53848.	51760.	53074.	47560.
TEXT	26072.	27325.	28821.	28509.	31195.	30170.	28708.	28264.	30582.	31248.	27430.	22517.
APPL	73580.	77789.	78277.	77981.	79536.	79434.	76620.	72352.	70453.	70635.	58398.	49276.
LUM&	14133.	13702.	15228.	16056.	13845.	14878.	15951.	15806.	15343.	16834.	14474.	12404.
PAPR	27728.	27257.	29011.	29698.	30762.	32085.	30545.	29076.	27532.	29483.	29669.	24818.
PRNT	34761.	35755.	37075.	39201.	38492.	42095.	42991.	42228.	42273.	43297.	44736.	44000.
CHEM	74945.	76550.	79183.	86054.	88398.	94373.	96441.	94413.	93963.	95223.	102393.	101012.
PETR	9808.	7758.	7167.	6573.	6584.	6930.	6286.	6478.	6380.	6672.	8883.	8967.
PRIM	28431.	29516.	30984.	32581.	30682.	31174.	30859.	26717.	25508.	26198.	24629.	21643.
FABM	58285.	57539.	61300.	65386.	66094.	67988.	66860.	59268.	58813.	61215.	60561.	54037.
MACH	59912.	63067.	67707.	74996.	75935.	76259.	73929.	63896.	64732.	68871.	66234.	64052.
ELMA	123707.	119739.	128261.	134681.	130783.	125873.	121983.	106471.	97866.	100323.	105038.	87357.
TRAN	35438.	36557.	35674.	33347.	31186.	32618.	28315.	25892.	25373.	26687.	23733.	23868.
OTHR	115955.	123135.	126667.	127702.	121509.	133420.	131906.	122977.	122003.	129494.	129357.	112023.
TCPU	150625.	152539.	158701.	156391.	157925.	160985.	171586.	168822.	166926.	170703.	180292.	172341.
WHRT	408107.	426735.	445511.	454185.	476262.	494095.	517238.	522536.	538431.	560945.	542117.	567171.
FIRE	97676.	101736.	104551.	106661.	111327.	113627.	117859.	120130.	126181.	133283.	131879.	131548.
SERV	485905.	511900.	544224.	581540.	612884.	635889.	665309.	683783.	716981.	750855.	776949.	799288.
GOVT	0.	0.	0.	0.	0.	0.	0.	0.	0.	0.	0.	0.
TOTL	0.	0.	0.	0.	0.	0.	0.	0.	0.	0.	0.	0.

STATE   1EMPLOYMENT PROJECTIONS
MODEL 1

	1980	1985	1990	1995	2000
AGRI	19937.	18328.	16823.	15737.	14651.
MINI	4692.	4453.	4214.	4037.	3860.
CONS	152297.	158237.	163905.	171698.	179464.
MANU	792999.	810822.	828647.	847726.	866768.
FD&K	50229.	48087.	46116.	44374.	42677.
TEXT	23007.	22187.	21404.	20690.	20006.
APPL	55265.	54580.	53923.	53152.	52437.
LUM&	13205.	12881.	12579.	12309.	12053.
PAPR	34709.	35306.	35956.	36683.	37381.
PRNT	50559.	51989.	54054.	55824.	57600.
CHEM	132554.	140276.	148565.	156751.	164786.
PETR	11777.	11411.	11087.	10802.	10531.
PRIM	25910.	24383.	22989.	21847.	20746.
FABM	62781.	63798.	64861.	65903.	66943.
MACH	72956.	73701.	74524.	75068.	75657.
ELMA	100513.	107270.	114482.	121797.	129015.
TRAN	27376.	28326.	26812.	26560.	26321.
OTHR	132157.	136628.	141294.	145966.	150615.
TCPU	209783.	223353.	237259.	251725.	266190.
WHRT	689051.	718572.	747242.	773673.	800103.
FIRE	159708.	173667.	188296.	203841.	219385.
SERV	993817.	1082290.	1178086.	1283464.	1388873.
GOVT	0.	0.	0.	0.	0.
TOTL	3022282.	3189722.	3364470.	3551898.	3739293.

	1980	1985	1990	1995	2000
AGRI	2677480.	2461450.	2259256.	2113463.	1967670.
MINI	706218.	670269.	634321.	607649.	580977.
CONS	4900851.	5092009.	5274399.	5525186.	5775095.
MANU	18384800.	18798016.	19211248.	19653584.	20095056.
FD&K	1542072.	1492756.	1453835.	1416177.	1377814.
TEXT	840737.	819791.	803190.	785962.	768814.
APPL	1178472.	1176827.	1180761.	1178218.	1175867.
LUM&	994324.	980731.	972646.	963439.	954367.
PAPR	665887.	684889.	708357.	731571.	754157.
PRNT	1149934.	1195615.	1262464.	1319870.	1377679.
CHEM	1002946.	1073186.	1154301.	1232917.	1311166.
PETR	177906.	174290.	171992.	169630.	167290.
PRIM	1170907.	1114185.	1066819.	1026337.	985904.
FABM	1525261.	1567216.	1618136.	1664390.	1710284.
MACH	2172802.	2219414.	2279152.	2324079.	2369535.
ELMA	1891976.	2041625.	2212812.	2383216.	2553764.
TRAN	1554259.	1626057.	1563106.	1567517.	1571488.
OTHR	2517321.	2631440.	2763675.	2890263.	3016946.
TCPU	5561355.	5921109.	6289758.	6673232.	7056706.
WHRT	18075984.	18850416.	19602512.	20295872.	20989232.
FIRE	4787700.	5206167.	5644735.	6110714.	6576692.
SERV	31555120.	34364272.	37405920.	40751824.	44098704.
GOVT	0.	0.	0.	0.	0.
TOTL	86649488.	91363696.	96322112.	101731504.	107140112.

COUNTY   1EMPLOYMENT PROJECTIONS
MODEL 1

	1980	1985	1990	1995	2000
AGRI	996.	916.	840.	786.	732.
MINI	294.	279.	264.	253.	242.
CONS	12549.	13039.	13506.	14148.	14788.
MANU	89044.	91046.	93047.	95189.	97328.
FD&K	3503.	3354.	3217.	3095.	2977.
TEXT	651.	628.	606.	586.	566.
APPL	4597.	4540.	4486.	4421.	4362.
LUM&	632.	617.	603.	590.	577.
PAPR	8176.	8317.	8470.	8641.	8806.
PRNT	2885.	2967.	3085.	3186.	3287.
CHEM	22099.	23387.	24769.	26133.	27473.
PETR	2649.	2566.	2494.	2429.	2368.
PRIM	5422.	5103.	4811.	4572.	4341.
FABM	6402.	6506.	6614.	6720.	6826.
MACH	6661.	6729.	6805.	6854.	6908.
ELMA	3950.	4215.	4498.	4786.	5069.
TRAN	3691.	3819.	3615.	3581.	3549.
OTHR	11466.	11853.	12258.	12664.	13067.
TCPU	19195.	20436.	21709.	23032.	24356.
WHRT	59942.	62511.	65005.	67304.	69603.
FIRE	7850.	8536.	9255.	10019.	10783.
SERV	79981.	87102.	94811.	103292.	111775.
GOVT	0.	0.	0.	0.	0.
TOTL	269851.	283863.	298437.	314023.	329606.

	1980	1985	1990	1995	2000
AGRI	18941.	17413.	15982.	14951.	13920.
MINI	4398.	4174.	3951.	3784.	3618.
CONS	139747.	145198.	150399.	157550.	164676.
MANU	703955.	719777.	735599.	752536.	769441.
FD&K	46314.	44336.	42511.	40902.	39334.
TEXT	22159.	21367.	20610.	19921.	19261.
APPL	50221.	49596.	48990.	48286.	47632.
LUM&	12462.	12156.	11869.	11612.	11370.
PAPR	26299.	26750.	27238.	27785.	28312.
PRNT	47254.	48587.	50508.	52158.	53813.
CHEM	109481.	115852.	122676.	129426.	136049.
PETR	9048.	8766.	8516.	8296.	8087.
PRIM	20307.	19109.	18013.	17118.	16253.
FABM	55883.	56784.	57720.	58643.	59563.
MACH	65710.	66377.	67107.	67591.	68116.
ELMA	95713.	102140.	108988.	115943.	122804.
TRAN	23476.	24289.	22986.	22769.	22563.
OTHR	119628.	123667.	127868.	132086.	136282.
TCPU	190588.	202917.	215551.	228692.	241834.
WHRT	629108.	656061.	682237.	706369.	730500.
FIRE	151858.	165131.	179041.	193821.	208601.
SERV	913836.	995188.	1083274.	1180171.	1277097.
GOVT	0.	0.	0.	0.	0.
TOTL	2752429.	2905858.	3066033.	3237873.	3409685.

```
   STATE      IEMPLOYMENT PROJECTIONS
MODEL 2
        1980       1985       1990       1995       2000

AGRI     18302.     15082.     11863.      8644.      5425.
MINI      4802.      4828.      4854.      4880.      4906.
CONS    139764.    140547.    141331.    142114.    142898.
MANU    730994.    709778.    688563.    667347.    646132.
FD&K     47249.     43373.     39496.     35620.     31743.
TEXT     22671.     22169.     21667.     21165.     20663.
APPL     43297.     32848.     22398.     11948.      1498.
LUM&     13064.     13100.     13136.     13172.     13208.
PAPR     33294.     34121.     34949.     35776.     36604.
PRNT     50774.     54884.     58995.     63105.     67216.
CHEM    135526.    149830.    164135.    178439.    192743.
PETR     11875.     12181.     12486.     12792.     13098.
PRIM     23107.     18842.     14578.     10314.      6049.
FABM     60116.     60059.     60002.     59945.     59888.
MACH     72676.     74864.     77053.     79241.     81429.
ELMA     71879.     52828.     33777.     14726.     -4325.
TRAN     21265.     14942.      8618.      2295.     -4028.
OTHR    124204.    125742.    127281.    128819.    130358.
TCPU    205903.    222108.    238313.    254518.    270723.
WHRT    706402.    791592.    876782.    961972.   1047162.
FIRE    156752.    175157.    193561.    211966.    230370.
SERV   1029604.   1189963.   1350322.   1510682.   1671041.
GOVT        0.         0.         0.         0.         0.
TOTL   2992520.   3249054.   3505588.   3762122.   4018656.
```

```
STATE      2EMPLOYMENT PROJECTIONS
MODEL 2
          1980        1985        1990        1995        2000

AGRI   2770170.    2650085.    2530000.    2409914.    2289829.
MINI    743047.     767243.     791438.     815634.     839829.
CONS   4626886.    4781451.    4936016.    5090581.    5245147.
MANU  17948528.   18457920.   18967328.   19476720.   19986112.
FD&K   1552202.    1560729.    1569257.    1577784.    1586311.
TEXT    844577.     856337.     868097.     879858.     891618.
APPL   1074129.    1021094.     968058.     915022.     861987.
LUM&    989575.    1014391.    1039207.    1064022.    1088838.
PAPR    639655.     666747.     693839.     720930.     748022.
PRNT   1090449.    1137117.    1183785.    1230453.    1277120.
CHEM    985905.    1069759.    1153614.    1237469.    1321324.
PETR    186289.     200701.     215112.     229523.     243934.
PRIM   1207040.    1197581.    1188122.    1178662.    1169203.
FABM   1492030.    1546328.    1600626.    1654924.    1709221.
MACH   2218188.    2371761.    2525334.    2678907.    2832480.
ELMA   1794418.    1905535.    2016652.    2127769.    2238886.
TRAN   1440531.    1340659.    1240787.    1140915.    1041044.
OTHR   2433585.    2569266.    2704948.    2840629.    2976311.
TCPU   5656797.    6284690.    6912583.    7540476.    8168369.
WHRT  18194864.   20093376.   21991904.   23890416.   25788928.
FIRE   4711753.    5276122.    5840492.    6404861.    6969230.
SERV  32488864.   37377984.   42267104.   47156224.   52045344.
GOVT        0.          0.          0.          0.          0.
TOTL  87140880.   95688848.  104236832.  112784800.  121332768.
```

COUNTY   1EMPLOYMENT PROJECTIONS
MODEL 2

	1980	1985	1990	1995	2000
AGRI	966.	858.	749.	640.	532.
MINI	266.	233.	201.	168.	135.
CONS	12178.	12905.	13631.	14357.	15083.
MANU	89420.	94377.	99333.	104290.	109246.
FD&K	4128.	4690.	5252.	5813.	6375.
TEXT	522.	388.	255.	121.	-13.
APPL	3765.	3060.	2354.	1649.	943.
LUM&	615.	607.	598.	589.	580.
PAPR	8903.	10157.	11412.	12666.	13921.
PRNT	2342.	2021.	1701.	1380.	1059.
CHEM	22429.	24648.	26866.	29085.	31304.
PETR	2987.	3371.	3756.	4141.	4526.
PRIM	4955.	4183.	3410.	2638.	1865.
FABM	7383.	8630.	9878.	11125.	12372.
MACH	8757.	11078.	13399.	15719.	18040.
ELMA	1805.	37.	-1731.	-3499.	-5267.
TRAN	3765.	3810.	3855.	3899.	3944.
OTHR	12059.	13476.	14893.	16309.	17726.
TCPU	21873.	26388.	30904.	35420.	39935.
WHRT	66166.	78291.	90415.	102540.	114665.
FIRE	8190.	9579.	10969.	12359.	13748.
SERV	86988.	104020.	121053.	138085.	155117.
GOVT	0.	0.	0.	0.	0.
TOTL	286047.	326651.	367254.	407858.	448461.

COUNTY   2EMPLOYMENT PROJECTIONS
MODEL 2

	1980	1985	1990	1995	2000
AGRI	17335.	14225.	11114.	8003.	4893.
MINI	4536.	4595.	4654.	4712.	4771.
CONS	127585.	127643.	127700.	127757.	127814.
MANU	641574.	615402.	589231.	563060.	536888.
FD&K	43122.	38683.	34245.	29806.	25368.
TEXT	22149.	21781.	21412.	21044.	20676.
APPL	39532.	29788.	20043.	10299.	555.
LUM&	12449.	12494.	12538.	12583.	12628.
PAPR	24391.	23964.	23537.	23110.	22683.
PRNT	48431.	52863.	57294.	61725.	66157.
CHEM	113097.	125182.	137267.	149352.	161437.
PETR	8888.	8809.	8730.	8651.	8572.
PRIM	18151.	14659.	11168.	7676.	4184.
FABM	52733.	51429.	50124.	48820.	47516.
MACH	63919.	63787.	63654.	63522.	63389.
ELMA	70074.	52790.	35507.	18224.	940.
TRAN	17500.	11132.	4764.	-1604.	-7972.
OTHR	112144.	112266.	112388.	112509.	112631.
TCPU	184030.	195720.	207409.	219099.	230788.
WHRT	640235.	713300.	786364.	859429.	932493.
FIRE	148563.	165578.	182592.	199607.	216622.
SERV	942615.	1085942.	1229269.	1372596.	1515923.
GOVT	0.	0.	0.	0.	0.
TOTL	2706472.	2924402.	3138332.	3354262.	3570191.

```
  STATE      1EMPLOYMENT PROJECTIONS
  MODEL 3
            1980        1985        1990        1995       2000

  AGRI     17737.        0.        15017.        0.       13256.
  MINI      4966.        0.         4476.        0.        4155.
  CONS    170783.        0.       184408.        0.      204567.
  MANU    875200.        0.       917533.        0.      972197.
  FD&K     57302.        0.        52795.        0.       49511.
  TEXT     25081.        0.        23417.        0.       22182.
  APPL     68017.        0.        66595.        0.       65608.
  LUM&     15652.        0.        14964.        0.       14533.
  PAPR     34574.        0.        35941.        0.       37858.
  PRNT     45742.        0.        49076.        0.       52993.
  CHEM    138767.        0.       156030.        0.      175167.
  PETR      8917.        0.         8424.        0.        8107.
  PRIM     33798.        0.        30094.        0.       27524.
  FABM     61847.        0.        64120.        0.       67060.
  MACH     83884.        0.        85989.        0.       88462.
  ELMA    126385.        0.       144443.        0.      164891.
  TRAN     26144.        0.        25697.        0.       25572.
  OTHR    149090.        0.       159947.        0.      172730.
  TCPU    239960.        0.       272281.        0.      309462.
  WHRT    686754.        0.       747209.        0.      810549.
  FIRE    162664.        0.       192418.        0.      227135.
  SERV   1037725.        0.      1234214.        0.     1474198.
  GOVT        0.        0.            0.        0.           0.
  TOTL   3195788.        0.      3567554.        0.     4015515.
```

	1980	1985	1990	1995	2000
AGRI	2679680.	0.	2261061.	0.	1969066.
MINI	705944.	0.	634059.	0.	580683.
CONS	4882366.	0.	5253896.	0.	5749993.
MANU	18302608.	0.	19122384.	0.	19989664.
FD&K	1535334.	0.	1447512.	0.	1371377.
TEXT	839006.	0.	801573.	0.	767093.
APPL	1165337.	0.	1167546.	0.	1162014.
LUM&	992576.	0.	971028.	0.	952745.
PAPR	666017.	0.	708477.	0.	753898.
PRNT	1155118.	0.	1268172.	0.	1383420.
CHEM	994796.	0.	1144595.	0.	1298139.
PETR	180822.	0.	174808.	0.	169947.
PRIM	1163430.	0.	1060059.	0.	979447.
FABM	1526559.	0.	1619532.	0.	1711132.
MACH	2162262.	0.	2268134.	0.	2357270.
ELMA	1865032.	0.	2181135.	0.	2515411.
TRAN	1556639.	0.	1565643.	0.	1573959.
OTHR	2499676.	0.	2744162.	0.	2993814.
TCPU	5531178.	0.	6254737.	0.	7013434.
WHRT	18078288.	0.	19602544.	0.	20978784.
FIRE	4784744.	0.	5640613.	0.	6568942.
SERV	31511216.	0.	37349792.	0.	44013392.
GOVT	0.	0.	0.	0.	0.
TOTL	86476000.	0.	96119072.	0.	106863920.

COUNTY　　1EMPLOYMENT PROJECTIONS
MODEL 3

	1980	1985	1990	1995	2000
AGRI	939.	0.	818.	0.	739.
MINI	223.	0.	207.	0.	197.
CONS	12370.	0.	13727.	0.	15576.
MANU	88745.	0.	95534.	0.	103469.
FD&K	3217.	0.	3047.	0.	2925.
TEXT	819.	0.	786.	0.	763.
APPL	4414.	0.	4443.	0.	4478.
LUME	765.	0.	752.	0.	748.
PAPR	4984.	0.	5313.	0.	5714.
PRNT	1522.	0.	1680.	0.	1858.
CHEM	24147.	0.	27819.	0.	31865.
PETR	811.	0.	787.	0.	775.
PRIM	6954.	0.	6338.	0.	5910.
FABM	3877.	0.	4132.	0.	4421.
MACH	6886.	0.	7253.	0.	7630.
ELMA	6693.	0.	7866.	0.	9190.
TRAN	3365.	0.	3394.	0.	3450.
OTHR	11564.	0.	12748.	0.	14080.
TCPU	15762.	0.	18384.	0.	21377.
WHRT	50754.	0.	56750.	0.	62969.
FIRE	7309.	0.	8893.	0.	10746.
SERV	79342.	0.	96969.	0.	118466.
GOVT	0.	0.	0.	0.	0.
TOTL	255445.	0.	291281.	0.	333538.

COUNTY MODEL 3 — 2EMPLOYMENT PROJECTIONS

	1980	1985	1990	1995	2000
AGRI	16798.	0.	14199.	0.	12517.
MINI	4743.	0.	4269.	0.	3958.
CONS	158413.	0.	170682.	0.	188991.
MANU	786454.	0.	822000.	0.	868728.
FD&K	53491.	0.	49198.	0.	46074.
TEXT	23996.	0.	22381.	0.	21184.
APPL	62905.	0.	61467.	0.	60457.
LUMB	14724.	0.	14055.	0.	13634.
PAPR	29265.	0.	30290.	0.	31790.
PRNT	43735.	0.	46873.	0.	50573.
CHEM	113362.	0.	126796.	0.	141726.
PETR	8017.	0.	7553.	0.	7252.
PRIM	26549.	0.	23494.	0.	21376.
FABM	57334.	0.	59327.	0.	61950.
MACH	76152.	0.	77867.	0.	79942.
ELMA	118379.	0.	135069.	0.	153988.
TRAN	22529.	0.	22057.	0.	21879.
OTHR	136016.	0.	145574.	0.	156904.
TCPU	224199.	0.	253896.	0.	288085.
WHRT	636000.	0.	690459.	0.	747580.
FIRE	155355.	0.	183525.	0.	216389.
SERV	958383.	0.	1137246.	0.	1355732.
GOVT	0.	0.	0.	0.	0.
TOTL	2940344.	0.	3276274.	0.	3681976.

```
    STATE      IEMPLOYMENT PROJECTIONS
  MODEL 4

             1980       1985       1990       1995       2000

  AGRI      16411.     13873.     12124.     10953.      9926.
  MINI       4238.      3850.      3551.      3340.      3149.
  CONS     144847.    147277.    150634.    156385.    162323.
  MANU     733790.    725565.    727113.    733567.    741984.
  FD&K      45924.     42147.     39357.     37151.     35187.
  TEXT      22238.     21058.     20062.     19214.     18440.
  APPL      48447.     45037.     42864.     41133.     39727.
  LUM&      12930.     12455.     12050.     11710.     11401.
  PAPR      33706.     33735.     33967.     34364.     34777.
  PRNT      53620.     56345.     59218.     61607.     63904.
  CHEM     139212.    149910.    160087.    169848.    179249.
  PETR      10050.      9059.      8421.      7947.      7556.
  PRIM      22277.     19571.     17690.     16311.     15123.
  FABM      58039.     56809.     56396.     56323.     56429.
  MACH      68849.     67593.     67088.     66670.     66466.
  ELMA      72239.     66540.     65011.     64934.     65465.
  TRAN      21716.     20258.     18012.     17063.     16327.
  OTHR     124542.    125049.    126889.    129291.    131935.
  TCPU     196146.    202865.    211869.    222093.    232670.
  WHRT     713885.    755896.    793086.    826343.    858769.
  FIRE     158333.    171532.    185577.    200586.    215623.
  SERV    1004240.   1098563.   1198944.   1308624.   1418148.
  GOVT         0.         0.         0.         0.         0.
  TOTL    2971887.   3119418.   3282895.   3461889.   3642590.
```

	1980	1985	1990	1995	2000
AGRI	2681006.	2465906.	2263955.	2118248.	1972397.
MINI	706672.	670873.	634984.	608346.	581689.
CONS	4908301.	5102970.	5287671.	5540500.	5792237.
MANU	18444032.	18883296.	19312816.	19767760.	20219872.
FD&K	1546387.	1498758.	1460712.	1423562.	1385500.
TEXT	841489.	820905.	804510.	787401.	770329.
APPL	1185342.	1186492.	1192054.	1190574.	1189017.
LUM&	994584.	981184.	973222.	964086.	955063.
PAPR	666863.	686377.	710198.	733683.	756498.
PRNT	1146751.	1190928.	1256662.	1313150.	1370121.
CHEM	996002.	1062550.	1140829.	1216960.	1292884.
PETR	179648.	176674.	174718.	172570.	170376.
PRIM	1174569.	1119120.	1072333.	1032154.	991859.
FABM	1530007.	1574224.	1626650.	1674047.	1720907.
MACH	2176885.	2225512.	2286582.	2332463.	2378705.
ELMA	1920630.	2083310.	2264150.	2442873.	2621124.
TRAN	1559982.	1634378.	1572347.	1577608.	1582216.
OTHR	2524903.	2642882.	2777853.	2906641.	3035270.
TCPU	5574993.	5941598.	6315149.	6702863.	7090227.
WHRT	18051152.	18813088.	19556672.	20243216.	20930576.
FIRE	4789075.	5208302.	5647455.	6113969.	6580454.
SERV	31544704.	34348016.	37385072.	40726688.	44069456.
GOVT	0.	0.	0.	0.	0.
TOTL	86699920.	91434016.	96403744.	101821568.	107236896.

COUNTY   1EMPLOYMENT PROJECTIONS
MODEL 4

	1980	1985	1990	1995	2000
AGRI	868.	752.	667.	608.	556.
MINI	223.	188.	166.	151.	139.
CONS	13097.	13857.	14505.	15308.	16092.
MANU	92528.	96122.	99132.	102062.	104867.
FD&K	4825.	5050.	5091.	5071.	5009.
TEXT	514.	428.	379.	345.	318.
APPL	3954.	3505.	3249.	3060.	2916.
LUM&	625.	581.	552.	529.	510.
PAPR	9601.	9985.	10284.	10570.	10836.
PRNT	2020.	1702.	1574.	1495.	1446.
CHEM	23239.	24072.	25163.	26305.	27469.
PETR	2503.	2264.	2111.	1998.	1904.
PRIM	4646.	3918.	3463.	3143.	2882.
FABM	8072.	8644.	9045.	9373.	9668.
MACH	12388.	15269.	17178.	18578.	19739.
ELMA	2402.	1979.	1814.	1732.	1687.
TRAN	4013.	4097.	3838.	3770.	3712.
OTHR	13705.	14627.	15393.	16095.	16770.
TCPU	25090.	29840.	33767.	37443.	40955.
WHRT	75479.	86810.	95557.	102992.	109868.
FIRE	9053.	10464.	11756.	13051.	14323.
SERV	94506.	110505.	125367.	140634.	155667.
GOVT	0.	0.	0.	0.	0.
TOTL	310845.	348538.	380917.	412249.	442466.

COUNTY   2EMPLOYMENT PROJECTIONS
MODEL 4

	1980	1985	1990	1995	2000
AGRI	15543.	13121.	11457.	10345.	9370.
MINI	4015.	3662.	3385.	3189.	3010.
CONS	131749.	133420.	136129.	141077.	146231.
MANU	641261.	629443.	627980.	631504.	637118.
FD&K	41098.	36894.	33946.	31679.	29724.
TEXT	21724.	20613.	19659.	18842.	18093.
APPL	44492.	41392.	39411.	37830.	36546.
LUM6	12305.	11850.	11464.	11139.	10844.
PAPR	24105.	23349.	23036.	22959.	22959.
PRNT	51599.	54574.	57546.	59994.	62326.
CHEM	115969.	124871.	133340.	141463.	149288.
PETR	7547.	6703.	6176.	5792.	5479.
PRIM	17630.	15495.	14009.	12919.	11980.
FABM	49965.	47818.	46782.	46209.	45883.
MACH	56459.	51710.	48829.	46624.	44936.
ELMA	69835.	64482.	63083.	63066.	63625.
TRAN	17702.	15996.	13933.	12995.	12278.
OTHR	110833.	109835.	110527.	111923.	113644.
TCPU	171055.	173025.	178101.	184451.	191714.
WHRT	638406.	669085.	697529.	723351.	748901.
FIRE	149280.	161068.	173821.	187535.	201301.
SERV	909733.	988059.	1073577.	1167990.	1262481.
GOVT	0.	0.	0.	0.	0.
TOTL	2661042.	2770882.	2901978.	3049641.	3200124.

Population References

Archer, W. "Improving Estimates of Local Population Through Census Public Use Samples." *Journal of the American Institute of Planners* 43 (July 1977): 242-46.

Bogue, D.J. *Principles of Demography*. New York: John Wiley and Sons, 1969.

Bjornstad, D.J. et al. *State Population Projections: A Comparative Review of National Series and Their Practical Usefulness*. Paper ORNL-UR-120, Oak Ridge, Tennessee: Oak Ridge National Laboratory, 1975.

Brown, L.; Horton, F.; and Wittick, R. "On Place Utility and the Normative Allocation of Intra-Urban Migrants." *Demography* 7 (1970): 175–183.

Carey, G; Zobler, L.; Greenberg, M.; and Hordon, R. *Urbanization, Water Pollution, and Public Policy*. New Brunswick, N.J.: Center for Urban Policy Research, Rutgers University, 1972.

Chapin, F.S., Jr. *Urban Land Use Planning*. Urbana, Illinois: University of Illinois Press, 1965: Chapter 5.

Greenberg, M. "A Test of Combinations of Models for Projecting the Population of Minor Civil Divisions." *Economic Geography* 48 (April 1972): 179–188.

Greenberg, M.; Krueckeberg, D.; and Mautner, R. *Long-Range Population Projections for Minor Civil Divisions: Computer Programs and User's Manual*. New Brunswick, N.J.: Center for Urban Policy Research, Rutgers University, 1973.

Harris, C.C., Jr. *The Urban Economies, 1985: A Multiregional Multi-Industry Forecasting Model*. Lexington, Mass.: D.C. Heath, 1973.

Herbert, J. and Stevens, B. "A Model for the Distribution of Residential Activities in Urban Areas." *Journal Of Regional Science* 2 (1960): 21–36.

Isard, W. *Methods of Regional Analysis*. Cambridge, Mass.: MIT, 1960.

Isserman, A. "The Accuracy of Population Projections for Subcounty Areas." *Journal of the American Institute of Planners* 43 (July 1977): 247-259.

Keyfitz, Nathan. "On Future Population." *Journal of the American Statistical Association* 67 (June 1972): 347–363.

Krueckeberg, Donald A. and Silvers, Arthur L. *Urban Planning Analysis: Methods and Models*. New York: John Wiley and Sons, 1974.

Lakshmanan, T. "An Approach to the Analysis of Intra-Urban Location Applied to the Baltimore Region." *Economic Geography* 40 (1964): 348–370.

Miernyk, W.; Shellhammer, K.; Brown, D.; Coccari, R.; Gallagher, C.; and Wineman, W. *Simulating Regional Economic Development.* Lexington, Mass.: D.C. Heath and Company, 1970.

Morrison, Peter A. *Demographic Information for Cities: A Manual for Estimating and Projecting Local Population Characteristics.* Santa Monica, Calif.: Rand Corporation, June 1971.

————. "An Overview of Population Forecasting for Small Areas" Santa Monica, Calif.: Rand Corporation, June 1975.

Newling, Bruce. *Population Projections for New Jersey to 2000.* New York, N.Y.: City College, 1968.

Pickard, J. *Dimensions of Metropolitanism.* Washington, D.C.: Urban Land Institute, 1967.

Piper, H.B. and West, G.L., Jr. *The Siting of Nuclear Reactors as Related to Urban Heat Supply.* Springfield, Va.: Clearinghouse for Federal Scientific and Technical Information (now National Technical Information Service), August 1970 (ORNL – HUD 11).

Pittenger, D.B. *Projecting State and Local Populations.* Cambridge, Mass.: Ballinger Publishing Co., 1976.

Schmitt, R. and Crosetti, A. "Short-Cut Methods of Forecasting City Population." *Journal of Marketing* (April, 1953): 417–424.

Siegel, Jacob S. "Development and Accuracy of Projections of Population and Households in the United States." *Demography* 9 (February 1972): 51–68.

U.S. Atomic Energy Commission. *Guide to the Preparation of Environmental Reports for Nuclear Power Plants.* Washington, D.C.: U.S.A.E.C., August 1972.

————. *Standard Format and Content of Safety Analysis Reports for Nuclear Power Plants* (Revision 1). Washington, D.C.: U.S.A.E.C., October 1972.

U.S. Bureau of the Census. *Handbook of Statistical Methods for Demographers,* by A. J. Jaffe. Washington, D.C.: U.S. Government Printing Office, 1951.

————. *Projections of the Population of the United States, 1975 to 2050.* Washington, D.C.: U.S. Government Printing Office, October 1975. (Current Population Reports, Series P–25, no. 601).

————. *Projections of the Population of the United States, by Age and Sex, 1975 to 2000, With Extensions of Total Population to 2025.* Washington, D.C.: U.S. Government Printing Office, February 1975. (Current Population Reports, Series P–25, no. 541).

————. *Illustrative Population Projections for the U.S.: The Demographic Effects of Alternative Paths to Zero Growth.* Washington, D.C.: U.S.

Government Printing Office, April 1972 (Current Population Reports, Series P–25, no. 480).

――. *Inventory of State and Local Agencies Preparing Population Estimates: Survey of 1969.* Washington, D.C.: U.S. Government Printing Office, December 1970 (Current Population Reports, Series P–25, no. 454).

――. *Preliminary Projections of the Population of the States: 1975–1990.* Washington, D.C.: U.S. Government Printing Office, March 1972 (Current Population Reports, Series P–25, no. 477).

――. *Projections of the Population of the United States, by Age and Sex: 1972 to 2020.* Washington, D.C.: U.S. Government Printing Office, December 1972 (Current Population Reports, Series P–25, no. 493).

U.S. Commission on Population Growth and the American Future. *Population and the American Future.* New York: New American Library, 1972.

U.S. Water Resources Council. *1972 OBERS Projections,* vol. 1, *Concepts, Methodology and Summary Data.* Washington, D.C.: U.S. Government Printing Office, 1972.

Zobler, Leonard; Carey, George; Greenberg, Michael; and Hordon, Robert. *Benefits from Integrated Water Management in Urban Areas – The Case of the New York Metropolitan Region.* Springfield, Va.: Clearinghouse for Federal Scientific and Technical Information (now National Technical Information Service), April 1969 (PB 184019).

Employment References

Alexandersson, G. *The Industrial Structure of American Cities*. Lincoln, Nebraska: University of Nebraska Press, 1956: Chapter 1.

Andrews, R. B. "Economic Studies". *Principles and Practices of Urban Planning*. Edited by William I. Goodman and Eric C. Freund. Washington, D.C.: International City Managers Association, 1968.

Ashby, L. D. *Growth Patterns in Employment by County, 1940–50 and 1950–60*. Washington, D.C.: U.S. Government Printing Office, 1965.

Brown, H.J. "Shift and Share Projections of Regional Economic Growth: An Empirical Test." *Journal of Regional Science* 9 (1969): 1-18.

Chenery, H.B. and Clark, P.G. *Interindustry Economics*. New York: John Wiley, 1967.

Executive Office of the President, Office of Management and Budget. *Standard Industrial Classification Manual*. Washington, D.C.: U.S. Government Printing Office, 1972.

Friedenberg, H. and Bretzfelder, R. "Tracking the BEA State Economic Projections." *Survey of Current Business* 56 (April 1976): 22–29.

Gass, Saul I. and Sisson, Roger L. Eds. *A Guide to Models in Governmental Planning and Operations*. Potomac, Maryland: Sauger Books, 1975.

Greenberg, M. R. "A Test of Alternative Models for Projecting County Industrial Production at the 2, 3, and 4-Digit Standard. Industrial Code Levels." *Regional and Urban Economics* 1 (February 1972): 397–417.

Greytak, D. "A Statistical Analysis of Regional Export Estimating Techniques." *Journal of Regional Science* 9 (December 1969): 387–395.

Haig, R.M. Major Economic Factors in Metropolitan Growth and Arrangement, vol. I, Regional Survey of New York and Environs. New York, 1928.

Hewings, G. "On the Accuracy of Alternative Models for Stepping-Down Multi-County Employment Projections to Counties." *Economic Geography* (July 1976): 206–217.

Holleb, D.B. *Social & Economic Information for Urban Planning*. Chicago, Ill.: The University of Chicago, The Center for Urban Studies, 1969.

Hirsch, Werner Z. *Urban Economic Analysis*. New York: McGraw-Hill, 1973.

Hoyt, J. *The Economic Status of the New York Metropolitan Region in 1944*. New York: Regional Plan Association, 1944.

Isserman, A. "The Location Quotient Approach to Estimating Regional Economic Impacts." *Journal of the American Institute of Planners* 43 (January 1977): 33–41.

James, F. J. and Hughes, J.W. *Economic Growth and Residential Patterns, A Methodological Investigation* New Brunswick, New Jersey: Rutgers University, Center for Urban Policy Research, 1972.

————. "A Test of Shift and Share Analysis as a Predictive Device." *Journal of Regional Science* 13 (1973): 223–231.

Krueckeberg, D.A. and Silvers, A.L. *Urban Planning Analysis: Methods and Models.* New York: John Wiley & Sons, 1974.

Kutscher, R.E. "Revised BLS Projections to 1980 and 1985: An Overview." *Monthly Labor Review.* Washington, D.C.: U.S. Government Printing Office, March 1976.

Lasuen, J.R. "Venezuela: An Industrial Shift-Share Analysis 1941–1961." *Regional and Urban Economics* 1 (August 1971): 153–219.

Lee, T.H.; Moore, J.R.; and Lewis, D.P. *Regional and Interregional Intersectoral Flow Analysis.* Knoxville, Tenn.: University of Tennessee Press, 1973.

Miernyk, W. *The Elements of Input-Output Analysis.* New York: Random House, 1965.

Morrissett, I. "The Economic Structure of American Cities.' *Papers and Proceedings of the Regional Science Association* 4 (1958): 239–256.

New Jersey Department of Labor and Industry. *New Jersey's Manpower Challenge of the Eighties.* March 1975.

New York State Department of Labor. *Manpower Directions, New York State 1965–1975.* Technical Supplement, December 1968.

Perloff, H.S.; Dunn, E.S.; Lampard, E.E.; and Muth, R. F. *Regions, Resources, and Economic Growth.* Baltimore, Md.: The Johns Hopkins Press, 1960.

Shapiro, A.K. *Input-Output Analysis as a Predictive Tool.* Washington, D.C.: U.S. Department of Commerce, 1972. (BEA Staff Paper No. 20 BEA-SP-72-020).

Sonenblum, S. "The Uses and Development of Regional Projections." *Issues in Urban Economics.* Edited by Harvey S. Perloff and Lowdon Wingo, Jr. Baltimore, Md.: The Johns Hopkins Press, 1968: 141–186.

Thompson, W. *A Preface to Urban Economics.* Baltimore, Md.: The Johns Hopkins Press, 1965.

————. "Internal and External Factors in the Development of Urban Economics." *Issues in Urban Economics.* Edited by Harvey S. Perloff and Lowden Wingo, Jr. Baltimore, Md.: The Johns Hopkins Press, 1968: 43–62.

Tiebout, C. M. *The Community Economic Base Study*, Supplementary Paper No. 16, Committee for Economic Development. New York: December 1962.

Ullman, E.L.; Dacey, M.F.; and Brodsky, H. *The Economic Base of American Cities.* Seattle, Washington.: Center for Urban and Regional Research, University of Washington Press, 1969.

U.S. Bureau of the Census, U.S. Department of Commerce. *Census of Business.* Washington, D.C.: U.S. Government Printing Office.

————. *Census of Manufactures.* Washington, D.C.: U.S. Government Printing Office.

————. *Census of Mineral Industries.* Washington, D.C.: U.S. Government Printing Office.

————. *Census of Population 1970*, Vol. 1, Characteristics of the Population, Part 1, U.S. Summary—Section 2.

————. *Census of County Business Patterns.* Washington, D.C.: U.S. Government Printing Office.

U.S. Bureau of Labor Statistics, U.S. Department of Labor. *Employment and Earnings.* Washington, D.C.: U.S. Government Printing Office.

————. *Employment and Wages.* Washington, D.C.: U.S. Government Printing Office.

————. *Monthly Labor Review.* Washington, D.C.: U.S. Government Printing Office.

————. *Monthly Labor Review.* Washington, D.C.: U.S. Government Printing Office, March 1976.

————. *Monthly Labor Review.* Washington, D.C.: U.S. Government Printing Office, November 1976.

————. *Patterns of the U.S. Economy* Bulletin 1672. Washington, D.C.: U.S. Government Printing Office, 1970.

————. *The Structure of the U.S. Economy in 1980 and 1985* Bulletin 1831. Washington, D.C.: U.S. Government Printing Office, 1975.

U.S. Department of Commerce. *1972 OBERS Projections.* Washington D.C.: U.S. Government Printing Office, 1972.

————. *1972 OBERS Projections.* Washington, D.C.: U.S. Government Printing Office, 1974.

Walderhaug, A.J. "State Input-Output Tables Derived from National Data." *Proceedings of the American Statistical Association: Business and Economics Statistics Section.* Washington, D.C., 1971: 77–86, 99–100.

Zimmerman, R. "A Variant of the Shift and Share Projection Formulation." *Journal of Regional Science* 15 (April 1975): 29–38.